Gambling Theory

And Other Topics
By
MASON MALMUTH

A product of Two Plus Two Publishing

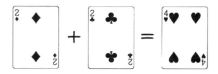

FOURTH EDITION

FIRST PRINTING: 1994

Printing and Binding
Creel Printers, Inc.
Las Vegas, Nevada

Printed in the United States of America

Table of Contents

Foreword

by David Sklansky

Several years ago on one of my periodic trips to California, I found myself playing in a moderate-size lowball game at one of the major poker clubs in Southern California. The game was what I would call a typical Southern California ace-to-five lowball game. Several players were quick to commit their chips, while a couple of other players were playing exceedingly tight. There was one exception, a quiet person who seemed to be playing at an expert level — that is, his game had the right mix of raises and calls — and there was no question that I was looking at a winning player.

Suddenly, one of the live players in the game began to complain about never being able to hit a draw. His complaint was answered by the quiet expert, who said, "When I am running bad, I take the cards and throw them at the dealer. I have found this to be very helpful." Needless to say, the whole table burst out laughing, and that was the first time that I encountered Mason Malmuth.

Since then, I have gotten to know Mason quite well and have discovered that he is one of the most serious thinkers in the gambling world. Fortunately for most of you, Mason has put many of his thoughts and highly original concepts in writing, and these are almost always ideas worth reading.

This is Mason's third book. The other two, *Winning Concepts in Draw and Lowball* and *Blackjack Essays,* are absolutely must reading for anyone interested in those games.[1] This book, *Gambling Theory and Other Topics*, is absolutely must reading for anyone interested in serious gambling, no matter what the game. Its central theme is what Mason calls "non-self-weighting strategies," which is one of the key concepts in all successful

---

[1]*Poker Essays* by Mason Malmuth was published in 1991.

gambling. Another theme that he brings out is that of statistical fluctuations. Most gamblers are just interested in how much they can win. But some of the material to follow will show that there is another parameter to look at. It is the standard deviation, a statistical measure of the fluctuations that a gambling event will produce. It turns out that in many cases, this measurement is as important as how much money can be won, which as stated is what most people concern themselves with.

In closing, I would like to mention that Mason and I, along with another friend, whom we refer to as the "Adventurer," often can be seen together in Southern California, where the super poker clubs are located, or in Las Vegas. When we are together, the conversations are probably some of the most enlightening in the gambling world. Fortunately for you, the reader, many of the concepts that the three of us have discussed are repeated in this book, so it seems to me that it is time to end this foreword and let you get to work.

Introduction

We all know that there are successful gamblers in the world, but striving to become a member of this unique group is not easy. Yet this extremely small group does exist. How is this so? What is it that these people do that enables them to achieve success, while so many other people have disastrous results? In fact, the typical person who becomes heavily involved in gambling usually gets himself in trouble. Let's see what sets the winners apart.

I believe there are several reasons why a small number of people are successful at gambling. First, they have a thorough understanding of gambling theory. This includes a solid foundation in general gambling concepts, as well as much specific knowledge in the appropriate game or area of interest.

Second, the successful gambler possesses the ability to develop a logical thought process and the willingness to continuously think about new gambling ideas and to review and update older ones. I am always amazed at how many active gamblers just go through the motions. Apparently, the thrill of betting is enough to keep many people active — that is until their money is gone.

Third, successful gamblers realize that gambling is a full-time commitment. It is actually a 24-hour-a-day activity. It includes not only our action at the "very exciting gaming tables,"[2] but many — if not all — of our decisions in everyday life. In fact, the successful gambler approaches many of these everyday decisions differently from most people. Some of the essays that follow will provide hints on how to approach this area.

Finally, there is an intangible quality that all successful gamblers possess. It has something to do with the willingness to take calculated risks, but these risks almost always have a much

---

[2]Actually, I don't find the gaming tables very exciting, but I do like to overuse this expression.

better chance of success than what a typical person would think. Many people refer to this quality as "heart" or "courage," but I have concluded that it is much more than that. It is true that heart or courage is involved, but the real experts are able to combine this attribute with a great deal of knowledge, and through the use of a logical thought process, seem to produce a series of decisions that just devastate their opponents.

Of course, being a gambler has its risks. Many of the most successful people, some of whom are very famous, have been broke at one time or another. Perhaps this was just part of their learning process, or perhaps a miscalculation occurred. But the bottom line is that in this business, a great deal of risk is involved. Consequently, gambling is an occupation for a special type of person.

But gambling can be highly rewarding. There is a special satisfaction not only in a large monetary return, but in the knowledge that you have successfully outplayed your opponents again, as usual. Also, a successful gambler has a level of freedom that the ordinary person does not enjoy. He often can choose his own hours to work (known as playing), can take extended vacations, and can say pretty much what he pleases. In other words, the opportunities to enjoy life are far greater for this intelligent risk taker than they are for just about everyone else.

The original version of *Gambling Theory and Other Topics* appeared in 1987, and it is now seven years later. During the intervening period, I received many comments on the book and I discovered that much of the material is more controversial than I assumed it would be. I also discovered how little most gamblers, even those who appear successful, really know. This leads me to two conclusions. First, many of the successful gamblers are instinct players who probably have been more lucky than good and can expect to struggle in the future. Second, few people really understand the amount of risk that is involved in a successful approach to gambling.

Why this is so is puzzling to me. But it appears that for many people, perhaps even for the majority of those who gamble seriously, the thrill of having money in action is stimulating enough, and thinking about the important gambling concepts is either too hard or just not interesting enough to make "the masses" want to improve their games. I have even given this book to a couple of friends who told me how terrific it is, but then at some future time asked a question that indicated they either did not read the book or did not think through what they were reading.

Perhaps this is why some people consider my writings controversial. I certainly don't. It is not my fault that many gamblers have so many misconceptions and try to avoid those subjects that will help them attain success.

The classic example of this is what is referred to as "money management." Some of the essays that follow explain why this is such a worthless subject and provide correct guidelines that are based on a solid mathematical footing.

My reason for deciding to revise and expand the original *Gambling Theory and Other Topics* was to make this the best book ever written on gambling. Although this book already was my favorite among all the books that I had been involved with, I believed I owed it to myself, to the people who have helped me, and to those who read my material to try to produce something special.

It may not be obvious to everyone, but a great deal of work has gone into this book, and I am very proud of its content. Almost all of the material stands on a solid mathematical foundation, even those ideas that at first do not seem to be related to mathematics at all. (A good example of this is the essay titled "Self-Weighting Disasters," which appears in the last section of this book.)

For those of you who have an earlier edition of the book, I suggest that you read this version completely as many essays have been updated and expanded. Also keep in mind that many ideas and concepts, though not explicitly mentioned, play a role in every essay that is included.

I also would like to point out that this work is not only about our favorite occupation, but about life itself. Many of the

3

ideas and concepts that I have found to be appropriate at the "very exciting gaming tables" I have found to be winning life concepts. I believe that if you give careful thought to what you are about to read, you also will discover this to be true.

Finally, many of the ideas in this book took a long time to create and develop, and I am indebted to many people for their assistance. These include David Sklansky, Mark Weitzman,[3] Steve Stamler, Mike Caro, Ray Zee, Ed Hill, Jerry Rancourt, and several others whose comments have been incorporated into this edition. I'd also like to thank Donna Harris for helping me with the proofreading and Lynne Loomis for her wonderful job in editing this manuscript. In fact, thanks to Lynne, you should not only be able to read this work, but to understand it as well.

---

[3]In fact, three of the essays that follow were written by Mark and are well worth reading.

4

Using This Book

This book provides a series of concepts and ideas that attempt to show how a thinking approach can help propel you to success in the gambling world. The book also contains many specific ideas applicable to certain games or situations. Even those of you who are only moderately knowledgeable probably will not agree with everything that is stated. In fact, some people will consider several of the ideas controversial. But their real purpose is to stimulate your logical thinking process. If you read something that you do not agree with, spend some time correctly thinking about it, and still disagree, this book has accomplished its purpose.

The book is a collection of essays organized by subject matter into six sections. Each essay was written to stand alone, so at a future time, you can return to just that essay and not have to reread a large section of the book. This makes for some redundancy among the essays, but as stated, this was done for your benefit.

I recommend that you first read the whole book. You may then want to return to those essays of interest for further study. Also, you should try to see how many concepts interact with each other and how this can lead to surprising conclusions.

Keep in mind that when either reading or reviewing this book, you should not take any idea or concept out of context. For example, one concept may tell you to do one thing while another concept may tell you to do just the opposite. Part of the trick to successful gambling is to be able to balance ideas and concepts, especially if they are new to your way of thinking. The essays should help some, but experience will play a major role in developing this skill.

Part One
Gambling Theory

Gambling Theory

Introduction

The key to successful gambling is simply to "get the best of it" and then to "make the most of it." However, this is not always easy to accomplish. In fact, most people who gamble a lot only rarely get the best of it, and their overall performance is almost always negative.

In 1975, when I was a young statistician at the United States Census Bureau, I learned that the correct way to design sample surveys was to make them "self-weighting." This ensured that the variance was kept to a minimum. However, it turns out that the way to design a statistical survey is not the way to gamble. Moreover, I believe the ideas and concepts that make one a successful gambler also can be applied to produce winning life strategies.

A Good Bet

The secret to all gambling is to identify a good bet. A good bet is when your expectation is positive, or put another way, when the return (assuming you win) is higher than the odds (that is, the inverse of the probability of winning minus one) multiplied by the amount of money bet. As obvious as this seems, many people don't apply it correctly. Let's look at an example.

Suppose you are able to identify the most likely horse to win a race. Is this horse a good bet? The answer is, not necessarily. If the odds of winning on this horse are 3-to-1, and it goes off at 2-to-1, it would not be a good bet. On the other hand, the worst horse in the race may be a good bet. If it goes off at 200-to-1 and it is a 100-to-1 horse, even though its chances of winning are small, you will show a profit on this type of bet in the long run.

This concept holds true in all gambling. It is why blackjack can be beaten and why craps and roulette cannot. It is also why some poker players are winners and others are not. Nevertheless, you should be wary of betting longshots, as short-term statistical fluctuations, which are discussed in detail in some of the essays that follow, will be large. This leads to another set of problems usually addressed under the heading of gambler's ruin. Consequently, the idea of statistical fluctuations is often as important as obtaining a positive expectation.

Remember, just because you have made a winning bet does not mean that you have made a good bet. It is your overall results in the long run that count, nothing more and nothing less.

Non-Self-Weighting Strategies

What is the most important gambling concept that there is? Which concept separates the winners from the losers? What is the one idea that permeates all successful thinking and theorizing on the subject of gambling? In my opinion, it is the little-known statistical concept of self-weighting versus non-self-weighting gambling experiences.

A self-weighting gambling experience is when your expectation and variance are the same from play to play. But what does this mean, and why is it so important? To answer these questions, let's start with a simple example.

Suppose you make a trip to Las Vegas, walk up to a craps table, and start betting $1 every time you roll the dice. You do this for 10,000 rolls, and then suddenly on the next roll you pull $1 million out of your pocket and put it all into action. Now how many times have you rolled the dice? Well, there are two answers, both correct. The mathematicians will say 10,001 times, but the statisticians will say one time simply because your results are all clustered around that one big bet. Notice that during the first 10,000 rolls of the dice, we were looking at a self-weighting gambling experience. But after that $1 million bet came along, we had a very non-self-weighting gambling experience. Incidentally, and this is important, all successful gamblers are statisticians, not mathematicians.

Why are all successful gamblers statisticians? To answer this, think about the games that can be beat. This includes poker, blackjack, sports betting, and progressive slot machines, just to name a few. It does not include roulette, craps, baccarat, super pan nine, and non-progressive slot machines. The reason the games in the first group are beatable is that successful non-self-weighting strategies are available. This is not true of the second group. Their self-weighting characteristics mean that the player will never have the best of it. To understand this, let's take a closer look at poker.

10

Suppose you are a Southern California poker player. Your game is high draw, jacks or better to open, played with a joker that either counts as an ace or can be used to complete straights and flushes. You are dealt a pair of aces. How should they be played?

The typical player plays this hand in a very straightforward manner. If no one has yet opened, he will open; If someone already has opened, he will call. Notice that this is a self-weighting strategy. In other words, there is very little difference in how this hand is played. Also notice that self-weighting players are very predictable opponents, and very predictable opponents are the easiest to beat. This is true in all forms of poker.

Now what about the expert high draw player? How does he play a pair of aces? Well, most of the time he will open when he is in an early position, but not all the time, especially if his other cards are small. (The small cards maximize the chances that someone else will be able to open the pot.) If someone else already has opened, the expert will call most of the time, but not all the time. If his opponent has opened very late, where most players are likely to play any minimum opener, such as a pair of jacks, he will raise. If a tight player opens early, the expert knows that he is (1) up against a quality hand and (2) less likely to be against a pair of aces, since the two aces in his hand reduce the chances that his opponent is also holding a pair of aces by 70 percent. (Not 40 percent as many people think. This is because there are 10 ways you can pick two aces out of five, while there are only three ways you can pick two aces out of three.) Consequently, there is a good chance the opener has a pair of aces badly beat. The expert player would throw his hand away in this situation, especially if several players still remain to act behind him.

It should be obvious from this example that the expert player is following a non-self-weighting strategy. Even though he does not play as many hands as his self-weighting counterpart, the expert still puts about the same amount of money in the pot.

This is because he gets full value for some of the hands he plays, while his typical self-weighting opponent does not.

By the way, it doesn't matter what kind of poker game it is. The expert players, who consistently take home the money, all follow non-self-weighting strategies.

One claim I've made is that the low-limit jackpot games in California can easily be beaten. Most people believe just the opposite, simply because the house takes a lot of money out of the pot to pay not only for the game, but for the jackpot as well. (For those readers unfamiliar with jackpot poker, a player wins the jackpot when he has a powerful hand beaten such as aces full or better in high draw or a six-four in lowball.) These jackpots become quite large, sometimes as high as $40,000 in certain games.

The jackpots have a unique effect on almost all players, turning them into self-weighting opponents. What happens is that typical players now have an incentive to play many more hands. Also, they don't want to make marginal (value) bets and raises — where the real money is won in limit games — simply because they are more interested in survival and shooting for the jackpot.

Remember, the more self-weighting your opponent is, the poorer he plays. An extension of this is that the more self-weighting opponents you have, the easier a game is to beat. As we have seen, in the typical jackpot game, almost everyone follows self-weighting strategies. This is why I argue that an expert player, who follows non-self-weighting strategies, can easily beat these games. The drop and the rake should be a small price to pay for the privilege of going home a winner. Summarizing, we see that in games with a jackpot, there are non-self-weighting strategies available that allow the expert player to compete with a positive expectation. The non-self-weighting player waits until he has the best of it and then takes maximum advantage of the situation. That is, he will make as big a bet as possible and take advantage of a very small edge if that is all the edge he has.

However, even though you have the best of it, this doesn't mean that you are going to win. In addition, following a non-self-weighting strategy has the statistical effect of decreasing the overall sample size. This leads to two related topics that will be covered in Part Two of this book: fluctuations, which every skilled gambler suffers from, and the "extremely silly subject of money management."

Non-Self-Weighting Strategies Revisited

Let's look some more at the idea of non-self-weighting versus self-weighting strategies. Quickly recapping, *self-weighting gambling strategies are those in which many plays are made for similar-sized bets, while successful non-self-weighting strategies attempt to identify where the gambler has the best of it and then to make the most of it.* As already noted, only non-self-weighting strategies, where appropriately applicable, are profitable for the gambler.

The previous essay gave some examples from poker. This essay offers examples from different games and from life in general. As I've stated, I believe you should live a non-self-weighting life to maximize success.

First, let's look at sports betting. What does the typical sports bettor do? Well, let's suppose it is football season. Every Sunday, the typical sports bettor places a bet on many games, if not on all the games. Although no individual bet is that large, all the bets together add up to a substantial sum. In addition, let's assume that the typical sports bettor knows exactly what the line should be. The problem with this is that the people who set the lines also know a great deal about spreads, which means that being knowledgeable is usually of no benefit. Consequently, in the long run, the sports bettor expects to be down his commission that he must pay to the bookie. That is, because he is following a self-weighting strategy, the typical sports bettor will slowly go broke.

But this game can be beat. How does the expert do it? He waits until he has the best of it and then makes a significant bet. Let's make up an example. Suppose the Los Angeles Rams make it to the Super Bowl. Since Las Vegas gets more visitors from Los Angeles than from anyplace else, a great deal of action will come in on the Rams. If the Rams win, the Las

Vegas books will lose a lot of money. Most books don't like to take this kind of "gamble;" they prefer the same amount of money bet on each team and are more than satisfied with their commissions. So the Las Vegas books have an incentive to get more money on the opponent of the Los Angeles team. This is easily done by just changing the line. Now a good bet has materialized, which the non-self-weighting expert will take advantage of.

I am told that these types of events occur often enough that a smart sports bettor, who follows a non-self-weighting approach, can make a living. He does not place nearly as many bets as his self-weighting counterpart, but in the long run, his total action is just as much. The only difference is that he expects to be ahead at the end of the year, not behind like most everyone else.

(I need to point out that a few expert handicappers are quite successful yet bet more games than seems logical. What they are actually doing is betting candidate games, which contain a subset that are good bets. Specifically, they know that certain characteristics are sometimes correlated with incorrect lines. That is, they have no edge in about half the games they bet but have a significant edge in the other half, enabling them to be overall winners. The problem is that they are not able to identify ahead of time which group a selection falls into. Thus they bet all the candidates, which, for example, might be as many as eight NFL games a week. See *Getting the Best of It* by David Sklansky for more information on some of these handicapping techniques.)

Here's another example. I have an acquaintance who regularly travels to Las Vegas for all the big fights, and he bets on almost every fight he sees. Because he follows a self-weighting strategy, he is slowly losing his money. But good bets in boxing do come along. A great example was the Gerry Cooney/Larry Holmes fight. So many tourists were in town that most books had to move their lines toward Cooney. The smart, non-self-weighting gambler would have recognized this and bet Holmes.

Now for a final sports betting example. The New York Mets had a terrific baseball team in 1986, and there was every reason to believe that the 1987 team also would be superior. When the playoffs came, the public, which is always interested in the playoffs, probably would have overbet the Mets (assuming they made the playoffs), forcing the books to move their lines. (This would have been especially true in the New York area.) Consequently, even though New York might clearly have been the better team, profitable bets against them could have been found.

Another extremely non-self-weighting game for which successful non-self-weighting strategies are available is blackjack. The skilled card counter is able to identify those situations where the deck is rich in high cards that favor the player. When this happens, he increases his bet. Notice that these big bets, which occur the minority of the time are the majority of the game. How the skilled card counter does on his big bets usually determines how he does overall, even though most of the time he is betting small. Also, the skilled card counter is willing to wait for the deck to become rich in high cards before making a big bet. He doesn't make large bets just because he needs to get even or because he has a hunch.

Let's change the subject and look at the stock market. One bit of advice that is constantly given is to diversify: "Don't put all your eggs in one basket." Clearly, this is a self-weighting strategy. Although diversification will enable you to do as well as the public in general, the expert will invest differently. He will carefully study the market and select, at most, a very small number of stocks and then invest heavily in them. If no stocks currently meet the non-self-weighting investor's standards, he won't buy any at that moment. An investment like a mutual fund or a company savings plan that invests in a lot of stocks won't even be considered. In addition, the non-self-weighting investor does a great deal of re-evaluating. This means that he is willing to buy and sell quickly if a profit or a loss materializes.

By the way, this statement about the stock market is apparently one of the most controversial in this book. I have received more comments — both positive and negative — about my opinion on not diversifying than on virtually anything else I have written. However, the statement is consistent with my view of the world. One of the things I will strive to show in this book is that the most profitable strategies, whether they deal with gambling or other life games, are associated with a great deal of risk. In addition, I claim that most minor details in life are just not very important. It is how you fare on the small number of significant events that really counts. (If you cannot afford to take a great deal of risk, these strategies may not be appropriate. As an example, if you are considering what to do with your retirement money, it may be best to give up some or most of your expectation if your risk is greatly reduced. In this case, a mutual fund or diversification can be more attractive.)

Let's change the subject again and look at nuclear war. First, what is a successful strategy for a conventional war? One successful approach is to identify where the enemy is weak and to hit these places very hard. Notice that this is a non-self-weighting strategy. The strategy for a nuclear war, known as Mutually Assured Destruction (MAD), is not like this. The idea is to have so many nuclear warheads in so many different locations that enough would survive any first strike by the enemy, meaning that the world would still be burnt to a crisp.

MAD is a self-weighting strategy. It is not designed to win. However, since each side has adopted it and neither side wants to lose, nuclear war has been averted. But if one side began to develop cleaner weapons (neutron bombs), more accurate delivery systems (MX Missiles), and a defense system (Star Wars), then a non-self-weighting strategy of just attacking the enemy's military positions could be followed. Fewer nuclear weapons would be required, the world would not be destroyed, and a nuclear war possibly could be won. (No wonder Mr. Gorbachev seemed very interested in arms control.)

Non-self-weighting strategies also carry over into life games, which are a constant gamble. Let's look at introverted versus extroverted people. The extroverted person usually has something to say about virtually everything. Obviously, this is a self-weighting strategy. The introverted person uses words sparingly. He doesn't say much, but when something is said, others usually listen.

A classic example of this occurred in November 1863 at Gettysburg, Pennsylvania. The highlight of the ceremonies commemorating the great Civil War battlefield was a lengthy speech by well-known orator Edward Everett. After the speech was over, one of the people in attendance, Abraham Lincoln, President of the United States, was asked to say a few words. In a few short lines, Lincoln defined equality and justice more clearly and precisely than had ever been done before. His extremely short speech is now known as the Gettysburg Address.

Societies also can follow self-weighting or non-self-weighting strategies. I believe this is why the Japanese have done so well in international markets. Without going into detail, it appears to me that their approach to industry and marketing is much more non-self-weighting than what has been typical for the United States. Specifically, their government seems to target certain industries for major development, which essentially discourages overdiversification.

Returning to the subject of gambling, I believe most successful gamblers are introverted. This is probably because they are using their minds and thinking instead of talking. It is true that there are some successful gamblers who appear loud and boisterous, especially in the poker world, but most of this is preplanned to manipulate their opponents into making mistakes. Virtually all of the top poker players I know happen to be quiet people who spend a good deal of time listening to what other people have to say.

One final thought. The successful non-self-weighting gambler is going to experience some extreme fluctuations, simply because he is willing to make large bets when he identifies that he has the best of it. Consequently, the idea of money management pretty much goes right out the window. This is much different from the foolish gambler who follows self-weighting strategies and usually either goes broke or loses a great deal of money. This idea, for the games I am most interested in, is further addressed in Part Two of this book.

Sequencing

A few years ago, a friend of mine approached me about a horse racing system that was based on sequencing. Let's define sequencing, determine how we can use it to our advantage, and then see how to apply it.

First, let's consider the following sequence of outcomes from some gambling event, where A denotes one possible outcome and B denotes its converse:

ABABABABABAB

Notice that a pattern has developed and we can predict that the next event will be an A. This type of sequence is non-random, since we can predict with certainty what the next outcome will be. Similarly, the following is also a non-random sequence:

AAAAAABBBBBB

Next, let's define a run to be a sequence of like elements. Notice that our first example contains the maximum number of runs possible (12), while the second example contains the minimum number of runs possible (2). The idea is that if these sequences were generated at random, the number of runs probably would not be close to either extreme. If this non-random condition exists, we would be able to predict the next event with certainty, and a sure bet could be made.

But what about something like this:

AABAABBABABBAABAAB

It is hard to tell if this sequence is randomly generated or not. Following is a test for random sequences. For those mathematically inclined readers, its source is *Statistical Theory And Methodology in Science and Engineering* by K. A. Brownlee.

Let m be the number of elements of type A, n be the number of elements of type B, and u be the number of runs. First compute the expected number of runs, E(u):

$$E(u) \ = \ 1 + \frac{2mn}{m+n}$$

Next compute the variance of the number of runs, V(u):

$$V(u) \ = \ \frac{2mn(2mn-m-n)}{(m+n)^2(m+n-1)}$$

Then the approximate unit normal deviate is

$$\frac{u+(\frac{1}{2})-E(u)}{V(u)^{\frac{1}{2}}}$$

If this number is greater than 2 or less than –2 be suspicious (95 percent confidence) that the sequence may be non-random; if the number is greater than 2.6 or less than –2.6 (99 percent confidence), perhaps you have something.

Let's return to our example:

AABAABBABABBAABAAB

Here m = 10, n = 8, and u = 12, and

$$E(u) = 1 + \frac{(2)(10)(8)}{10+8} = 9.89$$

$$V(u) = \frac{(2)(10)(8)((2)(10)(8)-10-8)}{(10+8)(10+8)(10+8-1)} = 4.12$$

Then the approximate unit normal deviate is

$$\frac{12+(\frac{1}{2})-9.89}{4.12^{\frac{1}{2}}} = 1.29$$

Consequently, we would conclude that the given sequence is random, and we cannot predict with certainty the next outcome.

The appropriate formulas for runs of three different elements — a, b, c (for example, red, black, and the zeros on a roulette wheel) — are

$$E(u) = \frac{2(ab+ac+bc)}{a+b+c} + 1$$

$$V(u) = \frac{(2(ab+ac+bc))^2}{(a+b+c)^2(a+b+c-1)} - \frac{2(ab+ac+bc)+6abc}{(a+b+c)(a+b+c-1)}$$

Then compute the approximate standard normal deviate as previously shown.

A word of caution. The approximation is not accurate for small values of m and n (or a,b,c). That is, you usually want at least 30 observations, and even if a sequence does test out as ✓ non-random, it may be difficult to predict the next value.

Also, keep in mind that this test will not determine situations unrelated to randomness, such as whether a roulette wheel, is biased. A wheel is said to be biased when one particular number (or group of numbers) comes up more often than its expected frequency. Note that even if this were the case, this "favorable" number (or numbers) would still appear at random.

Finally, how did the horse racing system work? I didn't get all the details, but the idea was to create a sequence of wins and losses based on post position. However, any variable could be used (a horse's weight, the jockey, and so forth). Then after enough data is collected, just apply the given test and hope for a non-random discovery. (Be cautious, though. If you do enough tests, something eventually will appear non-random due to statistical variance. In this case, it may be best to collect more data to see whether the pattern continues.)

Non-Self-Weighting
Poker Ideas

As I've noted, the idea of non-self-weighting strategies is a little-known but important concept that is extremely applicable in the world of gambling, especially if your game is poker. Once again, a self-weighting gambling experience is when your expectation and variance are the same from play to play. When this is not the case, the number of plays that are made is statistically reduced. That is, your risk is increased.

Let's look at some ideas on this subject as they apply to poker.

Idea No. 1: The non-self-weighting player. We all like to play against a "loose opponent,"which is usually defined as someone who plays too many hands. But this definition is not completely accurate. A true loose player also has a predictable and consistently passive style of play. Simply put, if he makes his usual call, he is probably weak; if he raises, he is probably strong. On the end, he will bluff only rarely, will not value bet much, will call frequently, and will be fairly easy to manipulate. In other words, a self-weighting player has just been described. Not only is he mathematically entering a lot of pots, but also statistically playing a lot of hands.

Occasionally, you will encounter players whose game may seem bizarre. They appear to play a lot of hands, and they raise and reraise when it doesn't seem warranted. On the end, they often can successfully bet hands that a "good" player would know to check. If you are up against one of these players and are not careful, you can find yourself calling raised and reraised pots with hands you normally would not play, as well as calling on the end with junk. As an example, how many of you California lowball players, when you've missed your draw, have called a player who raps pat and bets, only to discover that you were right about his hand being weak, but you still lost anyway.

What has happened is that you have run into a non-self-weighting player. Even though he has entered a lot of pots, statistically speaking, he is not playing that many hands since his results often cluster around those few hands where a lot of bets are made. Also notice that you are against a player over whom you have little control.

In an early issue of *Poker Player,*[4] the late, former World Champion Jack Strauss was quoted as saying that he plays many more hands than the poker books recommend. Somehow, I do not think Mr. Strauss fit the mold of the loose player you would want to invite to the Friday night poker game.

Idea No. 2: The non-self-weighting game. Many of these same ideas also apply to poker games. Consider straight limit games — that is, games where the bet on the end is the same as the initial bet. The structure of this game does not allow a player much creativity. Consequently, everyone is more predictable, and the overall game is roughly self-weighting. You can approach these games with a mechanical style and still have much success.

On the other hand, large no-limit games are very non-self-weighting. One or two successful plays a night can mean a large win for the skilled player. The self-weighting strategy of calling too many bets in these games can be disastrous. Similarly, be aware that games in which the stakes increase progressively or the pots can be killed are also non-self-weighting. Here your results often will cluster about the few big hands where you become "committed," or when you can get your opponent to chase in a situation where he has practically no chance of winning.

---

[4]Unfortunately, *Poker Player* ceased publication in 1987.

Idea No. 3: Non-self weighting bets. In limit poker, mistakes that cost you an extra bet or fail to get that extra bet for you are not always that important. It's true that these types of errors add up in the long run, but in reality, you are costing yourself only a mathematical fraction of a bet every time you commit one of these errors. However, mistakes that cost you a whole pot can be disastrous, and one of the major skills in poker is to get your opponent to make these types of mistakes against you while you do not make the same mistakes against him. An example from limit hold'em is to raise on the turn (fourth street) with a small pair and a flush draw, trying to get your opponent to fold. If your opponent does fold, he has made a significant non-self-weighting error. If your opponent calls, you have made only a small self-weighting mistake, since there are still a lot of cards that can make your hand.

Another thing to keep in mind is that these types of plays tend to confuse most of the people that you will be up against. This often means that your opponents will become less aggressive against you, which is the same as making your opponents more self-weighting. Obviously, this is a desirable result of your non-self-weighting strategy.

Final comment. As stated previously, non-self-weighting strategies are without a doubt the most important concept in all of gambling. The only games that can be beat are non-self-weighting games where successful non-self-weighting strategies exist. This includes blackjack, backgammon, pyramid games, and — of course — poker. There is another way of stating this important idea: The skilled poker player (or gambler) "makes the most of it when he has the best of it." This is what all serious gamblers, no matter what their game, should constantly be striving for.

Gambling Theory
Afterthought

As stated in the essays, the most important idea in all successful gambling is the concept of non-self-weighting strategies. There is not anything else that is even close. Yet my experience has shown that the typical gambler is more interested in being in action than in formulating a winning approach, and he will not take the time nor make the effort to become successful.

Also, as already pointed out in this book, winning play is not easy, simply because following a correct non-self-weighting approach can be outright boring at times. Being in action is much more fun than just watching, but it also can be costly. Always remember to think in terms of a non-self-weighting approach not only to gambling, but as the essays point out, to many life decisions as well.

In addition, be prepared to think through new ideas and to review and update old ones. Try to view the gambling world as a world of constant flux, where new ideas and updated old ones may present opportunities. But do understand that there is an underlying theme to successful gambling, and that theme is the concept of successful non-self-weighting strategies.

However, following correct non-self-weighting strategies can be frustrating due to the large amount of risk that is involved. Keep in mind that this approach has the statistical effect of reducing the mathematical sample size. This means, as we shall see in the next section, that the standard deviation — a statistical measure of dispersion — is often much greater than what most gamblers think.

Part Two
Theory in Practice

Theory in Practice

Introduction

Many things happen at the "very exciting gaming tables" that at first appear to be inconsistent with what we know should happen. For example, you can have much the best of it yet suffer a substantial loss. This is simply because risk is involved, and unless you have a good understanding of what the risk is, you are destined not necessarily to be a loser, but at least to get into trouble every now and then.

Other things happen that appear to defy logic. Some people always seem to win more than their share, while others, who should be big winners, have trouble holding on to their bankrolls.

This section discusses these ideas and helps explain why certain things happen all the time that many people believe should not happen at all. We will look not only at statistical reasons for why these events occur but at practical reasons as well.

I have been told on several occasions that it is "Impossible" to measure luck. Even though most gamblers believe this, statistical techniques are available that allow us to do exactly that. Specifically, luck can be measured, and these measurements — which are quantified by the statistical standard deviation — should play a major role in many of the decisions that we make.

Fluctuations

Suppose you are an expert gambler. Perhaps you are a poker player, perhaps you are a blackjack card counter, or perhaps you are highly skilled at some other game. It really doesn't matter where your expertise lies, but let's assume that you are good enough to win at a rate of $50 per hour in some hypothetical game. The problem is that you won't win $50 every hour you play. Sometimes you will do better, and sometimes you will do worse (and perhaps even lose). It so happens that there is another measure besides the expected win rate that should be important to you, the winning gambler. This measure is the (statistical) standard deviation.

The standard deviation is a statistical measure of dispersion, and most statisticians agree that for all practical purposes, the total population of possible results is contained within three standard deviations of the mean. For example, suppose your $50 an hour win rate is accompanied by a $500 per hour standard deviation. In this case, a $1,500 swing — either up or down — in an hour is not to be unexpected in your hypothetical game. No wonder some people seem incredibly lucky while others complain that they have been "running bad."

Let's now suppose that you, the expert, play your favorite game for 100 hours. Your expectation after this length of time should be $5,000.

$$5,000 = (50)(100)$$

However, as just seen, there is a good chance that you won't win exactly $5,000. You might do better or you might do worse. It turns out that the standard deviation of a sample mean is inversely proportional to the square root of the sample size.

That is, after 100 hours, we divide the per-hour standard deviation by 10 (the square root of 100) to get 50.

$$50 = \frac{(500)}{(10)}$$

This means that you could be losing as much as $100 per hour or winning as much as $200 per hour.

$$-100 = 50 - (3)(50)$$
$$200 = 50 + (3)(50)$$

Imagine you, the expert, playing for 100 hours and being down $10,000. Well, it definitely can happen.

Here's another example for the same hypothetical game. Suppose you have two break-even players, each of whom is experiencing this $500 per hour standard deviation. After 100 hours, it is actually possible for one of these players to be ahead $15,000 and for the other person to be behind by the very same amount.

Even though a $500 per hour standard deviation coupled with a $50 per hour win rate may appear high, these sorts of results are typical for expert gamblers who follow aggressive non-self-weightingstrategies available to them and who expect to do well in the long run. It's just a fact of life. If you correctly gamble for profit — and it doesn't matter whether your game is poker, blackjack, sports betting, real estate, stocks, commodities, backgammon, progressive slot machines, or something else — there will be times when your bankroll will jump up and down, and there isn't much you can do about it. In fact, we shall see that what is extremely important is the relationship between your expectation and the standard deviation that you are experiencing. Knowing one parameter without knowing the other often will lead to disastrous decisions, especially if just the expectation is known.

However, before addressing this, let's analyze one stream of thought that occupies much of the gambling literature dealing with this area. This concept is known as money management, but I prefer to call it "the extremely silly subject of money management." It is discussed in the next chapter.

The Extremely Silly Subject of Money Management

I see the silly words "money management" in print all the time. I'm sure you also have read that if you don't have good money management skills, you can't win and should expect to go broke. Also that money management will enable you to beat all sorts of games, such as roulette, craps, slot machines — you name it. That's what the majority of gamblers will tell you, and many pseudo authorities profess that this is the most important aspect of gambling. But as you will see, I don't agree with this. In fact, nothing could be further from the truth. Now I'm not the first to say it, but I hate money management. I hate it because it is a bunch of junk.

The theme of money management constantly seems to be on the minds of losers. But here is an absolute truth: If you are a loser and keep gambling, you will lose it all no matter how you handle your money. Anyone who tells you otherwise is wrong. If this were not the case, there wouldn't be so many large casinos in Nevada, in New Jersey, and throughout the world.

One well-known gambling book recommends in its large money management section only to play those games where the house has no more than a small advantage. The author "smartly" rules out games like roulette and keno. But if you play only games like craps and baccarat, and play them long enough, you are assured of losing. So why play them at all?

One possible reason for playing games with a low house percentage is that these bets really don't cost very much and you can maximize your time at the "very exciting gaming tables." But is this really true? Well, suppose you compare baccarat to keno. Where do you lose your money faster? At baccarat, the house has an edge of slightly more than 1 percent, while at keno the casino's advantage is approximately 30 percent. The problem is that you can get more bets down at the baccarat table in a specified period of time than you can sitting in a keno lounge. So it seems to me that you actually might be better off playing keno, even though the house edge in this game is astronomical.

Here are two other important facts. First, there is no mathematical formula that tells you when you have won enough money to quit, and second, there is no mathematical formula that tells you when you have lost enough money to quit. Nevertheless, these kinds of statements appear in print all the time.

Now at the poker table, I do use some guidelines to help me whether I should continue playing. Mike Caro has pointed out that when you are losing, your opponents no longer fear you and you can become a target. For example, someone who normally would almost never bluff may now take a shot that costs you a pot. The opposite is also true. When you are winning, your opponents will fear you more and play more predictably against you, making the game easier to beat. My experience agrees with this, and I use these powerful ideas to help me determine whether to stay in a particular game. If I am "running good" and appear to have good control in the game, but I'm not sure if the game is worth staying in anymore (perhaps a couple of weak players have been replaced by strong ones), I will continue playing. I will quit the game if I am losing, especially if it appears that I have lost control over my opponents. Notice that my decision is influenced by psychological reasons. I don't quit or stay because I have either lost or won some predetermined amount of money. I try to make an on-the-spot analysis of the game that I am playing, and in close decisions, my analysis is influenced by how I am doing.

Another money management concept is that you never should risk your entire bankroll at one sitting. It is often recommended that you split your bankroll into mini-bankrolls and risk only one of these mini-bankrolls at a playing session. But let's stop and think for a moment. Suppose you make a $10 bet. Does it matter whether you have $200 or $2,000 on the table? Of course not. (This is not completely true in poker,

35

especially in no-limit poker where a raise might jeopardize all your chips.) On the other hand, splitting your bankroll into several smaller "session" bankrolls is not incorrect. This is a personal matter. Lots of mini-bankrolls are neither better nor worse than one huge bankroll. It is true that the mini-bankroll approach might stop a player from "steaming," but the highly skilled players don't suffer much from this problem. That is, poor play — not a little bad luck — is usually the reason people steam.

Stop losses also can force your strategy into a "tournament mode." For example, suppose you are playing poker and are almost at your stop loss point. This means that you now may be compelled to play hands that your normal strategy would have you throw away, simply because you are afraid that if you don't play them, the blinds and antes may "eat you up." Consequently, the "extremely silly subject of money management" has stopped you from playing your normal best game.

The last money management idea that I want to attack is the concept that you need some minimum amount of money to play a particular game. It has been pointed out that there are two groups of gamblers, the plodders and the adventurers. Let's discuss them. (I'm not the first to write about the plodders and the adventurers. See *Caro on Gambling* by Mike Caro.)

A plodder is a conservative gambler who is satisfied with a small but steady income. An adventurer is a gambler with a lot of heart — a person who isn't satisfied with the status quo. Adventurers are also in and out of money. Sometimes they go broke, but sometimes they hit it big.

I tend to be a plodder. I don't like taking big risks, even though occasionally I will take a shot at something. I simply don't relish going broke. But many of the great and famous poker players are adventurers. Anyone who has read *The Biggest Game in Town* by A. Alvarez knows that some of the biggest names in poker have turned over literally millions of dollars. There is nothing wrong with this. It is obviously the way these people prefer to gamble.

Let me give an example. I have a friend who is extremely knowledgeable in the field of mathematical statistics. He also has become a fairly good poker player. In addition, he is quite an adventurer. A couple of years before hold'em and stud became legal in California, my friend found himself temporarily broke after a bad run in the $100-$200 lowball game at the Bicycle Club in Bell Gardens. This didn't bother him in the least. After resting for a day, he took $30 and started playing the smallest game in the house. My friend liked to say that he was probably "the only player in California who has played both the $100 blind and the $1 blind." After a couple of days, he took $250 into a $3-$6 lowball game and ran it up to $600. The next day, my friend was playing $15-$30 lowball. If you are much more conservative, which I recommend, you might want at least 10 times the amount of money my friend, The Adventurer, had to sit in a game this size. Yet being an adventurer, he was more than willing to take this risk. In just three weeks, he turned $30 into more than $12,000. Many of us told him that if he kept winning, he would have enough money to play the game that he was currently in.

The money managers would react to this story with horror. They would quickly point out that risking one's total bankroll at the $100-$200 level was a big mistake. Moreover, they would never allow someone to increase his bankroll by a factor of 400, which was exactly how much my friend's bank went up in three weeks from the $30 point. Although I don't recommend this type of adventurous approach, there is nothing necessarily wrong with it. Remember, the type of risk you want to take is purely a personal matter, so you should do what makes you feel the most comfortable. Just be able to face going broke if you do make large bets in relation to your bankroll.

One area where money management does come into play is in tournaments. It turns out that in poker tournaments, there are correct fast play/survival strategies that are in a sense related to money management schemes (see Part Four of this book). Also, Stanford Wong has shown in his excellent books on tournament craps and tournament blackjack that the correct

37

approach is again somewhat related to a money management scheme that causes you either to go broke quickly or to score a big win.

In conclusion, I do agree with a few ideas that the money managers espouse. For example, the bigger the game you play, the larger your bank should be in terms of betting units. This is because a wipeout at a high level is generally much more painful than a wipeout at a low level. Nevertheless, money risked is a personal matter, and there is nothing wrong with not following this advice. Let me put it this way: *Money management is not a "profit skill"* and *the serious gambler is much better off spending his time thinking about appropriate non-self-weighting strategies than worrying about the malicious "double M."*

We will talk more about some of these ideas later in this book and we will see how important it is to keep things "in balance," something that most money managers are not even aware of.

Special Note From Mike Caro

The following essay by Mason Malmuth will make you think about your bankroll in important new ways. The most frequent questions I am asked are "How much money does it take to win?" and "How big does your bankroll need to be?"

Tough questions. Yet to plan your bankroll requirements, you must decide what constitutes an acceptable risk. Do you seek almost absolute safety? A 95 percent chance of success? A 50 percent chance of success? Naturally, the smaller the degree of acceptable risk you choose, the more money you need.

Your bankroll requirements are determined by both the amount of money you expect to earn each hour and the degree of difference you reasonably can expect from one hour to the next. I recommend that you study Malmuth's explanation of this concept and pay close attention to the accompanying charts, which are very revealing.

There may be times when survival will mean more to you than increasing your hourly average. This means that you sometimes must sacrifice advanced techniques that add to your expectation in order to choose a safer, though less profitable, strategy.

If you don't have a winning expectation, there's no possibility of managing your money profitably. It most likely will require more money than you expect to guarantee survival.

There is one other fascinating truth that you should be aware of: A player who theoretically earns $45 an hour in a given game may have a better chance of survival than a player who wins $55 an hour. This is because in a game like poker, the expert's edge of that extra $10 an hour is achieved through tricks and techniques that carry a high risk. These may be image plays, or they may be extra raises that add only pennies to the overall expectation. In fact, the final advantages that a world-class player has over a lesser player are mostly high risk.

Think about this after reading Malmuth's essay. You'll see why great players sometimes need bigger bankrolls than good players just to survive.

How Much Do You Need?

At the Bicycle Club in Bell Gardens, California, they have a $30-$60 ace-to-five lowball game that I have played in many times. The game has a straddle structure. There is no ante, but there are three traveling blinds. The dealer puts up $10, the first person to the dealer's left puts up $20, and the second person to the dealer's left puts up $30. The bring-in bet is $60, all raises before the draw are in $30 increments, and all bets and raises after the draw are in $60 dollar increments. In addition, any player who has won two pots in a row must "kill the pot," or a player can look at the first two cards and then kill. For those of you unfamiliar with kills, let's just say for now that this effectively doubles the stakes. (For those interested in more information on the subject of killing the pot, see my book *Winning Concepts in Draw and Lowball*.) Finally, as in most lowball games in California, the deck contains a joker that counts as the lowest card not already in your hand.

What I have just described is a very volatile game. All players, whether they are skilled or not, will see large fluctuations in this or any other lowball game. So the question now arises of how much money you need to play. This question is asked over and over again, and usually leads to many irrelevant theories that come under the general heading of money management. Even though, I am not a fan of "the extremely silly subject of money management," this section will build on other ideas discussed previously and will attempt to answer the question of how much money is required to play a particular poker game. (Similar analyses could be applied to other forms of gambling.) As far as I know, at least for the game of poker, this type of analysis has never before been presented correctly in print.

The discussion that follows will benefit only those of you who are winning players. If you are a loser, and you keep playing, expect to go broke. As pointed out in the previous essay, this will happen whether you have stop loss rules, stop win rules, mini-bankroll rules, time limits, sleep requirements, and so on. The only way you won't lose it all is if you quit gambling. If you keep coming back, even though you may have some winning streaks, you can expect all of your money to eventually disappear.

The amount of money needed to play a particular game is predicated on two parameters and the appropriate relationship between them. The first is your win rate, and the second is your standard deviation in the game itself. Let's define these parameters in detail.

The win rate is simply your expectation over some period of time. It can be positive (if you are a winner) or negative (if you are a loser). Most people, including myself, like to measure win rates in hourly increments. As previously stated, even though your win rate may be some specific figure, you cannot expect to win that amount every hour. In fact, some hours you will do significantly better than your win rate, while (unfortunately) other hours you will do significantly worse. This leads to the next parameter, the standard deviation.

How much your results will vary from your expectation is measured by the (statistical) standard deviation, which is also the square root of the variance. As already noted, it turns out that one's results almost always will fall within three standard deviations of his expectation (for reasonably large sample sizes).

To estimate these parameters, you need to keep detailed records of your performance when you are in action. Many people have a fairly good idea of what their win rates are. Almost no one has any idea of what his standard deviations are, even though for many people, this parameter is just as important — or even more important than the expectation. Also, keep in mind that both parameters may vary based on your style of play, the rules that are enforced, and the skill of your opponents.

While playing at the Bicycle Club, where some of the best ace-to-five lowball action in California (or anywhere, for that matter) is continuously spread, Mark Weitzman kept meticulous records of his results in the big games. The standard deviation that he achieved for one-hour increments at the various lowball games is presented in Table I.

Table I: Standard Deviation For One-Hour
Increments at Various Lowball Games

Game	Standard Deviation
$15-$30	250
$30-$60	650
$50-$100	1,100
$75-$150	1,500
$100-$200	2,500

These are results obtained by a highly skilled player. Even though no two players will have the same results, most skilled aggressive players, who follow correct non-self-weighting strategies, should be in the same ballpark.

But how many hours must you play to guarantee that you will be a winner. To estimate this, you must know your win rate and your standard deviation, as well as understand that the standard deviation of a total is equal to the square root of your sample size multiplied by your standard deviation for the individual time increment. What does that mean? Let's look at an example.

Suppose you are a $30-$60 lowball player and have the standard deviation given in Table I — that is, $650 per hour — and your hourly expectation is $30. (By the way, you must be a fairly good player to win at the rate of $30 per hour, since this is your profit after paying collection and tips, which easily can cost up to $20 per hour in this game.) Then the number of hours that you need to play to assure a profit is given by the following equation:

$$(WR)(N) - (3)(\sigma)(N)^{1/2} = 0$$

where
WR is your win rate,
N is the required number of hours, and
σ is the appropriate standard deviation.

Solving for N, we get:

$$N = \left[\frac{(3)(\sigma)}{(WR)} \right]^2$$

And using the parameters mentioned, we see that you, a highly skilled player, need to play \$30-\$60 lowball for a total of 4,225 hours to assure a win.

$$4,225 = \left[\frac{(3)(650)}{(30)} \right]^2$$

This is easily more than two years of play and is without a doubt one of the most disturbing statistics I've ever seen. In short, you may be a highly skilled, winning player, but if you play ace-to-five lowball, it is possible to have a two-year losing streak. No wonder so many people complain about running bad.

Table II shows the different number of hours required to assure a win, given different win rates associated with different standard deviations.

Table II: Number of Hours Needed to Assure a Win

Win Rate	Standard Deviation				
	100	250	500	650	1,000
5	3,600	22,500	90,000	152,100	360,000
10	900	5,625	22,500	38,025	90,000
20	225	1,406	5,625	9,506	22,500
30	100	625	2,500	4,225	10,000
40	56	352	1,406	2,377	5,625
50	36	225	900	1,521	3,600
75	16	100	400	676	1,600
100	9	56	225	380	900
150	4	25	100	169	400
200	2	14	56	95	225

Table II: Number of Hours Needed to Assure a Win (Con't)

Win Rate	Standard Deviation				
	1,100	1,500	2,000	2,500	5,000
5	435,600	810,000	1,440,000	2,250,000	9,000,000
10	108,900	202,500	360,000	562,500	2,250,000
20	27,225	50,625	90,000	140,625	562,500
30	12,100	22,500	40,000	62,500	250,000
40	6,806	12,656	22,500	35,156	140,625
50	4,356	8,100	14,400	22,500	90,000
75	1,936	3,600	6,400	10,000	40,000
100	1,089	2,205	3,600	5,625	22,500
150	484	900	1,600	2,500	10,000
200	272	506	900	1,406	5,625

The next logical question to ask is, "How big must our bankroll be to assure that we don't go broke?" Let's look at the given equation in a slightly different form:

$$LL = (WR)(N) - (3)(\sigma)(N)^{\frac{1}{2}}$$

where LL is the lower limit, and all other symbols are the same as before.

What the equation provides is the lower limit of what our results may be. We need to find the correct number of hours, N, for a particular win rate and standard deviation, that minimizes (makes the most negative) the lower limit. Using some simple calculus, this is done by taking the first derivative of the equation with respect to N, setting it equal to zero, and solving for N. Then, once the correct number of hours is found, this number can be substituted back into the lower-limit equation, producing the desired result.

The first derivative of the lower-limit equation is as follows:

$$0 = WR - (3)(\tfrac{1}{2})(\sigma)(N)^{-\frac{1}{2}}$$

Solving for N, we get:

$$N = \left[\frac{(3)(\sigma)}{(2)(WR)} \right]^2$$

Again, looking at the example of the $30-$60 lowball player with a $30 per hour expectation and a $650 per hour standard deviation, we see that his maximum deficit can occur at 1,056 hours.

$$\frac{(3)(650)}{(2)(30)}\Bigg]^2$$

: lower-limit equation, we find
uired to assure oneself of never

$$5) - (3)(650)(1,056)^{\frac{1}{2}}$$

Table III gives bankroll requirements to assure a win for different win rates and different standard deviations.

Table III: Bankroll Required to Assure a win

Win Rate	Standard Deviation				
	100	250	500	650	1,000
5	4,500	28,125	112,500	190,125	450,000
10	2,250	14,063	56,250	95,063	225,000
20	1,125	7,031	28,125	47,531	112,500
30	750	4,688	18,750	31,688	75,000
40	563	3,516	14,063	23,766	56,250
50	450	2,813	11,250	19,013	45,000
75	300	1,875	7,500	12,675	30,000
100	225	1,406	5,625	9,506	22,500
150	150	938	3,750	6,338	15,000
200	113	703	2,813	4,753	11,250

Table III: Bankroll Required to Assure a Win (Con't)

Win Rate	Standard Deviation				
	1,100	1,500	2,000	2,500	5,000
5	544,500	1,012,500	1,800,000	2,812,500	11,250,000
10	272,250	506,250	900,000	1,406,250	5,625,000
20	136,125	253,125	450,000	703,125	2,812,500
30	90,750	168,750	300,000	468,750	1,875,000
40	68,063	126,563	225,000	351,563	1,406,250
50	54,450	101,250	180,000	281,250	1,125,000
75	36,300	67,500	120,000	187,500	750,000
100	27,225	50,625	90,000	140,625	562,500
150	18,150	33,750	60,000	93,750	375,000
200	13,613	25,313	45,000	70,313	281,250

Tables II and III give us the figures for when there is essentially no risk involved. But some winning players are willing to assume a small risk, perhaps 5 percent. These results are given in Tables IV and V. The difference is that 1.64 standard deviations is now used in the calculations instead of 3 standard deviations.

Table IV: Number of Hours Needed for a 95% Chance to Win

Win Rate	Standard Deviation				
	100	250	500	650	1,000
5	1,076	6,724	26,896	45,454	107,584
10	269	1,681	6,724	11,364	26,896
20	67	420	1,681	2,841	6,724
30	30	187	747	1,263	2,988
40	17	105	420	710	1,681
50	11	67	269	455	1,076
75	5	30	120	202	478
100	3	17	67	114	269
150	1	7	30	51	120
200	1	4	17	28	67

Table IV: Number of Hours Needed for a 95% Chance to Win (Con't)

Win Rate	Standard Deviation				
	1,100	1,500	2,000	2,500	5,000
5	130,177	242,064	430,336	672,400	2,689,000
10	32,544	60,516	107,584	168,100	672,400
20	8,136	15,129	26,896	42,025	168,100
30	3,616	6,724	11,954	18,678	74,711
40	2,034	3,782	6,724	10,506	42,025
50	1,302	2,421	4,303	6,724	26,896
75	579	1,076	1,913	2,988	11,954
100	325	605	1,076	1,681	6,724
150	145	269	478	747	2,988
200	81	151	269	420	1,681

Table V: Bankroll Required to Assure a 95% Chance to Win

Win Rate	Standard Deviation				
	100	250	500	650	1,000
5	1,345	8,405	33,620	56,818	134,480
10	672	4,203	16,810	28,409	67,240
20	336	2,101	8,405	14,204	33,620
30	224	1,401	5,603	9,470	22,413
40	168	1,051	4,203	7,102	16,810
50	134	841	3,362	5,682	13,448
75	90	560	2,241	3,788	8,965
100	67	420	1,681	2,841	6,724
150	45	280	1,121	1,894	4,483
200	34	210	841	1,420	3,362

Table V: Bankroll Required to Assure a 95% Chance to Win (Con't)

Win Rate	Standard Deviation				
	1,100	1,500	2,000	2,500	5,000
5	162,721	302,580	537,920	840,500	3,362,000
10	81,360	151,290	268,960	420,250	1,681,000
20	40,680	75,645	134,480	210,125	840,500
30	27,120	50,430	89,653	140,083	560,333
40	20,340	37,823	67,240	105,063	420,250
50	16,272	30,258	53,792	84,050	336,200
75	10,848	20,172	35,861	56,033	224,133
100	8,136	15,129	26,896	42,025	168,100
150	5,424	10,086	17,931	28,017	112,067
200	4,068	7,565	13,448	21,013	84,050

What does all of this mean? Well, if you are a professional player and bankroll preservation is of highest importance, a good chance exists that you are playing in a game too big for you, even if you are considered to be an expert at that form of poker. I believe this is why many skilled players go broke at different times during their careers and why so many other players who should be winners have problems controlling their emotions and constantly "steam" their money away.

Something else to keep in mind is that your win rate and standard deviation do not remain constant. For example, when you are running bad in a game, it usually encourages opponents to take shots at you, and these shots generally cost you money. That is, your win rate temporarily goes down, and your standard deviation temporarily goes up. The opposite also can happen. Notice that what I have just described is a non-self-weighting effect, and as already pointed out, non-self-weighting effects are statistically equivalent to reducing the sample size. In plain English, the numbers given in the tables may actually be too small. By how much I don't know, but the serious player may want to increase his bankroll allocations by 20 percent to 30 percent.

What about games other than lowball draw? Based on consultations with several knowledgeable people, I believe that the strong aggressive player would have about 75 percent of the fluctuations given in Table I when playing high draw, jacks or better to open; 100 percent to 180 percent of the fluctuations in seven-card stud, depending on the limit (the higher limits have a proportionately higher ante structure, which leads to greater fluctuations); 90 percent to 130 percent of the fluctuations in Texas hold'em;[5] 100 percent to 130 percent of the fluctuations in seven-card razz, depending on the limit; and

---

[5]This estimate is higher than that given in previous editions. The reason for this is that in some middle-limit hold'em games, a great deal of money goes into the pot before the flop. In these hold'em games, you will have higher fluctuations than in seven-card stud games of the same limit.

280 percent of the fluctuations in Omaha hold'em. These percentages refer only to limit games.

So if you play, for example, $30-$60 stud, you should experience a standard deviation approximately 40 percent higher than that given in Table I. Thus the estimated standard deviation is would be 910.

$$910 = (1.40)(650)$$

If your win rate in this game is $30 per hour, Table III tells us that you need less than $75,000 (the value that corresponds to a standard deviation of $1,000) to assure that you never go broke. Perhaps $65,000 would be about right. But remember that this estimate does not account for the non-self weighting effect. Consequently, a bankroll of at least $78,000 may be more appropriate.

Another point that needs to be made is that the various tables assume no removal of dollars from the system. So if you conclude that $5,000 is an appropriate bankroll and you now win $100, this $100 must not be removed from your bankroll. If you remove winnings, your level of risk will be higher. This is because some of the "paths" that allow you to stay in money take into account early wins, especially the tables that provide figures for a 95 percent chance to win.

What about pot-limit and no-limit games? No specific estimates of the standard deviations will be given, simply because there are so many variables that can come into play. But suffice it to say that the standard deviation for pot-limit games is significantly higher than for limit games, and the standard deviation for no-limit games is probably significantly higher than for pot-limit games. This is obvious when you realize that your results over a long period of time can be dominated by just one or two hands in which a major confrontation has occurred.

By the way, if you are an expert player, no-limit poker does not necessarily require a larger bankroll than limit poker. Remember, your required bankroll should be determined by the relationship between your expected win rate and your standard deviation. Specifically, if your win rate is significantly higher in no-limit than it is in limit, you actually may need a smaller bankroll than what some limit games require. (This is often the case for expert players, since the edges they can achieve over typical players are usually much larger.)

In summary, for the first time, you now should be able to estimate your bankroll requirements for most games that you are interested in playing. I'm sure that many people will discover they are playing in games where their bankrolls are at risk. But as stated earlier, this is a personal matter. Even so, many people who thought they were playing it safe will find out that they actually were in significant danger. Keep in mind that if bankroll preservation is important to you, many games that appear attractive from an expectation point of view may in fact be too dangerous to play.

What About the Losers?

The previous essay furnished bankroll requirements for winning players in different games. Put another way, it illustrated how badly a winning player can run in various poker games. The opposite is also true. A losing player can run good for reasonably short periods of time and will appear to be a big winner. Of course, the loser will lose it all in the long run. But for a given session or sessions, he actually can do quite well, and these winning periods can last a long time. The reason for this is that in all forms of poker (and in almost all other forms of gambling as well), the standard deviation is much larger than the absolute value of the expectation.

Suppose someone is playing in the $30-$60 lowball game discussed earlier, but instead of being a $30 per hour winner, he is now a $30 per hour loser. How well might he do in the short run? (Remember, this game has a $650 per hour standard deviation.) Since for practical purposes his results will be within three standard deviations of the mean, we have the following upper-limit equation for a short period of time:

$$UL = (WR)(N) + (3)(\sigma)(N)^{\frac{1}{2}} = 0$$

where
      UL is the upper limit,
      WR is your win rate,
      N is the appropriate number of hours, and
      σ is the appropriate standard deviation.

Assuming the loser plays a total of 10 hours, he can be ahead by as much as $5,866.

$$5{,}866 = (-30)(10) + (3)(650)(10)^{\frac{1}{2}}$$

If this person plays for 100 hours, he can be ahead by as much as $16,500.

$$16{,}500 = (-30)(100) + (3)(650)(100)^{\frac{1}{2}}$$

And if he plays for 1,000 hours, it is theoretically possible for him to be ahead by $31,664.

$$31{,}664 = (-30)(1{,}000) + (3)(650)(1{,}000)^{\frac{1}{2}}$$

Of course, if this person keeps playing, he eventually will become a loser. This is seen by the equation that follows, where he has played for 10,000 hours and the best he can expect is to be behind by at least $105,000.

$$-105{,}000 = (-30)(10{,}000) + (3)(650)(10{,}000)^{\frac{1}{2}}$$

What this means is that the standard deviation — especially for those games where it is large for relatively small periods of time compared to the win or loss rates that players achieve — can play havoc in the short run with the expected distribution of results. Also, as the equations show, it can take a very long time to get into the long run.

So how well can a bad player do? Tables I, II, and III give the upper limit, based on three standard deviations, for different loss rates and for different standard deviations. Table

55

I is for 10 hours of play, Table II is for 100 hours of play, and Table III is for 1,000 hours of play.

Table I: Upper Limit Based on 10 Hours of Play

Loss Rate	Standard Deviation				
	100	250	500	650	1,000
5	899	2,322	4,693	6,116	9,437
10	849	2,272	4,643	6,066	9,387
20	749	2,172	4,543	5,966	9,287
30	649	2,072	4,443	5,866	9,187
40	549	1,972	4,343	5,766	9,087
50	449	1,872	4,243	5,666	8,987
75	199	1,622	3,993	5,416	8,737
100	51	1,372	3,743	5,166	8,487
150	-551	872	3,243	4,666	7,987
200	-1,051	371	2,743	4,166	7,487

Table I: Upper Limit Based on 10 Hours of Play (Con't)

Loss Rate	Standard Deviation				
	1,100	1,500	2,000	2,500	5,000
5	10,386	14,180	18,924	23,667	47,384
10	10,336	14,130	18,874	23,617	47,334
20	10,236	14,030	18,774	23,517	47,234
30	10,136	13,930	18,674	23,417	47,134
40	10,036	13,830	18,574	23,317	47,034
50	9,936	13,730	18,474	23,217	46,934
75	9,686	13,480	18,224	22,967	46,684
100	9,436	13,230	17,974	22,717	46,434
150	8,935	12,730	17,474	22,217	45,934
200	8,435	12,230	16,974	21,717	45,434

Table II: Upper Limit Based on 100 Hours of Play

Loss Rate	Standard Deviation				
	100	250	500	650	1,000
5	2,500	7,000	14,500	19,000	29,500
10	2,000	6,500	14,000	18,500	29,000
20	1,000	5,500	13,000	17,500	28,000
30	0	4,500	12,000	16,500	27,000
40	-1,000	3,500	11,000	15,500	26,000
50	-2,000	2,500	10,000	14,500	25,000
75	-4,500	0	7,500	12,000	22,500
100	-7,000	-2,500	5000	9,500	20,000
150	-12,000	-7,500	0	4,500	15,000
200	-17,000	-12,500	-5,000	-500	10,000

Table II: Upper Limit Based on 100 Hours of Play (Con't)

Loss Rate	Standard Deviation				
	1,100	1,500	2,000	2,500	5,000
5	32,500	44,500	59,500	74,500	149,500
10	32,000	44,000	59,000	74,000	149,000
20	31,000	43,000	58,000	73,000	148,000
30	30,000	42,000	57,000	72,000	147,000
40	29,000	41,000	56,000	71,000	146,000
50	28,000	40,000	55,000	70,000	145,000
75	25,000	37,500	52,500	67,500	142,500
100	23,000	35,000	50,000	65,000	140,000
150	18,000	30,000	45,000	60,000	135,000
200	13,000	25,000	40,000	55,000	130,000

Table III: Upper Limit Based on 1,000 Hours of Play

Loss Rate	Standard Deviation				
	100	250	500	650	1,000
5	4,487	18,717	42,434	56,664	89,868
10	-513	13,717	37,434	51,664	84,868
20	-10,513	3,717	27,434	41,664	74,868
30	-20,513	-6,283	17,434	31,664	64,868
40	-30,513	-16,283	7,434	21,664	54,868
50	-40,513	-26,283	-2,566	11,664	44,868
75	-65,513	-51,283	-27,566	-13,336	19,868
100	-90,513	-76,283	-52,566	-38,336	-5,132
150	-140,513	-126,283	-102,566	-88,336	-55,132
200	-190,513	-176,283	-152,566	-138,336	-105,132

Table III: Upper Limit based on 1,000 Hours of Play (Con't)

Loss Rate	Standard Deviation				
	1,100	1,500	2,000	2,500	5,000
5	99,355	137,302	184,737	232,171	469,342
10	94,355	132,302	179,737	227,171	464,342
20	84,355	122,302	169,737	217,171	454,342
30	74,355	112,302	159,737	207,171	444,342
40	64,355	102,302	149,737	197,171	434,342
50	54,355	92,302	139,737	187,171	424,342
75	29,355	67,302	114,737	171,171	399,342
100	4,355	42,302	89,737	137,171	374,342
150	-45,645	-7,698	39,737	87,171	324,342
200	-95,645	-57,698	-10,263	37,171	274,342

The tables show many interesting things. One of them is that for very short periods of time, the standard deviation is much more important than your expectation in determining how you do. This can be seen from Table I (which is based on 10 hours of play), where the very bad player can do almost as well as anyone else. Another thing the tables show is that for many poker games, it may take a long time for what you expect to happen to begin to happen. (This is also true for many other forms of successful gambling.)

This fact results in some bad players thinking they are actually quite good. Consequently, they take their win, move up to higher stakes where the players are even better and their expectation is even worse, and quickly go broke. They never grasp the fact that they are losers. They just believe they were unlucky and cannot understand why they have suddenly done so poorly. They begin to think that the real reason they went broke was because of poor money management. And they fail to realize that in reality, they never had a chance.

One final note. Always keep in mind that the tables show the very best that a bad player can do. Results this good will happen only rarely. But the point is that because of the relatively large standard deviation that is present in almost all forms of gambling, all players — whether skilled or not — eventually will see their bankrolls go through some fairly large swings. This means that you need to be prepared for these swings, both monetarily and psychologically.

Computing Your Standard Deviation

Everyone plays poker differently, and no two poker games are identical. This means that no two skilled or unskilled players will have identical results. Specifically, no two players will have exactly the same win (or loss) rate, and no two players will have exactly the same standard deviation.

In the essay titled "How Much Do You Need?" standard deviations for different poker games were given based on one expert's playing results. You, the skilled player, should estimate your own standard deviation for the particular game or games that you play. In addition, this estimation should be updated every so often to account for natural changes — such as new players — that the games go through.

The easiest way I know to estimate your standard deviation is to use the following formula. This formula was derived by Mark Weitzman and is the maximum likelihood approximation for the standard deviation.

$$\sigma^2 = (1/N)\sum_{i=1}^{N} (X_i^2/T_i) - (U^2/N)\sum_{i=1}^{N} T_i$$

where
σ^2 is the variance,
N is the total number of plays,
X_i is the result of the ith play,
T_i is the length of time of the ith play,
U is the average result for one unit of time, and

$$U = \frac{\displaystyle\sum_{i=1}^{N} X^i}{\displaystyle\sum_{i=1}^{N} T^i},$$

the standard deviation is equal to the square root of the variance.

Now let's look at an example. Table I gives some results for 10 playing sessions. Incidentally, your standard deviation should be estimated from many more than 10 playing sessions. A good rule of thumb is to have at least 30 observations (playing sessions) for the estimate to be reasonably accurate. However, the more the better, unless for some reason you think the game for which you are trying to estimate your standard deviation has changed significantly over some particular period of time.

Table I: Results

Session	Result	Time
1	+48	3.5
2	+249	6.0
3	-71	4.5
4	+398	7.5
5	-173	2.5
6	-88	4.0
7	+301	5.5
8	+97	1.5
9	+229	4.0
10	-118	3.5

To compute the standard deviation, the following calculations are needed:

$$N = 10,$$

$$\sum_{i=1}^{10} X_i = (48+249-71+398-173-88+301+97+229-118) = 872,$$

$$\sum_{i=1}^{10} T_i = (3.5+6.0+4.5+7.5+2.5+4.0+5.5+1.5+4.0+3.5) = 42.5,$$

$$\sum_{i=1}^{10} \left[\frac{X_i^2}{T_i}\right] = \frac{48^2}{3.5} + \frac{249^2}{6.0} + \frac{-71^2}{4.5} + \frac{398^2}{7.5} + \frac{-173^2}{2.5} + \frac{-88^2}{4.0} + \frac{301^2}{5.5}$$

$$+ \frac{97^2}{1.5} + \frac{229^2}{4.0} + \frac{-118^2}{3.5} = 86,974$$

$$U = \frac{872}{42.5} = 20.52, \text{ and}$$

$$\sigma^2 = \left(\frac{1}{10}\right)(86,794) - \left[\frac{(20.52)^2}{10}\right](42.5) = 6,907.85$$

Consequently, the standard deviation is equal to 83.11, which is the square root of 6,907.85.

A few final notes. Let me first emphasize that 10 observations, as I have used in the example, is not enough to compute a reliable standard deviation. Use at least 30 observations. Second, for most poker games of any size, a standard deviation of 83.11 is not realistic. Expect a much larger number. Third, once you have computed your standard deviation, the techniques presented in the essay "How Much Do You Need?" can be applied to estimate what your bankroll requirements should be. Just remember to increase your estimate somewhat to account for the non-self-weighting effect. And fourth, remember to recompute your standard deviation every so often to account for changing game conditions.

Finally, although few people do these calculations, the results can be very important for most players. Admittedly, the calculations are a bit tedious, but I am certain you will find them most beneficial.

Win Rate Accuracy

Another related question that comes up is, "How accurate is my win rate?" I am constantly quoted very high win rates, some of which come from people who, in my opinion, don't play very well. Needless to say, statistically speaking, these win rates are never based on that many hours, so a large standard deviation is associated with them. My usual reply is, with the given win rate and the appropriate standard deviation associated with the game in question, "You still can be a loser."

Let's look at this question in more detail. Suppose a hypothetical player's win rate in some particular game is $30 per-hour, the estimated per hour standard deviation for this game is $500, and this person has a total of 400 hours of play. (This could be typical $20-$40 Texas hold'em results.) This means that the overall standard deviation based on 400 hours of play has been reduced to $25 per hour, since the overall standard deviation is inversely proportional to the square root of the sample size.

$$25 = \frac{(500)}{(400)^{\frac{1}{2}}}$$

Notice that even though it appears a lot of hours have been accrued in this game, the estimation of a $30 per hour win rate may not be even close. At three standard deviations, the true results are somewhere between losing at $45 per hour and winning at $105 per hour. At two standard deviations, representing a 95 percent confidence interval (two-tailed), we see that the correct result is somewhere between losing at $20 per hour and winning at $80 per hour.

Now suppose that this person wants to play more hours to cut his standard deviation in half. Since the overall standard deviation is proportional to the inverse of the square root of the sample size, four times the number of hours are needed. This is because the square root of four is two, and we now want to divide by an additional one-half. Specifically, to produce an overall standard deviation of $12.50 per hour, our hypothetical player would have to play an additional 1,200 hours, for a total of 1,600 hours in action.

Another related question is, "How many hours are needed to produce some particular overall standard deviation?" This can be found using the following equation:

$$N = \left[\frac{\sigma}{O(\sigma)} \right]^2$$

where
  N is the required number of hours,
  σ is the hourly standard deviation, and
  $o(\sigma)$ is the overall standard deviation.

Continuing with our example, if the hypothetical player wanted to reduce his overall standard deviation to $1 per hour, he would have to play 250,000 hours.

$$250,000 = \left[\frac{500}{1} \right]^2$$

We can conclude from this that (1) in some games, it may take a lifetime to find out exactly how well you play, and (2) just because you have had a good run does not mean that you have become an expert player. I also suspect that in many forms of poker, the expert player cannot win as much as many people think is correct.

What if You Play Blackjack?

The previous essays have shown that if you play poker, because of the relatively small expectation compared to the high standard deviation, large bankrolls are required to either assure survival or to give yourself a high probability of survival. The situation is similar for the game of blackjack (as it is for most forms of gambling). That is, for an expert card counter, blackjack has a high standard deviation compared to a relatively small expectation.

From Arnold Snyder's excellent book *The Blackjack Formula*, we know that the standard deviation for any given hand is approximately equal to the average bet size multiplied by 1.1, providing the betting spread is not too large. This information enables us to produce a lower-limit equation as follows:

$$LL = (ABS)(ADV)(N) - (3)(ABS)(1.1)(N)^{1/2}$$

where
      LL is the lower limit,
      ABS is the average bet size,
      ADV is the advantage, and
      N is the number of hands to be played.

Notice that the lower limit is being calculated at three standard deviations. This means that it is very unlikely for someone to do worse than this, since most statisticians agree that for practical purposes, the total population of possible results is contained within three standard deviations of the mean.

Let's suppose that a skilled player's average bet size is $25 and that he has a 1 percent advantage. If we set the lower-limit equation equal to zero and solve for N, we find that the number of hands that must be played to assure a win is achieved is 108,900.

$$0 = (25)(.01)(N) - (3)(25)(1.1)(N)^{1/2} \Rightarrow$$

$$N = \left[\frac{(3)(25)(1.1)}{(25)(.01)} \right]^2 = 108,900$$

Now suppose that our skilled player averages 100 hands per hour. This means that he must be prepared to play for 1,089 hours; otherwise, some possibility exists that he still can be a loser. Notice that this is about six months of full-time play.

Table I gives the different number of hours required, assuming 100 hands per hour, to assure a win. The size of the average bet does not matter.

Table I: Hours Needed to Assure a Win

Win Rate in %	Hours Required	Win Rate in %	Hours Required
0.1	108,900	1.0	1,089
0.2	27,225	1.1	900
0.3	12,100	1.2	756
0.4	6,806	1.3	644
0.5	4,356	1.4	556
0.6	3,025	1.5	484
0.7	2,222	1.75	356
0.8	1,702	2.0	272
0.9	1,344	2.5	174

As in the poker example, the next logical question to ask is, "How big must our bankroll be to assure that we don't go broke?" Again, let's take the first derivative with respect to N of the lower-limit equation, set it equal to zero, and then solve for N. This will give us the number of hands where our results can be at a minimum. Inserting this value for N back into the lower-limit equation will give us the desired information — that is, the bankroll required to assure that we don't go broke.

The first derivative, set equal to zero, of the lower-limit equation is as follows:

$$0 = (ABS)(ADV) - (3)(ABS)(1.1)(\tfrac{1}{2})N^{-\frac{1}{2}}$$

Solving for N, we get:

$$N = \left[\frac{(3)(1.1)}{(2)(ADV)} \right]^2$$

Looking at the example of the player whose average bet size is $25 per hand and who has a 1 percent advantage, we see that his maximum deficit can occur after 27,225 hands have been played.

$$27,225 = \left[\frac{(3)(1.1)}{(2)(.01)} \right]^2$$

Substituting this value into the lower-limit equation, we find that a bankroll of $6,806 is required to assure oneself of never going broke.

$$-6,806 = (25)(.01)(27,225) - (3)(25)(1.1)(27,225)^{1/2}$$

Table II below gives bankroll requirements to assure a win for different advantages and for different average bet sizes.

Table II: Bankroll Required to Assure a Win

Win Rate in %	Average Bet Size					
	1	2	5	10	15	25
0.1	2,273	5,445	13,613	27,225	40,838	68,063
0.2	1,361	2,722	6,806	13,613	20,419	34,031
0.3	908	1,815	4,538	9,075	13,612	22,688
0.4	681	1,361	3,403	6,806	10,209	17,016
0.5	545	1,089	2,722	5,445	8,168	13,613
0.6	454	908	2,269	4,538	6,806	11,344
0.7	389	778	1,945	3,889	5,834	9,723
0.8	340	681	1,702	3,403	5,105	8,508
0.9	303	605	1,513	3,025	4,538	7,563
1.0	272	545	1,361	2,723	4,084	6,806
1.1	248	495	1,238	2,475	3,713	6,188
1.2	227	454	1,134	2,269	3,403	5,672
1.3	209	419	1,047	2,094	3,142	5,236
1.4	194	388	972	1,945	2,917	4,862
1.5	182	363	908	1,815	2,723	4,537
1.75	156	311	778	1,556	2,334	3,889
2.0	136	272	681	1,361	2,042	3,403
2.5	109	218	545	1,089	1,634	2,723

Table II: Bankroll Required to Assure a Win (Con't)

Win Rate in %	Average Bet Size				
	50	100	250	500	1,000
0.1	136,125	272,250	680,625	1,361,250	2,722,500
0.2	68,062	136,125	340,312	680,625	1,361,250
0.3	45,375	90,750	226,875	453,750	907,500
0.4	34,031	68,063	170,156	340,313	680,625
0.5	27,225	54,450	136,125	272,250	544,500
0.6	22,688	45,375	113,438	226,875	453,750
0.7	19,446	38,893	97,232	194,464	388,929
0.8	17,016	34,031	85,078	170,156	340,312
0.9	15,125	30,250	75,625	151,250	302,500
1.0	13,613	27,225	68,063	136,125	272,250
1.1	12,375	24,750	61,875	123,750	247,500
1.2	11,344	22,688	56,719	113,438	226,875
1.3	10,471	20,942	52,356	104,712	209,423
1.4	9,723	19,446	48,616	97,232	194,464
1.5	9,075	18,150	45,375	90,750	181,500
1.75	7,779	15,558	38,893	77,786	155,571
2.0	6,806	13,613	34,031	68,062	136,125
2.5	5,445	10,890	27,225	54,450	108,900

Tables I and II provides answers when there is essentially no risk involved. But some winning players are willing to assume a small risk, perhaps 5 percent. These results are given in Tables III and IV. The difference is that 1.64 standard deviations is now used in the calculations instead of 3 standard deviations. (Again, remember that it is assumed that money for rent, expenses, or whatever is not being removed from the system. That is, these tables — especially Tables III and IV — apply for someone starting out who is trying to build a bankroll, but they don't apply as well for the "professional" who continually keeps his bankroll at a particular amount.)

Table III: Hours Needed for a 95% Chance to Win

Win Rate in %	Hours Required	Win Rate in %	Hours Required
0.1	32,544	1.0	325
0.2	8,136	1.1	269
0.3	3,616	1.2	226
0.4	2,034	1.3	193
0.5	1,302	1.4	166
0.6	904	1.5	145
0.7	664	1.75	106
0.8	509	2.0	81
0.9	402	2.5	52

Table IV: Bankroll Needed for a 95% Chance to Win

Win Rate in %	Average Bet Size					
	1	2	5	10	15	25
0.1	814	1,627	4,068	8,136	12,204	20,304
0.2	407	814	2,034	4,068	6,102	10,170
0.3	271	542	1,356	2,712	4,068	6,780
0.4	203	407	1,017	2,034	3,051	5,085
0.5	163	325	814	1,627	2,441	4,068
0.6	136	271	678	1,356	2,034	3,390
0.7	116	232	581	1,162	1,743	2,906
0.8	102	203	509	1,017	1,526	2,543
0.9	90	181	452	904	1,356	2,260
1.0	81	163	407	814	1,220	2,034
1.1	74	148	370	740	1,109	1,849
1.2	68	135	339	678	1,017	1,695
1.3	63	125	313	626	939	1,564
1.4	58	116	291	581	872	1,453
1.5	54	108	271	542	814	1,356
1.75	46	93	232	465	697	1,162
2.0	41	81	203	407	610	1,017
2.5	33	65	163	325	488	814

Table IV: Bankroll Needed for a 95% Chance to Win (Con't)

Win Rate in %	Average Bet Size				
	50	100	250	500	1,000
0.1	40,680	81,360	203,401	406,802	813,604
0.2	20,340	40,680	101,701	203,401	406,802
0.3	13,560	27,120	67,800	135,601	271,201
0.4	10,170	20,340	50,850	101,701	203,401
0.5	8,136	16,272	40,680	81,360	162,721
0.6	6,780	13,560	33,900	67,800	135,601
0.7	5,811	11,623	29,057	58,114	116,229
0.8	5,085	10,170	25,425	50,850	101,701
0.9	4,520	9,040	22,600	45,200	90,400
1.0	4,068	8,136	20,340	40,580	81,360
1.1	3,698	7,396	18,491	36,982	73,964
1.2	3,390	6,780	16,950	33,900	67,800
1.3	3,129	6,258	15,646	31,292	62,585
1.4	2,906	5,811	14,528	29,057	58,114
1.5	2,712	5,424	13,560	27,120	54,240
1.75	2,325	4,649	11,623	23,246	46,492
2.0	2,034	4,068	10,170	20,340	40,680
2.5	1,627	3,254	8,136	16,272	32,544

To use these four tables, you must know your average bet size and your advantage. Fortunately, this information is available in Arnold Snyder's *The Blackjack Formula*. Snyder notes that in a single-deck game, your average bet size is approximately four times your low bet added to your high bet, then divided by five. For a four-deck game dealt out 80 percent, the formula for average bet size is now seven times your low bet added to your high bet, then divided by eight. (See *The Blackjack Formula* for more discussion of this topic.) Also, in the September 1981 issue of *Blackjack Forum*, Snyder says that if you spread your bets from low to high instead of making a strict jump, you "should calculate as if you are using a smaller spread." Specifically, in a single-deck game, assume that your high bet is two-thirds of your actual high bet; in a multi-deck game, assume that your high bet is one-half of your actual high bet.

The estimate provided for the standard deviation is only approximate, and a more accurate estimate for when more than one bet size is used is to take the square root of the sum of the variances of the number of hands played at each bet size. A good discussion of this appears in the March 1981 issue of *Blackjack Forum*. However, for many situations, I believe the results given should be reasonably accurate. The exception is when you use a very large betting spread, causing a significant non-self-weighting effect.

As for estimating your advantage, this is a more complex problem that will not be addressed here. Fortunately, how to do this is also well explained in *The Blackjack Formula*.[6]

As the tables illustrate, if you are a professional player and bankroll preservation is of highest importance, a good chance exists that you are playing at a level too high for you, even if you are an expert card counter. I believe this is also why many aspiring card counters have gone broke.

In summary, you now should be able to estimate the bankroll requirements for most blackjack games you are interested in playing. As I've stated, I'm sure that many people will discover they are playing in games where their bankrolls are at risk. But there's nothing wrong with this, as the amount of risk one chooses to take is a personal matter. What is comfortable for one person may not be comfortable for someone else. Nevertheless, many people, who thought they were playing it safe, will find out that they actually were in significant danger.

---

[6]Also see *Beat the 1-, 2-, 4-, 6-, and 8-Deck Game* by Arnold Snyder.

Two Tales: The Bullfrog and the Adventurer

I. Introduction. I'd like to deviate a little from the rest of this book and tell you the stories of two people from the poker world. The first, whom I will call the Bullfrog, is someone whom many of us have had to sit with at the poker table on numerous occasions. The second, whom I will call the Adventurer, is without a doubt one of the premier poker players in California. (See the essays titled "The Extremely Silly Subject of Money Management" and "Free Bets and Other Topics," which appear in this section, and the essay titled "The Adventurer in Action," which appears in Part Six of this book.) The reason these stories are being told is that during a six-month period in 1986, both of these people won significant amounts of money. This was not surprising since both are very good players. The difference is that only one of them, the Adventurer, has managed to hold on to it. Thus, there are two lessons to be learned from these tales. The first is why the Bullfrog self-destructed, and the second is why the Adventurer will always be successful.

II. The Tale of the Bullfrog. The Bullfrog is a competent high draw, jacks or better to open, player who was making a decent living at the poker tables in Southern California. Unfortunately, part of the Bullfrog's game was built on what are known as angle shots and on irritating other players by trying to put them "on tilt." These strategies are not the way to maximize your winnings, as they tend to get the "live ones" out of a gambling mood and even to drive some of them out of the game. Although many of us tried to explain this to the Bullfrog, he persisted in his obnoxious behavior. However, the bottom line is that he knew how to play poker and was winning his share.

It's an interesting fact that in California poker, much more money is in the lowball games than in the high draw games, even though significant amounts of money can be won at both. At the Bicycle Club in Bell Gardens, California — where the biggest action was in the Los Angeles area during this time period — the largest high draw game regularly spread was a $25-$50 limit game — although a $50-$100 game did get down three or four nights a week. (This was before the legalization of stud and hold'em. Now conditions are much different, and almost no high draw is played.) On the lowball side, games as big as $200-$400 were regularly spread. Moreover, lowball games are bigger than high draw games. A $15-$30 lowball game, for example, is almost as big as a $25-$50 high draw game.

Well, as was inevitable, since the Bullfrog was doing well, he decided to take a shot at the bigger lowball games. After a couple of days playing at the $30-$60 level (which is a fairly big game by most people's standards), the Bullfrog found himself in a $75-$150 game, where he had a very successful session. He continued to play these games and soon won a substantial sum of money.

However, there were several things that the Bullfrog never understood. First, lowball is a poker game in which luck plays a large role in the short run. This is because, for the expert player, the relationship between the expectation and standard deviation in lowball is probably the poorest of almost all standard poker games. Although the best player expects to win in the long run, anyone can do exceptionally good or exceptionally bad in the short run. The Bullfrog never understood that he had been exceptionally lucky and that he was not playing significantly better than everyone else as he thought. In addition, since he was a new player to these large games, some of his opponents gave him excess action in an effort to run over him. This, coupled with his tight play, and an exceptional good run of cards, plus a significant tournament victory, produced a win of approximately $250,000.

But the Bullfrog had a major weakness, which, as some of us knew, would guarantee his self-destruction. This weakness was a gigantic ego. Soon the Bullfrog would play only in the biggest games in Southern California. Also, his constant ridicule of the live ones drove them away from these games.

Well, it soon turned out that the only games the Bullfrog played in were short-handed games against some of the best players in the world. In addition, his gigantic ego would not allow him to leave a game a loser, no matter how poorly he was doing. This meant that he was regularly playing 36- and 48-hour sessions, which might be all right once in a while but on an ongoing basis can be disastrous.

It took only about three weeks for the Bullfrog to be knocked out of the big games. The man had hit the big time and then blew it. He never understood the old poker adage: "If you sit down at a table and don't see any live ones, then *you* are the live one." Fortunately for the Bullfrog, he managed to stop before he was completely broke and returned to the games where he had started. This enabled him to still take some shots at the very large games. However, many of us suspected that it would be difficult for him to stay geared down in the future. Unless the Bullfrog changed his ways, there was a high probability that he eventually would be completely broke.

III. The Tale of the Adventurer. The Adventurer won a substantial sum in early 1986 and used most of his winnings to pay off some outstanding personal debts. But he made the mistake of not leaving himself enough money to play the big games he had become accustomed to playing. That is, he did not have enough money to survive a significant negative fluctuation, and after a couple of immediate losses in the big games, the Adventurer found himself temporarily broke.

Undaunted, he took a day off, and with an assist from myself and another friend, he began playing some of the smallest games in California. (He liked to say, "I am the only person around who has played in both the $1 blind and the $100 blind games.") After several days, the Adventurer had a bankroll of

$250 which he took into a $3-$6 lowball game. In a few hours, he ran this up to $600. He promptly quit the low-limit game and went to scout the $15-$30 lowball games.

After careful scouting, the Adventurer found a game that looked exceptionally weak, and since he was well-liked by the players, they welcomed him into the game and gave him plenty of good action. By the way, even though the Adventurer is an expert player, and even though the game was exceptionally weak, $600 is not very much money for a $15-$30 lowball game; that is, the Adventurer had a good chance of going broke again. But being an adventurer, this was the kind of risk he was willing to take.

As it so happened, my friend was exceptionally lucky, and when an expert player gets lucky in an easy game, a lot of money can be won. At the end of the day, the Adventurer was up almost $3,000, one of the largest wins that I have ever heard of in a game this size.

During the next few weeks, the Adventurer continued to win. Of course he had been lucky, but he also was very selective of the games he chose. In fact, the Adventurer and another well-known player even came up with a "Top Ten List." These were the ten weakest players who regularly played in the bigger games at the Bicycle Club. They knew when these people usually played and exactly what their weaknesses were. Of course, my friend's play became coordinated with the play of the live ones. In addition, the Adventurer was always polite and complimentary to these producers and it was not long before the live ones were trying to get into the same game with him.

Another trick the Adventurer used to maximize his profits was to always try to enter the game where his expectation was highest. This often meant that he did not play in the largest game. On several occasions, he skipped the $100-$200 lowball game because it was tough and played in the $75-$150 game because it was full of live ones. Apparently, when the $100-$200 lowball game was started, all the tough players — including the Bullfrog — immediately went to that game leaving the $75-$150 game very weak. But the Adventurer's ego was not a problem, so he would play in the smaller games. In addition, if a game went bad, he was able to leave a loser.

The Adventurer also knew that being nice to the live ones pays off. The best thing that can happen in poker is for a live one to request to get into your game because you are sitting in it. Needless to say, the Adventurer was certainly doing something right. He even would have dinner on occasion with some of his "friends," and the live ones often would inform him of when they were returning to the card room, so they all could play together again.

Contrast this to the situation created by the Bullfrog, who drove these players away. No wonder the best players in the world would play against the Bullfrog in short-handed games. They not only wanted his money, but wanted to get rid of him as well. In addition, because of the marathon sessions that the Bullfrog played, the other experts knew that he would be an easy target.

In about a six-month period the Adventurer won almost as much money as the Bullfrog did at his peak. The main difference is *not* that the Adventurer still has his win, but that it is much less likely for him to lose it than it was for the Bullfrog to lose his money. Since the Adventurer is willing to take some big risks, his money may disappear sometime in the future. But unlike the Bullfrog, the Adventurer won't lose his money because he does not have the best of it.

IV. Final Comments. I hope these two stories will be not only informative, but helpful as well. I don't recommend that someone put his whole bankroll on the table as the Adventurer is known to do, but I certainly recommend that many of his tactics be adopted. Because he played in an honest ethical way, the live ones knew they had a legitimate gamble. Most bad players know they don't have the best of it, but the thrill of the gamble is enough to keep many of them in action. However, ridiculing weak players and trying other tricks is often enough not only to drive them away, but to put you out of business as well. The Adventurer, even though he will have his ups and downs, will most likely always be successful at the poker tables. This certainly won't be true of some other knowledgeable poker players. Remember, it doesn't do any good to be the tenth best player in the world if only a certain nine players are willing to sit in the same game with you. Also, by driving the live ones out of the game, the relationship between your expectation and your standard deviation will deteriorate, thus increasing your risk — and no one needs that.

Free Bets and Other Topics

The winning gambler is always thinking about various things that may affect his results. In addition, he is always looking for new opportunities and is willing to change and update his ideas. What seems to be absolutely correct today may turn out to be totally incorrect tomorrow, and sticking with ideas that don't work can prove costly. Following is a discussion of free bets and other topics relating to opportunity and change.

Topic No. 1: Free bets. This is a dangerous idea, because it requires your bankroll to withstand very large fluctuations. That is, you will be making bets with approximately zero expectations but very high standard deviations. On the other hand, it is a successful strategy to use for obtaining comps from most casinos. This is how it works. Go to any major casino and place some large bets only on those options where the house edge is either very small or non-existent. Then introduce yourself to the pit personnel (if they have not already introduced themselves to you) and ask for a comp. Don't be bashful. Sometimes if you ask for the moon you can get it. This can include gourmet meals sent to your room, free tickets to the best shows in town with the best seats, and whatever else the casino may have to offer. By the way, when you are comped, you never have to stand in line. Here are some examples of free bets.

Blackjack. If you have mastered basic strategy and select a casino with good rules, the house edge will range from zero to .5 percent off the top of the deck, depending on the number of decks that are used. In addition, if you master a strong count and just use it for playing decisions, you can further reduce the house edge by a few tenths of one percent. Notice that you now can play blackjack (theoretically) virtually for free. If you make large bets (and can withstand the statistical fluctuations of the

81

game), you should be able to get the casino to treat you quite well.

Craps. Craps is another game where virtually free bets appear. The standard bet at craps gives the house an advantage of approximately 1.4 percent. (Some of the other craps bets give the house a significant advantage.) Although this 1.4 percent edge is small in comparison to that of other casino games, it is nowhere close to being free. But once a point is established, you can place an additional bet — known as taking the odds — which is essentially a free bet. Your wager is now doubled, and the house edge is cut approximately in half. But this is still not close to free by my standards. However, mainly because of competition, some casinos offer double and triple odds on your bets. This reduces the house edge by even more. In fact, several Las Vegas casinos offer much more than triple odds, sometimes even as much as ten times odds. This reduces the house edge, if you bet correctly, to about two-tenths of one percent. You now have a bet that is virtually free, which means that you can quickly generate a lot of action for only a nominal (expected) cost. For example, $10,000 of action will cost only on average $20, and $10,000 of action should easily get you plenty of comps from many casinos.

Baccarat. Baccarat is one of the simplest casino games. The house edge in this game is approximately 1.1 percent, but if the house did not take a 5 percent vigorish on the banker, the banker would have an edge of approximately 1 percent. This actually sometimes happens. I once watched my friend the Adventurer lose $3,000 playing baccarat. When he was done, he owed the house an additional $70, which the house told him to forget about. Apparently, especially if the amount owed is fairly small, after a player has incurred a significant loss, some casinos occasionally will tell the losing patron not to worry about the commission. What this means is that the skilled gambler may be achieving (essentially) free bets. (I doubt this situation occurs often enough to enable someone to play baccarat with a significant edge, but at casinos that are trying to attract high rollers, this occasionally may be the case.) Baccarat players are known to receive some of the best casino comps available.

Final note. Here is another true story about the Adventurer. When casinos first opened in Atlantic City, he had just accepted a job not too far away. Instead of getting an apartment, he took advantage of the then very favorable Atlantic City blackjack rules, made a bunch of free bets, and lived rent free for several months courtesy of an Atlantic City casino. My friend also took advantage of the hectic conditions that existed in Atlantic City at that time and did not really give the casino that much action. Today it would be much more difficult for someone to get away with something like this. On the other hand, making free bets is a strategy that more people could probably take advantage of.

Topic No. 2: A good game. All skilled gamblers try to identify a good game. You certainly don't want to play in a bad game, as the idea is to win as much as possible. But identifying a good game is much more complicated than it appears. (Incidentally, although a large proportion of my writings deal with poker, this topic concerns all forms of gambling.)

Most people think a good game is one where your expectation is highest. This may or may not be true. In reality, a good game exists when your expectation, your expected fluctuations (which are measured by the statistical standard deviation), and your current bankroll are properly balanced. Also, a good game is a personal matter. That is, what is a good game for one person may be a bad game for someone else. Let's discuss these parameters in more detail.

To begin with, your expectation is the average amount that you expect to earn over some period of time, perhaps an hour. This is usually all most people consider. They want to win as much as possible and try to select games where their win rates are as high as possible. Unfortunately, this can lead to some disasters. To understand why this is so requires a good understanding of the other two parameters.

Playing games with large fluctuations — as measured by the standard deviation — can result in prolonged losing streaks, even though you may be playing skillfully. An example is blackjack, where you are counting cards and have a significant edge over the casino but are making very large bet variations. Although these extremely large bets mean that your overall expectation is quite good, if you are unlucky and lose a high percentage of your big bets in a relatively short period of time, you can be a big loser for a session.

Another example is lowball draw poker. Based on an expert player's results at the tables, I have shown that a highly skilled player ($30 per hour expectation in a $30-$60 game) can be a loser after more than two years of full-time play. When this happens — and prolonged losing streaks are common in this game due to the poor relationship between the expectation and the standard deviation — the player often goes on tilt, steams much of his money away, and is no longer a good player.

An even more dangerous situation occurs when a weak player has a long positive fluctuation. Now he not only will think he is a good player but also will move up in stakes, where the competition to be faced will be much tougher. This means that the weak player will have a significantly greater negative expectation than before, and needless to say, this invites disaster. I sometimes wonder how many gamblers have fallen into this trap and then could not believe their "bad luck" when they quickly went broke.

Consequently, you would like to balance your expectation and standard deviation. The lower the standard deviation and the higher the expectation, the better off you are. However, there is also another parameter that comes into play: the size of your bankroll. Simply put, the larger your bankroll is, the larger fluctuations you can withstand. This is part of the reason why a good game for one person may not be a good game for someone else. Also, if your bankroll were infinitely large, there would be no requirement to reduce fluctuations, and only your expectation would count.

By the way, poker games like lowball, seven-card stud, and Omaha hold'em, which have high draw-out potential, produce much larger fluctuations than games like Texas hold'em[7] and high draw. At the tracks, bets on long shots and exotic bets (daily doubles and so forth) have larger fluctuations than standard straight win bets. In the stock market, options and penny stocks will have much larger fluctuations than conventional stocks and mutual funds. And for a final example, buying real estate in run-down neighborhoods for the purpose of rehabilitation is associated with much larger fluctuations than buying real estate in well-established, thriving neighborhoods.

But remember that just because a game has a large standard deviation doesn't mean that it's necessarily bad. What is important is the relationship between the expectation and the standard deviation, plus the size of your bankroll coupled with how much risk you are willing to assume.

This brings up an interesting point: the concept of trying to balance your bankroll against your expectation and standard deviation. This leads to the conclusion that there is always some "best" game for you to play, which seems to contradict the idea of plodders and adventurers. Someone who constantly adventures will end up with a smaller bankroll in the long run than someone who attempts to always keep his play in balance. This is because constant adventuring eventually will lead to a disaster, thus leaving you with less money than someone who always plays in his best game.

Again, I want to emphasize how important this idea is. It may be the most significant gambling concept that I will ever write about. Simply put, some people don't make what they should because they constantly play in games too small for their abilities and bankrolls, and some people don't make what they should because they constantly play in games that are too big

---

[7]As previously stated, in some middle-limit hold'em games, a great deal of money goes into the pot before the flop. When this is the case, you will have higher fluctuations than in seven-card stud games of the same limit.

for their bankrolls, even though they have the ability for a positive earn. Don't let this happen to you.

Topic No. 3: A good player. Most people will tell you that a good poker player is someone who wins more on his good hands and loses less on his bad hands. While there is some validity to this, it is a long way from being correct. In reality, a good player is someone who wins a great deal of money on his marginal hands. He does this by getting the most out of any small edge that he may have.

What about a great player? Obviously, he does what a good player does but even more so. I believe a great player not only makes the most of his marginal edges, but also manages to take situations that are losers for most people and turn them into winners. This is done through superior deceptive strategies, correct evaluation of his opponents, and understanding exactly how his opponents perceive him. But this does not come for free. The price paid to become a great player is higher fluctuations.

Here is an example. Suppose your expectation is $30 per hour and your standard deviation is $650 per hour. (This may be typical of a good player at the $30-$60 lowball game that is spread in Southern California.) To assure that you won't go broke, not counting any non-self-weighting effect, you need a bankroll of approximately $32,000 (3 standard deviations). Now suppose you are able to increase your expectation by 10 percent, but it causes your standard deviation to double. To assure that you don't go broke — again, not counting any non-self-weighting effect, you need a bankroll of approximately $115,000. Notice that the relationship between the expectation and the standard deviation significantly deteriorated. (The calculations are not shown, but those readers interested should see the essay titled "How Much Do You Need?" which appears earlier in this section.)

Is this 10 percent increase worth the price? I'll let you decide, but I would like to give an example. I have a very good friend who is without a doubt one of the best poker players around. Yet many of his opponents just think he plays tight, because in certain situations, he has decided to reduce his standard deviation. Of course, this also reduces his expectation. But my friend never plans on going broke, and so far, after many years of gambling, he has always managed to stay in money.

Finally, there is one other conclusion that we can draw. It is simply that great players are more likely to go broke than good players. Somehow this just doesn't seem right, but that's the way it is in the poker world.

By the way, the concept that a great player is more likely to go broke than a good player has generated a lot of discussion. But it's true, provided that the great player and the good player both start with the same size bankroll. A corollary to this is that if you are playing on a small bankroll, it is wise to be somewhat more conservative than what is optimal to assure survival. (This concept was first proposed by David Sklansky, who recommends tighter play than what normally would be correct when playing in a great poker game at stakes too large for your bankroll.)

Topic No. 4: The ideal game. An ideal game for the expert player is when the coefficient of variation (c.v.), which is the expectation divided by the standard deviation, is equal to .1 or 10 percent. I believe this enables the expert to win fairly consistently but still allows enough fluctuations to keep weak players hooked.

When examining poker, it seems as though the game of razz (seven-card lowball) is probably the closest to a c.v. of 10 percent for the expert, providing his opposition is weak. However, razz has gotten a great deal of bad publicity over the years (dealing with cheating), and this has scared many players away from the game. The c.v. for seven-card stud, Omaha, and draw lowball should be below 10 percent for the expert, meaning that these games may be too much of a gamble for someone trying to make a living, especially if his bankroll is limited or he is interested in playing the bigger games.

On the other hand, the expert's c.v. for Texas hold'em may be above 15 percent (and even higher against very weak opponents).[8] However, hold'em has certain characteristics, such as "any two cards can win," that make the game seem much more of a gamble than it really is. Consequently, even though the c.v. is frequently too high in this game by my criteria, it may be the ideal game to master.

Topic No. 5: Idiots and maniacs. We all should want to compete against weak playing opponents when playing poker. However, many people claim that they prefer games where their opponents play fairly tight and that they do better in these games than in games where their opponents play loose. I believe such claims are made because these players fail to properly adjust their strategy when they are against "idiots" and/or "maniacs." This section defines these two types of live ones and discusses how to play against them and what it means to have them in your game.

The very best opponent to have at the poker table is what I refer to as "an idiot." Simply put, this is a very loose player who not only plays too many hands, but also plays in a predictable and passive manner. That is, he will usually call, rarely raise, rarely bluff, and rarely bet for value. Notice that he is following a self-weighting strategy.

Unfortunately, there are not that many idiots around, because these players either go broke or learn to play better. However, when a tourist sits down in the card rooms of Nevada, he often plays like an idiot.

A maniac is a different kind of opponent. Like the idiot, he plays too many hands. But the problem is that he almost always will raise, whether his hand warrants it or not. Even though maniacs eventually will go broke, their style of play can be disastrous for those players who are not able to make the

---

[8]Again, as previously stated, this estimate is probably too high for some middle-limit hold'em games.

appropriate adjustments. The maniac's approach is not correct, but its non-self-weighting characteristics make it far superior to the approach followed by the idiot.

Specifically, some poker hands play well against many opponents, while other hands play well against a small number of opponents. And by raising all the time, the maniac reduces the number of players that are in the pot. So even though the maniac may be blowing off a lot of money, the skillful player must reduce the number of hands that he is willing to play. (Notice again that the game has become more non-self-weighting.) But when a hand is played, it should be played very aggressively, unless you think the maniac is likely to bluff.

Nothing can be more frustrating in a poker game than being forced to throw away a lot of hands while some maniac is blowing off his chips. But getting in there with marginal hands, which is usually worth doing with an idiot, can become an expensive proposition in this case.

A maniac also causes the standard deviation of a game to increase dramatically, because every pot that you play has the potential to become a major confrontation. Consequently, if you are on a small bankroll, it may be best to avoid games that contain known maniacs, even though your expectation may be much higher than normal. In other words, the risk of going broke may not be worth the extra money that you expect to earn.

Another problem with maniacs is that they tend to make other loose opponents tighten up. Now the maniac has caused your opposition to become tougher.

By the way, some expert players are capable of "changing gears" and playing like a maniac for short periods of time. Needless to say, this type of opponent is very dangerous.

Topic No. 6: Making opponents happy. Depending on the situation, you may want to make your opponents either happy or unhappy. Why is that? This question can be answered by noticing certain characteristics of happy and unhappy opponents, especially if they are not sophisticated players.

Happy players tend to want to gamble. That is, the thrill of gambling will make them play many hands and use strategies that they know are costing them money. Changing a happy player's mood can be expensive for you in the long run.

Unhappy opponents are usually in no mood to gamble, although some very unhappy players will go on tilt and steam a good deal of their money away. Sometimes, steaming opponents begin to play like maniacs in a desperate attempt to get even. I know many players who are small winners most of the time but significant losers overall because of the brief periods when their unhappiness becomes so severe that they tilt.

What does this mean to the skilled player who, of course, does not suffer from these tendencies? Let's look at an example. Suppose an opponent bets into a large pot, and mathematically, or strategically, or logically, you can reason only that calling is a close decision. You should now consider how your call will affect this player's state of happiness. If he is already unhappy and a successful call might cause him to tilt, the call may become correct. On the other hand, if he is happy and ready to "gamble it up," your folding may cause him to quit gambling if he has really made a hand. Thus, it might be best to call, even if you are convinced that you have slightly the worst of it.

I realize that I have not given any specific advice on what the skilled player should do. But this is something else to consider in developing your overall strategy at the poker table.

Topic No. 7: Winning edge is the wrong parameter. Suppose you are trying to compare two systems, or approaches, to your gambling interest. The first approach wins at a rate of 1 percent, while the second approach wins at the rate of 10 percent. Which approach is better? Based on the information that I have supplied, you do not know enough to answer the question.

When you are trying to evaluate which method is best, the parameters of interest should be the expectation and the standard deviation. These parameters are discussed in detail elsewhere in this book, so I won't go into them here. But notice that your expectation is the product of the amount of action that the system achieves and the winning edge. This means that if the system with the smaller winning edge generates a lot more action than the system with the higher winning edge, the former may be better. Of course, the expert gambler also needs to look at the standard deviation. The system with the higher expectation (not winning edge) may be less desirable for some people if it has a much larger standard deviation, and if the user has a small bankroll relative to the relationship between the expectation and the standard deviation. This would be especially true if the user not only has a limited amount of money, but is also concerned about going broke.

Topic No. 8: Small-ante versus large-ante games. There are essentially two classes of poker games: small-ante games, where the total ante when compared to the initial bet is relatively small, and large-ante games, where the total ante compared to the initial bet is relatively large. Which game is better to play?

This question is easily answered by understanding that small-ante games favor those players who are more mathematically inclined, as there is usually not enough money in the pot to compensate an otherwise skillful player for any strategy mistakes that he may make. For example, from a mathematical point of view, the area of psychology in small-ante games cannot make up for unsound playing decisions.

The opposite is true in high-ante games. Now many mathematical errors can be tolerated, simply because the other skills that a top poker player needs — such as psychology, reading opponents, manipulating opponents, understanding what your opponent is probably thinking, and so forth — become much more important. The large ante has somewhat neutralized the mathematics of the game.

An interesting aside is that most small- and medium-stakes games are small-ante games, while most big games are played with a large ante. This means that many mathematically inclined players who do extremely well in games at a $10-$20 to $30-$60

91

level will perform poorly in high-limit games. The skills required to beat the mid-level games are not nearly as important in the bigger games, because games at the higher limits usually have much larger antes in proportion to the initial bets. That is, at the very high limits, the ability to play other players becomes much more important than the ability to play cards.

Skills Required to Hit the Big Time

It is probably every poker player's dream to hit it big and be able to regularly play in the very large games. But as Topic No. 8 in the previous essay pointed out, achieving success in the big games, because of the proportionately larger ante size and the smaller number of players participating, requires a different set of skills than it does in games at the medium and low stakes. Few players are able to make the move up in limits successfully, although some players who fail to make the transition can win regularly at the medium levels and are recognized by their peers as being among the best players around. This essay discusses some of the skills needed to be successful at the higher-stakes games. (I need herewith to reference Doyle Brunson's book *Super/System*, which was especially helpful in putting these ideas together.)

Skill No. 1: Willingness to gamble more. This idea isn't quite what it seems. Since the antes are larger, any time an opponent throws a hand away that he shouldn't, it becomes a costly mistake for him and a profitable play for you. Consequently, you should be more willing to make "plays" at your opponent if there is some chance that he will give up or if you might be able to knock someone else out of the pot.

For example, in hold'em, with more cards to come, raising with a hand like an inside straight draw may be good strategy. Because of the size of the pot, it actually may be correct in some instances to draw to these hands, especially if you think that there will be no raise behind you. If there is an additional chance, even a small one, that your opponent will throw his hand away if you raise, then this "semi-bluff" should be made. In a smaller game — that is, one with a smaller proportionate ante — the chances that your opponent will throw his hand away, coupled with your chances of getting "lucky," may not be large enough when considering the size of the pot for this type of play to be the best approach.

Skill No. 2: Ability to identify steal situations. Let's give an example. Suppose you are in a small-ante hold'em game, a ragged flop comes, a tight player bets, and you have nothing. Can you continue playing? The answer is no. First, if many players are in the pot, even though your opponent is unlikely to play two small cards, there is still some chance that he has something. Also, even if the initial bettor is on a steal, a reasonable chance exists that someone else will be able to play with him.

But what if this same situation came up in a short-handed, high-ante game? Now the circumstances are different. Fewer players will make it more likely that your opponent is trying to steal, and there may not be anyone left (after you) to defend the pot. Now the correct play may be either to raise and attempt to win the pot right there or to just call and attempt to win the pot on a later betting round.

Notice that what I have described is a defensive steal. It is rarely ever correct to make this play in a small- or medium-limit game. But in the large games, the most successful players are masters at this type of maneuver.

Skill No. 3: Understand that hands change value. Suppose your starting hand has flush potential. To play this hand, there are two requirements: First, you want enough money in the pot to make the play initially correct, and second, you would like to have enough opponents so that someone will still be around to pay you off if you make your hand.

In both small-ante and large-ante games, the initial starting pot often will be correct. The small-ante games are usually played at full tables, and more players are generally in the initial pot, which compensates for the small ante. The large-ante game may have enough money in the pot just based on the antes to make the hand appear playable. But the difference

94

occurs when the hand is over. The small-ante game may still have enough players remaining to pay you off. The same is not necessarily true in the big games, which are often played short-handed, thus producing a lot of heads-up pots.

This means that many hands change value. Specifically, hands that play well against a small number of opponents (pairs and high cards) go up in value in the large-ante games, while hands that play well against a large number of opponents (mainly the drawing hands) have lost some of their value.

Skill No. 4: Take advantage of tight play. Many players who enter the larger games are just taking shots at them and have not correctly adjusted their play. This means that they do not call enough, especially on the first betting round. Consequently, a skillful player who doesn't always wait for a strong starting hand will be able to pick up a lot of antes. (Be careful if the players whom you are trying to steal from "play back" a lot.) Because of the large ante structure, these pots become significant in the long run.

Picking up the antes also will enable you to take the worst of it when you are called. (See the no-limit hold'em section in Doyle Brunson's book *Super/System*.) Now when you occasionally draw out, you will appear lucky to some of your opponents who don't understand what you are doing, and they may make mistakes against you in situations that appear similar but in reality are somewhat different.

Skill No. 5: Make sure you have an out. From the skills described so far, it appears that you will be playing quite recklessly in the larger games. In some sense, this is true. Compared to your style of play in the smaller games, you will be taking many more chances. But the secret is not to take these chances when you feel like it, but when they have the greatest probability of being successful. This means that you usually must have an out. For example, if you recognize a steal situation, don't just automatically raise. It may turn out that your opponent really has something. However, if your hand is weak but also has some potential, such as an inside straight draw or a small pair, then your "reckless" play may become correct.

Skill No. 6: Know your opponents. In the smaller games ($30-$60 limit and below), there are often enough people in a pot and you have enough knowledge of the boards that it is safe to put someone on a hand. The same is not true in the bigger games. The larger ante structure, coupled with fewer opponents, means that it is more likely someone will be putting on a play. Consequently, that knowledge of your opponents' habits becomes extremely important. Knowing who is more likely to bluff and who is more likely to start with a weaker hand can make the difference between winning a pot or saving several bets. (For example, you may want to reraise with what appears to be an inferior hand either to knock other players out of the pot or to possibly "steal back.") This idea is, of course, important in all levels of poker, but in the bigger games, it comes up more often.

Also, you need to know who the very strong players are and which people play in a way that negatively affects your strategy. Needless to say, you should stay away from these opponents as much as possible. When you do run up against them, make sure to mix up your play. (Against a weak opponent, mixing up your play is not necessary — and may even be costly.)

Skill No. 7: Know who is on a short bankroll. Many of your opponents in the very large games, especially in the side action at the major tournaments, cannot afford to play at that level. Playing the biggest games is an ego trip for them. This means that they will get off their normal best game, because their risk of going broke often will be high enough to stop them from extracting the maximum profits when they hold a strong hand or cause them to throw away hands that are correct to play.

The expert player will recognize this and take advantage of it. Specifically, it will be less likely that this opponent is on a steal, it will be more likely that he will fold when you attempt to steal, and it will be more likely that he has the hand he is representing.

By the way, poker writer Mike Caro has pointed out that players on a short bankroll often are scared out of playing enough hands. In other words, when playing short-handed, especially if the ante is large, you cannot wait for a strong hand; you must defend your stake in the pot. In a full game, especially if the ante is not proportionately large, "rocks" who do not play enough hands usually don't hurt themselves very much. However, this is not the case in the high-limit games.

Skill No. 8: Isolating players who are currently playing badly. These could be either opponents who are currently on tilt or players who just play poorly. Due to the large ante, it is sometimes worth taking somewhat the worst of it if you can assure yourself of being able to get into a heads-up situation with someone who is currently playing poorly. This may include raising with the second-best hand or calling with a long-shot draw when the pot odds do not seem to justify it (but the expected action if you make your hand may justify the play).

This situations also comes up in the smaller games. But with many more players to shut out of the pot and the smaller ante making it somewhat less profitable, it does not often make sense to attempt these kinds of maneuvers. However, in the big games, they are a major part of your winning strategy.

One word of caution, though. Opponents who are temporarily playing badly usually recover their skills after winning a couple of pots. In a short-handed game, this can happen quickly. Always keep in mind that the opponent who was on tilt 20 or 30 minutes ago may now be playing quite well. That is, you can expect to see dramatic mood swings in some players.

Skill No. 9: Changing gears. Changing gears is the idea of playing fast for a while — that is, making every possible bet and raise — and then switching to more conservative play, usually for a longer period of time. This skill is important in all levels of poker, but it is especially important in the bigger games. The reason is that with a small number of players in the game, your opponents have fewer players to focus on, and thus it is easier for them to get a line on your play than it is in a full ring game. Another advantage of switching gears, as Doyle Brunson points out in *Super/System*, is that at the right time, this can give you the image of a loose action player. However, in high-limit seven-card stud and high-limit Texas hold'em, I don't believe this is the appropriate image to have, since stealing pots in these games plays an important role in most winning strategies. (See *Hold'em Poker For Advanced Players* by David Sklansky and Mason Malmuth, or see *Seven-Card Stud For Advanced Players* by David Sklansky, Mason Malmuth, and Ray Zee.)

Final comments. Of course, there is much more to playing in the big games than this essay covers. But the topics discussed are some of the more important considerations. In addition, you must be able to put your head into your opponent's head and determine what he's thinking. Keep in mind that otherwise excellent medium-limit players who are not able to make the necessary adjustments will not enjoy long-run success when they attempt to "hit the big time."

Traps to Avoid

Successful gambling is not easy, partly because a high level of skill is required to master the many beatable games that exist. However, achieving success is also difficult due to the many traps that await the semi-prosperous gambler. This essay discusses some of these traps and tries to explain why they are so dangerous for someone attempting to be successful in this field.

Trap No. 1: Marathon sessions. One of the most dangerous traps that a skilled gambler can fall into is playing marathon sessions, that is, playing too long without any sleep. For example, I have seen some people regularly play poker for 48 hours or more at a time. Obviously, a player's skill level and judgment begin to drop off after staying awake for so long.

But another problem also occurs. Most players indulge in marathon sessions because they have been losing and don't want to leave a loser. This creates a desire to attempt to win their money back quickly, and they are willing to take somewhat the worst of it if there is a chance that a particular play will produce a large win. Statistically, they become interested in high-standard-deviation plays, no matter what the expectation is, and they begin to take chances that they normally would never take. No wonder so many marathon players go broke.

However, as long as you are able to maintain control, marathon sessions sometimes make sense when the game is so good that even if you are not playing at your optimal skill level, your expectation should be high. In poker, this may be when some exceptional "live ones" are at the table and they still have a good deal of money to lose. In blackjack, this may be during a special casino promotion when the house is giving up much more than it realizes.

Trap No. 2: Ego problems. The highly skilled gambler knows he is good at what he does and has complete confidence in himself. On the other hand, he does not let his ego get the best of him. Because of the large short-term standard deviation (when compared to the expectation) present in almost all gambling games, the skilled (or unskilled) gambler can have periods of time when his results are spectacular. As has been shown, these periods of time may last longer than seems reasonable.

Such runs of good luck sometimes can turn a winning player into a loser by convincing him that he is much better than he actually is and by encouraging him to take chances that he normally would not take. This includes overbetting his bankroll and taking an unacceptable risk of ruin, as well as playing in games where the opponents are too tough or the rules and/or conditions are not favorable.

Another consequence of having an ego problem at the poker table is that it causes many players to dislike you. This means that weaker opponents who like to gamble will not make their loose plays against you. Most people who gamble know they are losers, but the thrill of being at the tables is enough to keep them going. However, when the experience is no longer enjoyable, they will lose their gamble and begin to play much better. This reduces the expectation not only of the irritating player with the gigantic ego, but also of all other skilled players at the table.

Trap No. 3: Playing unethically. Another area that can get the semi-skilled gambler in trouble falls under the heading of unethical play. This includes things like passing or betting out of turn at the poker table to get information that you are not entitled to. In blackjack, an example of unethical play is pretending that your six-card total of 22 is really a total of 21 and trying to get paid for it. Unless you are against very unsophisticated opponents, these types of maneuvers only occasionally work. But they do alert your opposition, whether

100

it is other players or a casino, that you need to be watched very closely.

If you are a blackjack player, not only will you come under close observation, which can be disastrous for someone trying to count cards, but the casino may not be willing to take any chances and might reduce the quality of its game. This usually translates to less deck penetration, longer and more thorough shuffling procedures, or the constant arrival of new decks. In addition, it may now be tougher to get comped. Worse yet, if you make a couple of unethical moves, the pit personnel may conclude that you are a cheater and will take what they consider is appropriate action.

If you are a poker player, the most likely result of unethical behavior is that the action players who enjoy losing their money will no longer enjoy losing it to you. This means that against you, and perhaps against everyone, they will tighten up their play because they are no longer in a gambling mood. At the very least, your win rate may be significantly reduced; at the very worst, you may be kicked out of the game. (If you are playing in a home game, you may not be invited back.)

I'm sure that these ideas carry over into other gambling games as well. It's important to understand that even though an unethical play may increase your immediate profits, the long-term effect on your overall expectation can be disastrous.

Trap No. 4: Playing bigger to recover a loss. Suppose that you have just suffered a substantial loss in a game where your expectation should have been very positive. One trap that many otherwise skilled players fall into is moving to a higher stakes game or significantly increasing their bets in an effort to catch up. This basically puts you at the mercy of the standard deviation. Consequently, the skill that the game requires becomes less meaningful, especially if you don't have much money left. In other words, you are now simply gambling and are almost in the same position as the typical gambler.

The skilled gambler should never put himself in this type of situation. The expert wants to balance his expectation against the standard deviation, which means that he would like his expectation to be as high as possible and his standard deviation to be as low as possible. In reality, this balance is almost never achievable, so the skilled gambler should look for a compromise, where he is satisfied with his expectation and can live with the standard deviation that the particular game is offering. Accurately estimating the standard deviation is one reason why it's so important to keep meticulous records.

Supplemental Skills

The successful gambler not only needs to be highly skilled at a particular game, or games, but also must acquire a few supplemental skills that sometimes can make the difference between winning and losing. Yet many players, who otherwise would do quite well, don't give these supplemental skills much thought.

Skill No. 1: Gearing down. Many people become accustomed to playing at a certain level where the size of the bets forces them to play at their best, and as a result, they expect to do very well in the long run. But sometimes they are not able to play at this level. Perhaps the game is currently not available, perhaps they don't have enough money with them to play their usual game, no seats may be available, or their usual game is much tougher than they expected. Consequently, they find themselves playing in a smaller limit game where the size of the bets are not that meaningful to them.

Many people discover this to be a costly experience. They have a great deal of trouble gearing down and playing their usual quality game. To get around this problem, try to think you are playing with chips — not money — and your goal is to win all the chips that you can. If this doesn't help, it may be best not to play in the smaller games at all. Also, if you suffer from this problem, don't think a few chips here and there don't really matter. Over a long period of time, they definitely add up.

Skill No. 2: Looking for good games. The ability and desire to search out and find the better games is one of the most important skills a successful gambler employs. A good game may translate to weak opponents for the poker player, good deck penetration for the blackjack player, and a slightly better line for the sports bettor.

Good games have two benefits for the skilled player. First, they produce a better win rate. That is, over some specified period of time, you expect to be ahead by more than what a typical game would produce. Second, good games often result in a smaller standard deviation. In some respects, as previous essays in this book have attempted to show, this may be the more important parameter. A smaller standard deviation means that you do not need to risk as much money to gain success. It also may mean that you can take a shot at a larger stakes game than you normally would play.

The drawback to looking for good games is that the search can take up a fair amount of your playing time. But I believe this is a small price to pay if you can substantially increase your expectation while at the same time significantly decrease your standard deviation.

Skill No. 3: Leaving stuck. One of the hardest things for most gamblers to do is to leave a game a loser. No matter how bad conditions may be, some people continue to play if they are not winning. Even if you are tired, there are many reasons to keep playing. These can include weak opponents in poker, or exceptional deck penetration or a high bet-spread tolerance in blackjack. But being a loser is not a reason to stay in a game. The skilled gambler tries to determine whether the expectation and standard deviation warrant his staying in a particular game. If the answer is yes, he usually should keep playing; if the answer is no, it generally is best to quit. (The exception to this is when you have lost so much that your bankroll is now in jeopardy.)

By the way, the opposite situation also occurs. That is, some gamblers will quit a game when they get ahead, especially if they are satisfied with the size of their win. They are known as hit-and-run players. (An exception is in blackjack where it may be best not to stay too long in any one casino.) Of course, for the same reasons as just given, this is no reason to stop playing. Remember, if the game is good, it is best to keep playing, especially if you have good control over your opponents. But if the game is no longer good, you should quit. Your overall results should have very little to do with your decision.

Skill No. 4: Self-evaluation. Although it is important, it is very difficult for most people to accurately evaluate their own playing abilities. Some people do well as long as their competition is not tough, but they are still losers overall. Part of the reason for this is that they overrate their skill level and are quick to jump into games that are too tough for them. This is true no matter what form of gambling they specialize in. Knowing your own abilities and limitations is one of the keys to success in this field. Also, being able to accurately compare your abilities to those of your competition can be crucial to gambling success.

Special note: The following essay, due to the legalization of stud and hold'em poker in California, became obsolete shortly after it was written. However, the ideas that the essay contains are still worth thinking about, which is why it is included in the book.

California or Nevada?

In the world of poker, there are two places where serious players can play: California and Nevada. I am referring, of course, to public cardrooms.[9] If home games were considered, there would be many other locations.

The differences between California and Nevada are great, primarily because of the strange California gambling law. Due to the way this law is interpreted, only forms of draw poker are legal in California. What this means is that many different forms of lowball are played everywhere around the state, and high draw, jacks or better to open, is played in the very large clubs.

In Nevada, all forms of poker are legal. However, only seven-card stud and Texas hold'em are played everywhere, with a few of the larger cardrooms spreading some other variations of these two games. However, at the major tournaments, many other games are spread, especially Omaha eight-or-better, seven-card stud eight-or-better, and no-limit deuce-to-seven lowball.

So the question now arises, where is the skilled player better off playing? The answer is not that simple. Following are my observations and thoughts on this subject, along with some discussion.

---

[9]This is no longer true. Serious poker is now being played in public cardrooms in Mississippi and Atlantic City and at numerous Indian reservation/casinos across the nation.

Observation No. 1: Players are more skilled in Nevada. There is no question that a typical player in Nevada is more knowledgeable than a typical player in California. However, this is not necessarily an advantage for the expert in California, as in games like lowball, the edge that a skilled player has over his opponents is small. In Nevada, the expert player — especially if his game is hold'em — will have a big edge over a slightly better than average opponent.

Observation No. 2: There are more live ones in California. Perhaps it has something to do with the large population base, but a higher percentage of terrible players seem to be present in California cardrooms than in Nevada cardrooms. However, due to the small edge present in most California games, the expert needs more terrible players to assure a decent income. I suspect that the effect of bad players in both states is about the same, although there are perhaps three times as many on the West Coast than in Nevada.

Observation No. 3: You need a large bankroll in California. In California, you are playing games where the antes are proportionately higher than those in Nevada and in which your edge is not as great. (This is especially true if you compare hold'em to lowball.) Consequently, to achieve some appropriate win rate, the expert player needs a bankroll significantly larger than that required in Nevada, because the relationship between his expectation and the standard deviation is much poorer. How much larger is "significantly?" Based on the essay titled "How Much Do You Need?" which appeared earlier in this section, "significantly" usually means a bankroll as much as five times larger for the California games, especially if you specialize in lowball. (If you play high-limit seven-card stud in Nevada, your bankroll requirements will be more in line with those of California.)

Observation No. 4: Expect more fluctuations in California. This is a function of the proportionately larger antes and the smaller edge that these games offer. This means that in the long run, the expert player might win as much (or even more) in California as in Nevada, but he can experience some tremendous fluctuations along the way. These fluctuations affect different people in different ways. Some people thrive on them, while others have trouble coping with them and are constantly flirting with going on tilt every time they hit a bad streak. On the other hand, from a win/loss point of view, the games in Nevada are boring since your results tend to be more consistent day in and day out and you are less likely to experience a really big win or loss.

Observation No. 5: You can play half-asleep in California. Although this is a slight exaggeration, the games in California are simpler to play. This is especially true of lowball. Also, the California games, being forms of draw poker, don't have a board to keep track of, meaning less memory work is required. In addition, two rounds of betting are less mentally taxing than four or five betting rounds so those of you who like to play for exceptionally long periods of time (marathon players) should favor California.

Observation No. 6: Most of the big tournaments are all in Nevada. Even though both states offer many small tournaments, all the major tournaments, with the exception of the Bicycle Club's Diamond Jim Brady Tournament, are held in Nevada.[10] One of the attractions of the tournaments is the tremendous side action that is generated. However, I feel that this aspect of tournaments is overrated. It is true that some very large games are spread during tournaments, but most people can't afford to play in them and you often will find some of the best players in the world sitting at these tables.

---

[10]There are now other major tournaments in California, including the L.A. Poker Classic held every year at the Commerce Casino.

Observation No. 7: The big games are in California. With the exception of some extremely large (limit and no-limit) games spread a couple of times a year in Las Vegas, usually at tournament time, California consistently spreads bigger games, especially at the large clubs. At the major clubs in the Los Angeles area, games at the $200-$400 limit and higher are spread almost every day. Games of this size are virtually non-existent in Nevada.[11]

Observation No. 8: Small games are cheaper in California. The small games in Nevada, usually the $1-$3 and $1-$4 seven-card stud games have a very high rake. The rake is generally 10 percent up to either $3 or $3.50, and in some places up to $4. I understand that about three out of four pots reach the maximum limit. With about 30 hands played per hour, this comes to approximately $75 per hour (per table). The drop (or collection) for the small games in California comes to half this amount, which makes the games in California a bargain when compared to their counterparts in Nevada.[12] (I am not counting the additional drop in California for the jackpot, since this money is returned to the players.)

Observation No. 9: Big games are cheaper in Nevada. The most that any cardroom in Nevada takes from a table is usually $75 per hour. This is substantially less than what the bigger games cost in California. For example, in a $30-$60 lowball game, each player pays $8 every half-hour in the Los Angeles area. With eight players at the table, this comes to $128 per hour. A $75-$150 lowball game can produce $160 per hour for the

---

[11]With the opening of the poker room at The Mirage in Las Vegas, big games are now regularly being spread in Nevada.

[12]This is no longer the case. Since the legalization of hold'em and stud, most California cardrooms are now raking more at their smaller limits.

cardroom, assuming the table is full. Needless to say, big games are a bargain in Nevada when compared to California.

Observation No. 10: You can play any time in California. At the big clubs in California, games of all sizes go around the clock. So if you feel like playing poker at some odd hour, a game is usually available. In Nevada, many games start in the afternoon and tend to break up by the early morning hours. Consequently, if you want to play a game like $10-$20 hold'em or $15-$30 stud, you may not find one readily available.[13] An exception to this occurs at tournament time when many of the side games go around the clock.

Observation No. 11: The large California clubs offer a big selection of games. A requisite skill of an expert poker player is having the knowledge and ability to pick the very best games to play in. In the large California clubs, there are usually many games to choose from, even at the higher stakes. For example, at the Bicycle Club in Bell Gardens, I have seen as many as four $30-$60 lowball games going at one time. In the few Nevada cardrooms that offer moderately large games, it is rare to find more than two games to choose from at the medium limits, and at the higher limits more than one game is virtually unheard of. (Of course, during a major tournament, this is not true.) This means that sometimes the skilled player will decide that it is best not to play.

Observation No. 12: Other forms of gambling are available in Nevada. I am mainly thinking of sports betting, which many poker players also participate in. Most Nevada casinos have recognized this and have located their poker rooms close to their sportsbooks. Of course, this option does not exist in California.

---

[13]With the opening of The Mirage room, many games at the middle limits do go around the clock.

Observation No. 13: Your other expenses are much less in Nevada. A poker player's profit is the difference between his winnings and his expenses. Needless to say, Nevada is much less expensive than California. This includes virtually everything from housing to meals. This brings up another interesting point. Even though bigger games are regularly played in California, you don't need to play as big in Nevada to maintain the same standard of living simply because you don't need to win as much.

Observation No. 14: You can eat meals at the table in California. One advantage of playing in California is that you can eat meals at the table. Since the more an expert player plays the more money he makes, your meals can become a profitable experience. However, there are disadvantages to having meals served at the table. First, eating players tend to slow the game down, and this reduces an expert player's win rate. Second, players who are eating tend to gamble less. That is, they are often too busy eating to play hands that have only long-shot potential. (This can also be advantageous, since it is now more likely for an eating player to have a legitimate hand and he may become easier to read.) Third, some players don't play while they are eating, which causes other players who don't like to play short-handed to stop playing. (I have even seen games break up because someone orders a meal.) And fourth, the cards sometimes get messed up.

Observation No. 15: The big tournaments tend to leave other Nevada games weak. Earlier, I mentioned that the side action in the major Nevada tournaments attracts many top poker players. This has the effect of diluting the opposition at the cardrooms where the major tournaments are not being held. Consequently, very good games at the medium limits often can be found around tournament time in the non-participating cardrooms. This situation does not exist in California.

Observation No. 16: Stud and hold'em are more interesting. In my opinion, the extra betting rounds in stud and hold'em, and the developing boards, make these games more interesting, and more sophisticated strategies are required to be successful at them. This doesn't mean that games like draw and lowball are not interesting but that the degree of skill required to play well is greater in stud and hold'em. On the other hand, a game like lowball can be quite exciting when many outcomes hinge on the one draw card.

Observation No. 17: There are more angle shooters in California. An angle shooter is someone who will try to gain an edge through unethical means. This can range from something very mild, such as acting out of turn, to outright cheating. I am not exactly sure why there are more angle shooters in California, but I suspect that it has something to do with the fact that until recently, most of the games were dealt by players. This may have encouraged a small number of players to develop strategies that are based on getting favorable decisions from floor personnel. Fortunately, this situation has improved. With the introduction of house dealers in almost all games, angle shooting is not as prevalent as it used to be. But it is still much more of a problem in California than in Nevada.

Final comment. Of the seventeen observations given, nine favor Nevada and eight favor California. So the decision of which is the better place to play is not easy to make. In addition, many more legitimate observations probably can be given, but I hope this essay will be helpful to those of you who are considering playing in a different location.

Jacks-Back

The California poker game that produces the most action, yet is without a doubt the most frustrating, is jacks-back, also known as "high back to low." The game is a combination of high draw, jacks or better to open, and ace-to-five lowball.

The rules are as follows. Everyone antes and a round of high draw, jacks or better to open, is played. If no one opens, the player to the dealer's left puts in a blind bet, and the game becomes ace-to-five lowball. The deck contains a joker that counts as an ace or can be used to complete straights and flushes when the game is opened high; the joker becomes the lowest card not already in your hand when the game goes low.

Jacks-back has two characteristics, already mentioned, that set it apart from most other games in California. First, it is extremely frustrating, because the pot is often opened for high when you hold a terrific low hand. For example, suppose you hold a pat six, everyone passes to the dealer, and he now opens with a pair of jacks. Anyone who regularly plays jacks-back experiences this, and it can be irritating at times.

The second characteristic is the high level of action that the game offers. There are two reasons for this tremendous action. First, many players tend to open for high with marginal hands, much more than they would in regular draw poker. They are afraid that no one will open and that they won't be able to play when the game goes low. In fact, some opponents who are habitual sandbaggers in standard draw poker just about never pass a hand in this game.

The second reason for more action is that when the game goes low, many players will play virtually anything. The frustration of having so many good low hands wasted when the game is opened high takes its toll, and when it does go low, many opponents who normally play reasonably well become complete live ones.

The rest of this essay discusses some specific concepts that should help you achieve winning play in this game. However, it is assumed that you are experienced at both high draw, jacks or better to open, and ace-to-five lowball. If this is not the case, I suggest that you stay away from jacks-back.

Concept No. 1: Sandbag more. From the introduction, it should be obvious that if many opponents are opening more in this game than they would in a standard jacks-or-better-to-open game, you should sandbag more. For some reason, players who are habitual sandbaggers in standard jacks-or-better games will open very liberally in a jacks-back game. This does not mean that in an early position you should pass every strong hand that you hold. A good guideline is to open one seat later with hands that you normally would pass from an early position.

Concept No. 2: Identify players who open weak. Many players who normally pass and call with weak hands will now open, since they are afraid the hand will go low. You should identify these players and be prepared to raise them with medium-strength hands that you normally would call with or perhaps even throw away. This is especially true if you think that your raise will limit the pot to just the two of you or that the opener may fold.

You especially should identify those players who always open on anything when they are in the blind position (first person to the left of the dealer). Against these opponents, be prepared to raise on a pair of aces and any two pair. Also be prepared to value-bet many medium-strength hands after the draw.

Concept No. 3: Open slightly more liberally in late positions. In standard draw poker, one reason not to open is that when everyone passes, the antes are still on the table and you have another shot at them. In jacks-back, this is not the case. When everyone passes, the game becomes lowball, meaning that if you hold a high hand, your interest in the antes is lost. As a result, it becomes correct to open a bit sooner with very marginal hands. For example, I normally require a pair of queens to open next to the dealer in a standard high draw game. In jacks-back, especially if it is a typical game with little sandbagging, it is usually correct to open on a pair of jacks in this spot. By the way, most players understand this, but many people overreact and begin to open on virtually everything, no matter what their position.

Concept No. 4: Open on kings in the blind. The most common mistake players make in this game is to open on anything in the blind position. This is done due to the fear that the hand will go low and the person under the gun not only will have an unplayable hand, but must put a forced bet into the pot as well. However, with a full table of players, opening on anything will leave you too vulnerable to raises. Also, some of the more observant players will correctly begin to raise you very liberally.

The correct solution is to compromise. That is, open more liberally in the blind, but don't open with everything. This typically means that a pair of kings is correct for your minimum opening hand. Also open with all two-pair hands unless your two pair and offcard are all small.

Concept No. 5: Identify those players who don't adjust when in the blind. Another small group of people who play the blind exactly as though they were under the gun in a standard draw game. That is, they are very selective of the hands they open with. These players are also easy to identify. They rarely open when in the blind position and never open on a pair of face cards. Obviously, you should play tight against this type of opponent, just as you would in a regular draw game.

Concept No. 6: Pass many hands with low potential. Almost all players realize that a hand like a six-high straight should be passed for low. What they don't realize is that many other low hands also should also be passed. For example, suppose you are dealt a pat ace-king flush that is also a one-card draw to a good seven. Clearly, the ace-king flush is a better hand for high than the draw to a good seven is for low. But even if only two or three players remain to act behind you, it is still best to pass the hand. The reasons for this are that (1) someone may still open and you might have the opportunity to trap several players, and (2) if the game goes low, you still have a hand with value. Also, notice that in standard high draw, you almost never would want to pass this hand in a late position.

Concept No. 7: When a player check-raises from a late position and then stands pat, he almost always has a small straight. Let's look at an example. Suppose the dealer opens, you call, an opponent in a late position now check-raises and stands pat. It should be obvious that this player's most likely hand is a small straight and it was passed in the hope that the contest would go low. This means that if you make a hand like a nine-high straight, it is generally correct to go for a raise. This concept also applies if the blind is pat.

Concept No. 8: Play slightly looser lowball. Most players, out of frustration, play much too loose on those occasions when the hand goes low. However, there is a mathematical reason to play looser. Low hands in jacks-back have a much larger ante structure than in standard ace-to-five lowball. This is because each pot begins with a high draw ante, which is roughly double that used for lowball, before the blind bet is added. For example, in a single-blind $10-$20 lowball game, there is usually $18 in starting money including the blind. When a $10-$20 jacks-back game goes low, because of the larger high draw ante that stays in the pot, there is now $26 to be fought for.

This is a significant difference that indicates much looser play. However, there is also a counter-balancing force. When the pot is not opened for high it usually indicates an absence of high hands, which means that some of your opponents likely hold quality low hands. This information clearly implies that you should play tighter than what would be correct for a normal lowball game.

So what's the verdict? Do you play tighter or looser when the hand goes low in jacks-back? Based on the discussion just given and my own experience in the game, I believe that correct play on the low side in a jacks-back game should be slightly looser than correct play in a standard ace-to-five lowball contest. By the way, if you follow this advice, you will be playing much tighter than many of your typical opponents, who out of frustration are now playing virtually anything when a hand goes low.

Concept No. 9: Choose your opposition carefully. Unfortunately, there is one major drawback with jacks-back: It is an ideal game for cheaters, because the dishonest player has two sets of hands to work with, high hands and low hands. So even though jacks-back is an action-packed game, be especially sure that the game is honest before you get into it. I believe most jacks-back games are honest, especially those spread at the major clubs. But if you have any doubts, it might be better to play a conventional game.

Seating and the Interclass Correlation Coefficient

One question often asked by beginning poker players is where should they sit at the table. The typical answer is that the cards don't know where anyone is sitting, meaning that it doesn't matter which seat you take. While I agree that the cards are not knowledgeable, I will show in this essay that there are good statistical reasons, derived from a knowledge of your opponents, to determine the best and the worst seats.

The interclass correlation coefficient is a statistical measure of homogeneity (that is, similarity) when clusters are sampled from a given population. For example, suppose you are conducting a sample of housing units and your sample is composed of all housing units on certain selected blocks. If the characteristics of houses within blocks are similar (and this is usually the case), this would produce a positive interclass correlation coefficient. In other words, knowledge of one house will provide information on other houses in the block. Consequently, the sample is statistically smaller than a mathematical count would indicate.

On the other hand, if all the housing units in a block were different, there would be a heterogeneous population, which produces a negative interclass correlation coefficient. Here, knowledge of the characteristics of one house on the block is of no help if one is interested in information about the neighborhood. But the interesting thing is that knowledge of all the houses in this block will most likely produce good information on the overall population. Consequently, the sample is statistically larger than a mathematical count would indicate.

Now let's look at where one should sit at the poker table. Keep in mind that in most poker situations, it is better to act

118

late, or last, than to be in an early position. So we need to find the seat that is statistically, but not necessarily mathematically, ideal. That is, you may have more players behind you than in front of you, yet you still would be in a statistically late position.

First, let's consider loose players. One characteristic of all loose players is that they play a lot of hands. But these hands can differ greatly from player to player. Some players will open with almost anything. Others are afraid that they will be raised and are selective when opening, but they often will call with weak hands. Still others love to play "come" hands, no matter what the odds or how live their hand may be, and in games like high draw and lowball, which are usually played with a joker, this card is enough to get them into the pot. I probably could go on and on, but the bottom line is that loose players are a heterogenous group that produces a negative interclass correlation coefficient. Thus there are statistically more of them than you can mathematically count, meaning that they should be seated to your right so you can act after they do.

Now let's look at aggressive players. They also exhibit differences in their play. Some will habitually check-raise. Others will raise with marginal hands instead of folding. Some will raise on second-best hands, especially in games like hold'em and stud, trying to limit the pot to just a few players. Others will raise trying to get a free card on a later round, and another subgroup often will bluff.

Again, I could go on and on, but the bottom line is that this is also a heterogeneous group producing a negative interclass correlation coefficient, meaning that there are statistically more aggressive players than you can mathematically count. Consequently, you also want aggressive players seated on your right, especially if they are skillful players. (In fact, if they play very well, you may want them as far away from you as possible so you interact with them as little as possible.)

Finally, let's look at (non-aggressive) tight players, which we like to call "weak tight."[14] To be a tight player, you must be selective when deciding which hands to play. Consequently, tight players generally play only strong hands. Also, these "rocks" tend to bluff very little, play drawing hands only when the odds are correct, and rarely bet a marginal hand for value when all the cards are out.

As in the two previous examples, I could go on and on, but the bottom line here is different. This is a homogeneous group producing a positive interclass correlation coefficient. Thus, there are statistically fewer of them than you can mathematically count, meaning that they should be seated on your left.

Final comment. Several years ago, I attended a poker seminar sponsored by one of the major cardrooms in Las Vegas. The "expert" who was speaking was asked which seat is best. His answer had something to do with comfort and "knocking knees." Obviously, at least in this area, the speaker either was not much of an expert or chose not to share his knowledge with the audience.

---

[14]I first heard the term "weak tight" many years ago when talking with world-class player Ray Zee. I believe the first time this term appeared in print was in *Hold'em Poker For Advanced Players,* which I co-wrote with David Sklansky.

Betting and Game Theory

In poker, if your opponent is playing "correctly" in a game-theory sense, his bluffing and calling frequencies should be dependent upon the pot size in relation to the bet size. The optimal bluffing and calling frequencies are thoroughly discussed in David Sklansky's book *The Theory of Poker*, and their development will not be repeated here. But there is a question that I would like to address: What is the optimal betting frequency? (Remember that few players actually play in an optimal game-theory fashion.)

Many of the ideas that follow are either based upon or are extensions of those given by Norman Zadeh in his excellent book *Winning Poker Systems*. Some of this material is extremely complex and may be difficult for many readers to follow. But what is important are the conclusions at the end, not the mathematics. Incidentally, I'd like to thank my friend Mark Weitzman for helping me put these ideas together.

When trying to determine your betting hands, Zadeh gives the following criteria (slightly modified):

1. Each player's minimum betting hand should be such that it doesn't matter whether the hand is bet or not.
2. Each player must bluff at a game-theory frequency.
3. Each player must bluff whenever it is profitable to do so, and he must not bluff when it is not profitable to do so.

We also will assume here that when the first player bets, his opponent will not raise. That is, the second player to act will either call or fold. (By the way, against some opponents or in certain situations, this can be a very dangerous assumption.)

So the question is, what is the minimum betting hand? Or what is the hand that does just as well if you bet or pass? First, if you bet this hand, your expectation is as follows:

$$Ex = (1)(C-B1) + (-1)(B1)$$

where

    C is the correct calling frequency (based on the bet size and the size of the pot),

    B1 is the minimum betting hand (as a rank in percent),

    $(1)(C\text{-}B1)$ represents those bets that you win when your opponent calls and loses, and

    $(-1)(B1)$ represents those bets that you lose when your opponent calls with a better hand.

Now suppose you check this same hand. Your expectation is as follows:

$$Ex = (-1)(B1) + (1)(B2-B1) + (1)(BL2)$$

where

    B2 is the minimum betting hand of your opponent,

    BL2 is the percent of hands that your opponent will bluff with,

    $(-1)(B1)$ represents those bets that you loose when your opponent bets a better hand,

    $(1)(B2\text{-}B1)$ represents those hands that you win when your opponent bets a weaker hand, and

    $(1)(BL2)$ represents those bets that you win when your opponent bluffs.

Notice that your opponent's minimum betting hand is actually the midpoint between your minimum betting hand and your minimum calling hand (based on the correct calling frequency). This is because the second player to act, unlike you, does not have to worry about bluffing if you check. Hence, B2 is equal to the following equation:

$$B2 = \frac{B1 + [1 - (B1)(1 - C) - B1](C) + B1}{2}$$

In addition, BL2 is equal to the following:

$$BL2 = (B2)(1 - C)$$

Substituting these formulas into our expectation equations and then setting them equal to each other produces the following table of betting frequencies, dependent upon the correct (game theory) calling frequencies.

Betting Frequency Table (%)

Calling Frequency	First Player Betting Frequency
.40	.074
.50	.133
.60	.222
.70	.346
.75	.424
.80	.513
.90	.729
.95	.857

What does this table mean? Let's look at an example. If it is correct for your opponent to call 50 percent of the time (.50 X 100), then you should bet 13.3 percent (.133 X 100) of your hands. (This is the same example that Zadeh gives in the appendix of his book.)

In addition, the table shows something very interesting. For small calling frequencies, you should check your weaker value hands. For example, we just noticed that if your opponent will call with his best 50 percent of hands, your weakest betting hand is 13.3 percent. This is true even though hand 24 percent can still be bet for value. However, checking is the best strategy, as these hands do better in this situation when they are available to pick off bluffs.

But the table shows that the opposite is true for the higher calling frequencies (which are typical for most limit games due to the relatively large pot size in comparison to the bet). That is, you should bet hands that seem to actually cost you money in the long run. This is because when the pot becomes large, it is sometimes more expensive to give your opponent the opportunity to bluff than it is to make losing bets.

To conclude, I want to add two cautions. First, these ideas apply when your opponent does not raise. If you can be raised, you probably should bet slightly fewer hands. Second, these guidelines are beneficial when you are not sure how your opponent plays. If you have a good line on him or her, then this might dictate a different strategy. For example, if you know your opponent is a habitual bluffer, it might be best to almost always check and call, no matter how big the pot is.

Which Count Is Best?

One question that I am often asked by aspiring blackjack players is, "Which counting system is best to use?" A great many counting systems are available on today's market. Some appear in the many books on blackjack and consequently cost little to obtain, while others still sell at a premium. (A few years back, almost all the better counting systems, plus some that weren't so good, sold for very high prices.)

Over the past several years, my opinion has changed dramatically. I used to think it was important to use a count that would win at the highest possible rate and put the most money on the table. In fact, I thought this second consideration, which was supposed to maximize my expectation, was the most important of all, and I was convinced that the more complicated counts identified many more favorable situations, thus making these counts the best. Moreover, I couldn't understand why many proponents of the simpler blackjack systems didn't also see it this way.

However, before discussing this idea in detail, let's look at two representative counts. The first is best known as Hi-Opt I. It is an extremely simple counting system. The threes, fours, fives, and sixes are counted as plus 1, all ten-valued cards are counted as minus 1, and every other card is ignored (that is, they receive a count of zero). More advanced players also can keep a side count of aces to adjust their betting decisions. In addition, detailed strategy tables are available for those players who want to do better than just play basic strategy. Since no card is assigned a point value greater than plus one or less than minus one, Hi-Opt I is known as a level one count.

The second example is known as the Uston Advanced Point Count. This is a much more complicated counting system and is consequently much tougher for some people to master. In this system, the deuces and eights are assigned a point value of plus 1, the threes, fours, sixes, and sevens are assigned a point

125

value of plus 2, the fives are plus 3, the nines are minus 1, and all ten-valued cards are assigned a value of minus 3. In addition, a player can keep a side count of aces to adjust his playing decisions, and there are (of course) detailed strategy tables to memorize. The Uston Advanced Point Count is known as a level three count.

For a long time, it was known that the higher level counts produced higher win rates, but the interesting thing was that these win rates were only slightly higher than those produced by the simple systems. Consequently, some authorities argued that players were probably better off using the simple counts if it meant that the propensity for making errors was reduced. I, for one, didn't buy this argument. I believed that if the more complicated counts found more favorable situations, meaning that a player could put more money on the table in the long run, they were still much superior. In fact, I didn't even think it was close.

One of the reasons I believed this comes from Ken Uston's book *Million Dollar Blackjack*. On page 102, Uston states that during the winter of 1979-1980, his team, which used a complex count, averaged $350 per hour, while another team, which used a simple count, averaged only $100 per hour, and that both teams each played for about 1,000 hours. This seemed like a huge difference to me. So obviously, the extra work to learn a more complex counting system was well worth it.

However, blackjack authority Arnold Snyder countered with a strong case of his own. His results, which are based on computer simulations by Dr. John Gwynn, show that in the long run, the simpler counts put approximately the same amount of money on the table as the much more complicated systems.

So what about the Uston experience? What happened is that the standard deviation — a statistical measure of dispersion (also known as short-term luck) — is so large in blackjack, especially if you are using large betting spreads, that even this difference was not statistically significant. That is, Uston came to the wrong conclusion, because he just happened to be much luckier than someone else. Even though much of my writings warn against this type of mistake, I fell into the trap.

Consequently, we can conclude that the simpler counts are superior to the more sophisticated counts. Simple counts have approximately the same expectation, but since they are much easier to use, a skilled player should make fewer errors and should be able to play for longer periods of time.

So which counting system is the best to use? In my opinion, it is Arnold Snyder's "Zen Count," which is available in his book *Blackbelt in Blackjack*. As Snyder says in his book, "This is an advanced card counting strategy for blackjack players who are willing and able to devote the time and effort necessary to mastering it. Even so, it is far simpler to learn and play than any other advanced blackjack strategy, because it has been streamlined for maximum efficiency with minimum effort."

Tipping

Believe it or not, tipping is a controversial subject. The reason is that no two serious gamblers will agree on how much is correct to tip. Some virtually never tip, while others tip so much that their tipping, not their bad play, makes them overall losers. This essay takes a closer look at tipping and suggests what I believe is an optimal strategy.

Let's first consider the person who would be classified as a big tipper. These people generally tip more when they are winning and less when they are losing, but nevertheless still tip a lot. In fact, as already stated, some people would be winners if only they would cut down on their tipping. Because the standard deviation for most gambling games is large when compared to the expectation, many big tippers do not think they are tipping excessively. That is, when they are running good, it does not seem that they have given away much money; when they are running bad, they reason that they would have been losers anyway. What they fail to consider is that in the long run, if they had never tipped, their overall performance would have been significantly better.

This seems to be an argument for never tipping, but being a "stiff" also can cause problems. What happens if you never tip is that you become known as someone who never rewards the dealers for good service. This means that when disputes arise, the casino or cardroom may be more likely to rule against you, simply because you are disliked. For example, a poker or blackjack dealer may reconstruct the dispute differently from the way it actually happened, forcing the floorman to rule against you. If this occurs only a few times, not tipping becomes very costly.

Consequently, the conclusion is to tip some but to keep tipping to an acceptable minimum. Exactly what this acceptable minimum should be is hard to say. It depends on many variables, including how well you are currently doing, how you have done in the long run, and the people with whom you are dealing.

I'd like to address one final aspect of tipping: giving timely tips in an effort to obtain a particular favor. This is often recommended in the gambling literature. As an example, the reader is advised to place a bet for the blackjack dealer or to tip him in an effort to encourage him to deal out more cards. Another example is to tip a poker room floor person in an effort to be put in a game before someone else.[15]

While this idea may have some merit, I do not subscribe to it. Moreover, in my opinion, the amount of these "bribes," to be truly worthwhile, would not prove cost effective. Yet this advice is given all the time, and many otherwise knowledgeable gamblers tip to get special favors. I suspect this is quite costly for most of them in the long run. (For more discussion on this subject, see my book *Blackjack Essays*.)

---

[15]Years ago, in the cardrooms of California, this was a very common practice. In fact, at times it was the only way that you could get a seat. However, today this is no longer the case. I know of no cardrooms in either California or Nevada that will tolerate this practice.

Theory in Practice

Afterthought

Always keep in mind that the standard deviation is your friend, not your enemy, as it allows losers to sometimes walk away from the tables as winners. It is this fact that makes many gambling games worthwhile. That is, there needs to be some hook that keeps the losers coming back, and allowing them to occasionally leave a winner is just what the skilled players need.

However, this does not mean that you should neglect the skills that achieve a high positive expectation. Just the opposite is, of course, true. But as some of the essays have show, practical actions as well as technical skills can influence your win rate. In fact, if the wrong actions are followed, a winner can expect to become a loser.

Also, remember that what is good for one person may not be good for another. Specifically, to gamble optimally, you need to appropriately balance your expectation against your standard deviation. This is done by also considering the size of your bankroll and the amount of risk that you are willing to take. This idea is extremely important, as are the many practical concepts that should influence your decisions.

Part Three

Pseudo Theory Exposed

Pseudo Theory Exposed

Introduction

Many of the ideas already developed, especially those dealing with the standard deviation and how it works, are not well understood by some of the writers in the vast field of gambling. This causes a great deal of advice to be given under what I call "pseudo theory." Even though many of these authors have good intentions, much of their advice will prove to be costly.

In addition, though they probably don't realize it, the pseudo theorists also preach self-weighting strategies. They would have us believe that winning opportunities occur all the time, are easy to identify, and are easy to take advantage of. Unfortunately, as we shall see, this is not the case.

Lottery Fallacies

With the recent increased interest in state lotteries, especially since the introduction of a lottery in the state of California, much literature has been produced discussing how these games are played and which strategies are supposed to produce profits. Unfortunately, even though there are a few occasional "big" winners, your expectation is always negative, no matter how these fixed-percentage games are approached. (An exception to this may exist based on strategies using unpopular numbers. See William Ziemba's book *Dr. Z's 6/49 Lotto Guidebook*. Another exception would be when there is a large carryover from a previous drawing.) That is, in the long run, you should expect to lose a lot of money. The purpose of this essay is to discuss and examine, from a "rational" point of view, some of the fallacies and misconceptions that have appeared in print.

Fallacy No. 1: Wheeling the numbers lowers the odds. The example I saw was as follows. Out of a possible 40 numbers, 11 were chosen. Then out of these 11, a different grouping of six numbers was selected for each game, with the argument being that it was easier to hit if 11 numbers were selected instead of six. Let's examine this concept.

First, in how many ways can exactly six out of 40 numbers be selected? This is solved by the mathematical theory of combinatorial analysis and is given by the following equation:

$$\binom{n}{k} = \frac{n!}{k!(n-k)!}$$

where

$$\binom{n}{k} \text{ is read } n \text{ choose } k, \text{ and}$$

$$n! = (n)(n-1)(n-2)...(3)(2)(1)$$

For our problem, $\binom{40}{6}$ is equal to the following:

$$\binom{40}{6} = \frac{40!}{6!(40-6)!} = \frac{(40)(39)(38)(37)(36)(35)}{(6)(5)(4)(3)(2)(1)} = 3,838,380$$

That is, there are exactly 3,838,380 ways in which six different numbers can be chosen out of 40. Taking the inverse of 3,838,380, we see that the probability of success is .000000261.

$$.000000261 = \frac{1}{3,838,380}$$

Now let's look at the wheeling method. First, let's assume that the 11 numbers do contain the six selections. Using similar analysis to that just given, we see that the probability of selecting these six numbers out of 11 is .002164502.

$$\binom{11}{6} = 462, \text{ and}$$

$$\frac{1}{462} = .002164502$$

The next question to ask is, what is the probability of picking 11 numbers out of 40 that will contain the six selections? For simplicity, let's assume that the first six numbers in the group of 11 are the selected six and that the remaining five are any of the 34 non-selected numbers. Now the probability of the first number being good is simply 6/40. The probability of the second number being good is 5/39, since there are five good numbers left out of the remaining 39. Continuing in this manner, we will exhaust the six good selections, leaving 34 numbers, all of which are bad, meaning that the probability of selecting a bad number is now 1 (after the six good numbers have been removed).

Returning to the general case, we see that it doesn't matter in which order the six good numbers are selected and that the overall probability of selecting any particular set of 11 numbers that contain the six numbers is the same. (You can see this for yourself by working a few examples, with the order of the good hits different from the example given.) Now we are back to asking how many ways a set of 11 can contain a particular set of six, (or 11 choose six) which as before is 462. Consequently, the probability of picking 11 out of 40 that will contain the six selections is .000120363.

$$.0001206363 = \frac{(6)(5)(4)(3)(2)(1)(34)(33)(32)(31)(30)}{(40)(39)(38)(37)(36)(35)(34)(33)(32)(31)(30)}$$

And since the probability of selecting the correct six numbers, given that the larger group of 11 contains them, is .002164502, the overall probability of success is .000000261.

$$.000000261 = (.002164502)(.000120363)$$

Notice that this is the same probability as when the numbers were not wheeled. Consequently, the idea that wheeling can reduce the odds against you is completely worthless.

Fallacy No. 2: Go with the hot numbers. The idea here is that certain numbers are currently hot and therefore should be selected. (This could happen if there was some flaw in the selection device, causing some number to have a greater probability than normal to be selected, or if non-random events were taking place. For those interested in information on non-random events, see the essay titled "Sequencing" in Part One of this book.) Similarly, the lottery player should stay away from other numbers that are cold. For example, in the August 1985 issue of *Gambling Times,* a frequency table was given for 26 consecutive weeks of the Maryland State Lottery, which chooses six numbers out of 40 each week for its "Lotto Game." Sure enough, one number was never hit during this entire time period. Should this number not be played? To answer this, let's compute the probability for a number not being selected and then decide how reasonable or unreasonable this probability is.

First, what is the probability of not selecting a number in a particular week? Since six out of 40 balls are chosen, the probability of not selecting the number on the first try is 39/40. On the second try, assuming the number is not hit on the first attempt, the probability of not being selected is 38/39, as one ball has been removed. This process is continued until six selections are made, producing a probability of not being hit of .85.

$$.85 = \frac{(39)(38)(37)(36)(35)(34)}{(40)(39)(38)(37)(36)(35)}$$

For 26 games, the probability of a number never being selected is .85 to the 26th power, since each game is statistically independent of all the others. This computes to .0146. In other words, approximately 1.5 percent of the time, a number will not hit for 26 games. With 40 numbers available, the expected number of balls that will never be selected is 0.584.

$$0.584 = (40)(.0146)$$

Consequently, it seems reasonable that one number was not selected.

On the high side, from the same frequency table, we see that three numbers were each hit a total of 7 times. Was this unusual? To compute this probability, we need to use what is known as the Binomial Theorem. It tells us that (when we are sampling with replacement) the probability of a number being selected exactly k times in n trials is equal to the following formula:

$$\text{Probability} = \binom{n}{k} p^k q^{n-k}$$

where
    n is the number of trials,
    k is the number of selections,
    p is the probability of success, and
    q is the probability of failure.

Suppose we were interested in the probability of exactly three selections for some particular number in our example. Our variable values are: n is 26, k is 3, q is .85 (from above), and p is 1 - .85 or .15, since the total probability of all events is 1. This means that the probability of selecting a number exactly three is .2089 or approximately 21 percent.

$$.2089 = \binom{26}{3}(.15)^3(.85)^{23}$$

Table I gives the probability for a different number of selections out of 26 trials with p = .15.

Table I: Probability of Frequency Selections in 26 Trials

Number	Probability	Number	Probability
0	.0146	6	.1016
1	.0671	7	.0512
2	.1480	8	.0215
3	.2089	9	.0076
4	.2119	10	.0023
5	.1647	20	----

To answer our question, the probability of seven or more selections is simply 1 minus the probability of having zero, one, two, three, four, five, and six selections. This computes to .0832.

$$.0832 = 1 - (.0146 + .0671 + .1480 + .2089 + .2119 + .1647 + .1016)$$

Without showing any further calculations, it easily should be seen that the two extremes of zero selections and seven selections are not really extreme at all. Consequently, the idea that this game can be "handicapped" is not mathematically justified. In fact, the game appears to be performing as the laws of probability would have us believe it should.

Fallacy No. 3: Double hit ratio. The idea here is to determine those numbers which, when they are selected, have a high propensity to hit again the very next game. Let's look at an example. In the March 1985 issue of *Gambling Times,* we are told that in the New York Lottery, which contains 44 numbers, that on 52 occasions where #10 was selected, given that it was not selected the previous week, this number immediately hit again 17 times (four triple hits plus 13 double hits). The question arises whether this "double hit ratio" is out of line. (We are assuming that the series did not end on a live hit. If that were the case, the following probabilities would be slightly different.)

To answer this, using similar analysis to that given in Fallacy No. 2, it can be shown that the probability of any number not being selected is .8636, which means that the probability of being selected is .1364. Now given that this number was selected 52 times without a preceding hit, it means that there were 52 opportunities for it to hit again. Table II gives the probabilities for different number of successive hits when there are 52 opportunities.

139

Table II: Probability of Frequency Selections in
52 Trials

Number	Probability	Number	Probability
0	.0005	11	.0450
1	.0040	12	.0243
2	.0161	13	.0118
3	.0425	14	.0052
4	.0822	15	.00212
5	.1246	16	.000758
6	.1542	17	.000254
7	.1600	18	.000078
8	.1422	19	.000022
9	.1098	20	.000006
10	.0746	21	.000001
		22+	.------

Again, using similar analysis as in Fallacy No. 2, the probability of 17 or more successive hits (based on Table II) is .000361. With 44 numbers to be selected, once they each have had 52 opportunities for successive hits, the expectation for 17 or more double hits is approximately 0.0159.

This is actually a very low expectation. In fact, you would expect this to happen only once in every 63 sets of 52 trials (on all 44 numbers). Consequently, this number could be a candidate for some sort of bias. Does one exist?

On further examination of the article, we find that the New York Lottery used to have 40 numbers instead of the current 44. Table IIA is supplied to give the same results based on a total of 40 balls being eligible instead of 44.

Table IIA: Probability of Frequency Selections in 52 Trials (40 Balls)

Number	Probability	Number	Probability
0	.0002	11	.0667
1	.0020	12	.0402
2	.0088	13	.0218
3	.0260	14	.0107
4	.0561	15	.0048
5	.0950	16	.0020
6	.1314	17	.000732
7	.1524	18	.000251
8	.1512	19	.000079
9	.1305	20	.000023
10	.0990	21	.000006
		22	.000002

This table shows that the probability of 17 or more hits is approximately .0011. Again, once all 40 numbers have each been selected 52 times, the expectation for 17 or more successive hits is .0484. Now we need only 21 sets of 52 trials for the expectation to be 1. This is still a small probability but not as extreme as the other result. In truth, the result is probably between these two extremes, as the number of balls changed. But an expectation in the range of .0159 to .0484 is not unrealistic, since we are looking at a large volume of data, and a situation where one number appears off would eventually occur. (For example, an expectation such as .0001 would be very strong evidence.) Also, upon examination of the table on page 79 of the March 1985 issue of *Gambling Times,* there is no other number out of line. (Another example is given below.) Consequently, since everything else is behaving as it should, it is not surprising in a large sample of data points to find one that at first appears not to be from the hypothesized population. However, until more evidence is accumulated, it is unwise to make this assumption.

Similarly, #6 also had 52 opportunities (one triple hit plus three double hits plus 48 single hits). From Table II, the probability of four or fewer follow-up hits is almost 15 percent. Table IIA also gives a highly significant number. Obviously, this example, which appeared in the same article, is well within the expectation of normal probability, and there is no reason to believe that when #6 is selected, its probability of not being selected the next week is reduced. Enough said.

Fallacy No. 4: Skip-and-hit patterns. The idea for "skip-and-hit" is that when numbers go cold, they can become very cold. Suppose we are dealing with a 44 number Lotto game where six balls are selected. From Fallacy No. 3, we know that the probability of any number not being selected for any particular game is .8636. For two consecutive games, the probability of any number not being selected — since the games are "statistically independent" of each other — is simply .8636 X .8636, or .7458. Similarly, for three consecutive games, the probability of no selection is .8636 X .8636 X .8636 or .6441. Table III gives the probability of "cold streaks" for different number of games.

Table III: Probability of Cold Streaks

Consecutive Games Without a Hit	Probability	Consecutive Games Without a Hit	Probability
1	.8636	13	.1486
2	.7458	14	.1283
3	.6441	15	.1108
4	.5562	16	.0957
5	.4804	17	.0827
6	.4148	18	.0714
7	.3583	19	.0617
8	.3094	20	.0532
9	.2672	25	.0256
10	.2307	30	.0123
11	.1993	35	.0059
12	.1721	40	.0028

Again, trying to keep the mathematics brief, Table III shows that extended cold streaks for a few numbers out of the total 44 numbers is not unusual, but expected. This doesn't mean that these particular numbers are "cold," but that the selections, which are governed by the laws of probability, are behaving as expected. That is, in the very next game, the probability of a cold number being selected is the same as the probability of a hot number being selected.

Fallacy No. 5: Companions. Do numbers really make friends with other numbers and make an effort to be hit together? Or do the laws of probability tell us that with a large selection of numbers to begin with, it is expected that a few other numbers will appear to hit when a particular number is selected? That is, their previous companionship has no effect on future selections. Obviously, the second conjecture mentioned is true.

For example, suppose in a 40-number Lotto game that some particular number is selected. What is the probability that a second particular number also will be selected? First, notice that given the first number is picked, there are only five opportunities for some other number to be selected. Consequently, the probability of this second number not being selected is .8718.

$$.8718 = \frac{(38)(37)(36)(35)(34)}{(39)(38)(37)(36)(35)}$$

This means that the probability of the second number being selected is .1282. Now suppose the first number is selected on 30 different occasions. Using analysis similar to that previously given, Table IV shows the probability of different frequency distributions of a companion number.

Table IV: Probability of Companion for a
40-Number Lotto Game with 30 Opportunities

Number	Probability	Number	Probability
0	.0163	7	.0494
1	.0720	8	.0209
2	.1534	9	.0075
3	.2106	10	.0023
4	.2090	15	.000001
5	.1598	20	.----
6	.0979	25	.----

As can be seen from Table IV, along with some further analysis not shown, the probability after 30 opportunities for some number to be a companion eight or more times is .0307, or slightly more than 3 percent of the time. This means that with 39 companions available, there usually would be another number that is "friendly." But it does not mean that some number, which does not appear friendly, has any less chance of being a companion in the future than any other number.

Final comments. I suspect that a lot of people are spending many hours charting and handicapping their Lotto numbers. Instead, they could go to the local zoo and ask the first monkey they see to make their selections, and the probability of becoming a winner would be exactly the same. The idea that numbers have personalities and other human traits is just plain silly. Anyone who suggests this is extremely ignorant of probability theory and the appropriate mathematical laws that govern selection of these numbers.

The only bit of advice that I have seen with any merit is to try to select numbers that are not popular with most players. This way, if you do win, you won't have to split the money pool with as many other people. (Again, see the Ziemba book.)

Finally, lotteries do provide an opportunity to win a large amount of money for a very small investment. But trying to play a lottery for profit is not realistic. (As Ziemba's book notes, even when you can buy a ticket based on unpopular numbers that has a positive expectation, the standard deviation on this ticket is still extremely large.) I don't care how many winning tickets are in someone's desk or how many times some Bulgarian mathematician's name is mentioned. If selecting winning lottery numbers were actually possible, we all would be doing it.

Dangerous Ideas

One problem that the aspiring gambler must cope with are the many dangerous ideas that appear throughout the gambling literature. These ideas are dangerous in the sense that if you follow them, they have the ability to quickly deplete your bankroll. Some of the ideas are put forth by well-meaning people who don't fully understand the subject matter that they are grappling with. Unfortunately, however, many ideas are proffered by individuals who are just trying to make a quick buck and don't mind ripping off their customers to do so. For example, I know of two self-proclaimed gambling "experts" who also claim to have Ph. D.s in mathematics. In my opinion, they can barely add and subtract, yet many of their ideas have received much publicity at times. Some of these dangerous gambling ideas are discussed in this essay.

Dangerous Idea No. 1: Blackjack biases can be exploited. In his book *The Theory of Blackjack*, Peter Griffin says that if you take a brand-new deck (where the cards come in a particular preset order) and give it five perfect shuffles, the house will have a huge advantage. This is because the results of the shuffles are now "deterministic" instead of being "probabilistic."

I have done something similar. (See my book *Blackjack Essays*.) On my computer at home, I started with a deck of cards ordered ace to king, ace to king, ace to king, and ace to king, used a crude non-random shuffle (that I programmed), played basic strategy against Las Vegas Strip rules, and had a loss rate of more than 2 percent when the expectation was to break even. That is, I obtained a result that was completely unexpected.

Notice that in both of these examples, it appears that a dealer bias has developed. Also, it seems logical that if dealer biases can develop, then player biases can develop. But does this mean that a skilled player can go into a casino and exploit biases to his advantage?

In the last few years, several systems have come on the market that recommend this approach. The player walks into a casino and tries to correlate certain table/playing characteristics with those of an ongoing player bias. If the correlation is successful, then a profitable situation should be found, even if conventional card counting techniques predict otherwise.

My research indicates that I was able to create a dealer bias because I began with the deck in a particular order and used a very crude shuffling procedure. But in a casino, the decks will never be ordered to such an extreme; even a new deck will quickly change. In my experiment, a new deck was brought into play every set of shuffles. Obviously this will not happen in a casino, plus the typical casino shuffle is much more unpredictable than what I used. In addition, my attempt to correlate a bias with the number of statistical "runs" in a deck was unsuccessful. (Again, see *Blackjack Essays.*) The conclusion is that while biases do exist, they are not only few and far between, but extremely weak as well. Consequently, the idea that you can walk into a casino and play winning blackjack by appropriate table selection just doesn't make much sense.

In 1987, a paper by John Gwynn and Arnold Snyder that examined the differences between casino blackjack and computer-simulated blackjack was presented at the 7th International Conference on Gambling and Risk Taking in Reno, Nevada. In their study, Snyder and Gwynn simulated non-random shuffles and attempted to see whether a poor shuffle can be exploited as the basis of a winning system.

Snyder and Gwynn had no luck. Even though they collected "voluminous" data, their conclusion was that the basic strategy player could not tell the difference between simulated dealer shuffling and random shuffling.

Dangerous Idea No. 2: Random numbers come in predictable patterns. This is part of the pseudo-theory that lottery system sellers use to manipulate the naive public. Lotto is similar to keno. Every week, a subset of numbers is selected from a larger population of numbers, and it often happens that some numbers, if you consider past games, have been selected much more than other numbers. Does this mean that some numbers are hot and others are cold? The lottery system experts would have you believe so.

In reality, this sort of (number) distribution is expected. Probability theory tells us that if you repeat sampling a small group of numbers out of a larger group, it is expected that some numbers will be picked more than their fair share, while others will be picked less than their fair share. This is exactly what happens in weekly lottery games.

But probability theory also tells us that even though these patterns seem to appear from a historical standpoint, they actually do not exist. This is because if each number were to be selected exactly its fair share, the selection procedure would not be random. Consequently, each number has the same chance of selection in the next game no matter what its performance in previous games may have been. Moreover, other ideas — such as skip-and-hit patterns, companion combinations, and wheeling techniques — will not help you select winning combinations.

Ironically, these ideas won't hurt either, in the sense that if you follow them, your chances of success won't be diminished. But if they encourage someone to play the lottery who otherwise would not have played, they become expensive. In addition, I suspect that some of the people who peddle these worthless ideas have made a lot of money. Somehow, this does not seem right.

Dangerous Idea No. 3: It's better to be lucky than good. This statement is heard from participants in all forms of gambling, and many players truly believe it. However, your results are actually predicated on two parameters. The first is the win rate, which is your expectation for some period of time. (Note that the win rate can be positive or negative.) The second parameter is the standard deviation, which is a statistical measure of the natural fluctuations of the game. Some people refer to these natural fluctuations as "luck," either good or bad.

It turns out that in many forms of gambling, if you participate for only a short period of time, the standard deviation is the parameter that dominates your results. That is, in the short run, it probably is better to be lucky than good. But what happens if you gamble regularly, as does the poker player who plays every day or the sports bettor who visits his favorite book several times a week? Now your overall expectation will begin to dominate your results, and the luck factor will become less significant. This is known as getting into the long run, and in some forms of gambling, it can take a very long time.

So if you are just an occasional gambler, or if you plan to play for only a short period of time, then it is better to be lucky than good. The problem is that you won't know until after the fact what your luck will be. On the other hand, if you plan on playing for a long time, or if you are willing to make a significant investment, the luck factor should eventually become minimal. This means that you must be good, otherwise, you can expect to ultimately go broke.

Dangerous Idea No. 4: Gambling occurs in the short run. This is related to Idea No. 3, but I frequently have seen it used by blackjack system sellers who were arguing against conventional card counting techniques. The argument claims that card counting techniques work on computers where millions of hands are simulated and the shuffle is totally random, but that other means are required for short-term casino sessions.

What this argument shows is that the proponents do not understand the concept of statistical fluctuations as measured by the standard deviation. In other words, even though you may have a certain expectation in a game, large fluctuations in your results can appear. This is also true from a casino's point of view. For example, in a large casino, it would be expected that there are a small number of tables where the dealer has gone over a total of 21 much more than was expected in some recent period of time. But this does not mean that the next hand dealt at one of these tables is any more likely to be a dealer bust — unless, of course, other specific information is known about the distribution of cards in the deck. Yet the proponents of "short-run gambling" make this claim.

By the way, if gambling was really a series of short-run experiences, numerous typical short runs easily could be reproduced on a computer, thus producing long-run results. The researcher would then look at these long-run results and draw appropriate conclusions about the short run. This is exactly what I did (see Idea No. 1) and is precisely why I do not support these claims.

Dangerous Idea No. 5: Always try to walk away a winner. I recently heard this remark from a poker acquaintance (who, by the way, is a very weak player). "Mason," he said, "I was ahead $1,500. Why didn't I quit before I lost it all back?" Needless to say, this is the type of silliness that the money managers propose. It is easy to say after the fact that you should have quit, but to say it ahead of time is another matter.

It seems to me that the money managers are looking for a way to tame the standard deviation that a particular game might offer. Of course, this cannot be done. But in truth, the standard deviation is not something that the skilled gambler wants to tame, because the natural fluctuations inherent in most forms of gambling enable the overall losers to score some occasional wins. This means that these players return to compete again, usually to make a deposit, not a withdrawal. Also, notice that if losers can occasionally score some wins, it is inevitable that winners will sometimes lose. In fact, winners should sometimes have significant losses. But in the long run, they expect to do quite well.

Another thing to keep in mind, as has already been mentioned, is that more powerful strategies, which can increase your expectation only slightly, often have significantly higher standard deviations. Consequently, the better you are, the more losses you may have, although your long-run performance may be closer to optimal. This is because you are attempting to squeeze the maximum amount of profit out of very marginal situations.

Dangerous Idea No. 6: Winning poker is just statistical analysis. I wish only that this were true, for if it was, I have no doubt that I would be one of the very best players around. However, winning at poker requires a knowledge of many things, such as basic probabilities, advanced mathematics, psychology, logic, reading hands and opponents, shifting gears, strategic concepts, and much more. The beginning poker player tends to think that it is necessary to learn only the basic probabilities. But someone who has a detailed knowledge of the basic probabilities will enjoy at best only a very small advantage against someone who has a good intuitive feel for the same statistics. (I am assuming that the two players are equal in the other areas of the game.)

This does not mean that a beginning poker player should neglect the basic mathematics of play. Just the opposite is true, as the basic probabilities of poker are the foundation upon which the expert player builds his game. But poker is a marvelous blend of many attributes that must be mastered to become an expert player, and unless this is done, you can expect to be a loser for life.

Incidentally, typical players, even those who visit public cardrooms regularly, never fully realize the gap in skill that exists between them and the real experts. This is probably why so much nonsense is published about luck. In fact, the very best players are aware of — and successfully use — strategies (such as game-theory techniques) and counterstrategies that the typical player doesn't even know exist. (See *Sklansky on Poker* by David Sklansky for more discussion on this subject.)

Dangerous Idea No. 7: Home computers make gambling easy. I have often read that computers make gambling an easy undertaking, and many people believe this is true. One young lady even claimed (in print) that she bought a home computer, quickly taught herself the Basic language, and then programmed about twenty different blackjack systems to help her determine which was the best. Even though I suppose this is possible, I don't know anyone, including myself, who has this ability.

By the same token, several of my friends and acquaintances have requested a visit to put everything they know about poker or some other form of gambling into my computer. They have no idea what a difficult task this would be, and that such a major undertaking could require several years to complete, especially if an attempt to program sophisticated strategies was made.

Let's look at home computers and gambling from a realistic point of view. First, a computer is a significant investment. Not only is it expensive, but the basic computer is not powerful enough to do the type of computations that such sophisticated research requires. You might need to add memory expansion chips, special processing chips to speed up calculations, appropriate software, a modem (for communications), and a hard disk to increase storage space. These extras don't come for free.

Second, you will need to learn an appropriate computer language. Unfortunately, Basic won't do. It is too cumbersome to program in and too slow to do the number of simulations that gambling research requires.[16] One good language is Pascal and other excellent languages are also available. Related to the language that you choose is the need for a thorough knowledge of your system, as some languages have features that work on some systems but not on others.

And third, you need a complete knowledge of what it is you are trying to resolve, since many research problems — especially those related to poker — are complex.[17] Just having

---

[16]This no longer may be accurate. New versions of Basic are now available that are much more versatile and flexible.

[17]In fact, a great deal of inaccurate computer results relating to poker have been published. Many of these authors need to recognize that their opponents do not play random cards and do not automatically go to the end.

an idea of what you want done is not good enough. An exact understanding of the specific circumstances is an absolute requirement.

This was not written to discourage you from doing gambling research. In fact, there is no question that home computers are marvelous tools, and because of them, much enlightened research has recently been done. But this endeavor is not as easy as some "experts" have claimed it to be.

Dangerous Idea No. 8: Experienced gamblers know what they are doing. Just because someone has been gambling for many years does not mean that he knows what he is doing. To assess a gambler's ability, you first must consider the games he plays. If he plays craps or some other house-percentage game, then he is a loser no matter what he may claim, no matter how knowledgeable he may be about the game, and no matter how successful he may appear to be at it.

On the other hand, suppose he plays a beatable game like poker or participates in sports betting. Here again, having a great deal of experience does not mean that he is a winner. The reason is that many people, even though they may have years of playing experience, believe that all gambling games are luck-oriented. They are dominated by the natural fluctuations that are present in almost all forms of beatable gambling, and they never set out to discover and master those skills that can make someone a winner in the long run.

By the way, just because someone tells you he is a winner doesn't mean that it's true. In fact, I suspect that most gamblers who believe they are winners are actually losers. They blame their losses on bad luck and fail to recognize that a lack of skill is causing their problems. Moreover, their occasional big wins reinforce the false belief that they are winners. Of course, readers of this book will recognize that the large standard deviation inherent in most forms of gambling fools the typical risk taker, which is another example of why the standard deviation is the skilled gambler's friend.

153

Dangerous Idea No. 9: Great players regularly can be found in low-limit games. This is an idea that is frequently heard in the poker world, but I suspect it applies to other forms of gambling as well. Suppose you are a small-stakes poker player and you are able to win at a rate of $5 per hour. Wouldn't you be tempted to move to a bigger game where you could perhaps double or triple your win rate? Well, virtually every winning poker player does this, and there are two consequences. First, the larger games become tougher, and second, many players move up to a level where they no longer can win.

But what about the great small-limit player? Does such a person actually exist? Is it possible that the greatest players in the world might be playing $1-$2 limit instead of $100-$200 limit? I think this is extremely unlikely. First, the lure to move up is just too great for most people. A second reason — often overlooked by the proponents of this idea — is that since most of the better players do move up, the quality of competition is not that strong at the smaller limits, and to become a great player, you need to go up against quality competition. Consequently, I cannot believe that some of the greatest players to ever participate in the game play only for small stakes.

By the way, it is not my intention to criticize or degrade anyone for playing small stakes. I believe someone should play at a level where he is comfortable. In addition, if you are a serious player who has trouble winning at the higher stakes, you are certainly better off playing small. In fact, because the high-limit games are so much tougher, you frequently can expect a higher win rate at the smaller limit. (Even though this is often true, few professional players follow this advice.) What size game you decide to play should be a personal matter, but don't let ego or other extraneous factors determine the stakes.

Dangerous Idea No. 10: It is not necessary to read the books. Again, I am thinking primarily of poker, but I'm sure this idea carries over into other forms of gambling. Winning poker is not only the process of accumulating knowledge, but also the art of applying the right knowledge at the most opportune time. In other words, a winning poker player uses the knowledge gained from books (and other sources), plus acquires a great deal of playing experience. This combination can make you an expert.

Unfortunately, the vast majority of poker books (and books on other forms of gambling) are not very good. In fact, most are illogical and are filled with misleading advice. One skill the expert player has is the ability to distinguish between good and bad literature. Following are a few questions I ask myself to determine whether what I am reading is good.

1. Does the author or "hero" of the book constantly make great unbeatable hands?

2. Does the author play against "dumb, fat" opponents who like to give their money away, or is the quality of competition considered tough?

3. Is the author considered to be an expert, or is he someone who can even win on his "occasional trips to Las Vegas"?

4. Does the author consider other factors, such as position, potential pot size, impact of past plays, and so forth, when giving advice?

5. Is the author specific or vague in his advice?

6. Given that the advice is specific, are the author's recommendations based on sound detailed research and/or playing experiences, or do they just seem to materialize?

7. Does the author advise readers just to play tight, or does he understand what a tight but aggressive approach is?

8. Does the author claim that poker is easy, or does he recognize the many complexities and subtleties of the game?

I once asked one of my favorite gambling authorities his opinion of a certain book pertaining to sports betting. "Well," he said, "80 percent of what that book says is correct, and 20 percent of what that book says is wrong. The problem is that you won't be able to tell the 20 percent from the 80 percent." Of course, this doesn't mean that all books on sports betting are like this, but it does mean that you should be certain the advice you are following is absolutely correct.

Dangerous Idea No. 11: I'll win it all back tomorrow. One of the great misconceptions in all of gambling is that the skillful player can quickly make up his losses. Furthermore, winning players who do not understand this can get into a lot of trouble if they press trying to recoup what they have lost. Let's look at an example.

Suppose you are a $30 per hour winner in a game that has a $500 per hour standard deviation, and your typical playing session is five hours. Thus, your overall expectation for the session is $150. (These numbers are typical for many forms of gambling.) The first question to ask is, how often will you be a loser? This is determined by solving the following equation:

$$0 = (30)(5) + (X)(500)(5)^{1/2}$$

X turns out to be −.13, which is the number of standard deviations below the mean — that is, the $150 expectation — required to break even. (See the essay titled "How Much Do You Need?" in Part Two for a fuller explanation of the math.) From a normal distribution table, we see that −.13 standard deviations corresponds to the 44.83 percentage point. This means that with the parameters given you should expect to be a loser in about 45 percent of your five-hour playing sessions.

Some of these losses will be small, and some will be substantial. Your median loss will occur at the 22.815 percentage point, which (again from the table) corresponds to

.74 standard deviations below the mean. Consequently, your median loss is given by the following equation.

$$Median\ Loss = (30)(5) + (-.74)(500)(5)^{\frac{1}{2}}$$
$$= 677.35$$

This means that half of your losses, given that a loss occurs, will be greater than $677.35. Also, remember that your expectation is just $150 per session. Hence, it could be many sessions before a loss is made up.

This is why it is crucial for the serious gambler to be willing to "grind it back," even though it may be frustrating to do so. Many players, when they get "stuck" for a lot of money, abandon this style and try to play in such a way that enables them to quickly get even. This usually translates into taking chances that are incorrect but that can recoup a large portion of their losses if they are successful. An example is to draw to an inside straight in poker when the pot odds don't warrant it, or to double down in blackjack when it is incorrect to do so. It is true that this approach, because of the increased standard deviation that comes with it, may give you a better chance of breaking even in a short playing session. But you usually decrease your expectation, and some players who would be long-run winners become long-run losers because of this practice.

Dangerous Idea No. 12: Luck exists and is a tangible quantity. In reality, the results you obtain at the gaming tables are governed by probability or skill or a combination of both. The idea that certain people are inherently lucky or that you can create your own luck is just plain silly. But sometimes certain people appear to be lucky or unlucky, because many gambling games have large statistical fluctuations. This means that over a fairly long period of time, a small number of people will do much better than expected, and a small number of people will do much worse than expected. These individuals thus will appear either lucky or unlucky.

What is important is to make your opponent think you are lucky, even though you are no more lucky or unlucky than anyone else. Here is an example. Suppose you are a skilled blackjack player. One major problem is that the house may figure out you have the skill to beat the game. If pit personnel conclude, correctly, that your capabilities are this strong, they most likely will alter their game or perhaps even bar you. However, if you can convince the pit that you are just lucky and that your wins are not a result of skill, there is a better chance that you won't receive any heat. (One way to help achieve this is to talk about your big wins at other games, such as craps and keno.) Always keep in mind that many opponents including casino personnel are luck conscious, and this is what the skilled gambler can exploit. He cannot exploit the idea of luck itself.

Dangerous Idea No. 13: Always play at stakes you are comfortable with. This is a concept usually aimed at poker players, but it carries over to many forms of gambling. Of course, most of us agree that we don't want to risk the rent money. The pressure would be too great and would prevent us from making the correct decisions all the time. But what does being comfortable mean? To me, it means gambling with money that won't matter if I lose. My experience is that if the money does not matter, the thrill of gambling begins to dominate the decision-making process. This will cause the poker player to play too many hands, the blackjack player to play in casinos with poor rules and/or poor deck penetration, and the sports bettor to bet too many games.

The conclusion is that the successful gambler plays with money that (1) he can afford to lose but that (2) losing it will be unpleasant and actually may hurt him a little. This is the balance that I believe produces optimum results. For example, when waiting to get into my regular poker game, I used to pass the time at much smaller limits. Even though I was successful in the bigger games (which were much tougher), I found myself losing at the small limits. The amount of money risked in these little games was just not meaningful enough to make me play well.

Dangerous Idea No. 14: Examine large volumes of data. This has to do with sports betting and the large amount of statistical data that can be collected. Any competent statistician will tell you that you first should form a hypothesis and then collect data to either (statistically) confirm or reject the hypothesis. You should not collect the data first and then look for patterns or trends to exploit, because with a large body of data, pseudo-patterns that are logically flawed will appear. For example, you might discover that a certain team performs very well, as long as it is five days after a win and it was raining the day the win occurred. Clearly, this trend is totally illogical, but with lots of data available on lots of teams, I see this type of information in print all the time. (For instance, many tout sheets have a section on the latest "angles.")

A great example of this type of flawed analysis was baseball's All Star Game during the '70s and 80s. Even if the National League was far superior to the American League, it was not expected to win such a large percentage of the All Star games during this time frame. The reason for this is that no baseball team can produce the type of control over the game that will allow it to win virtually every time against reasonable competition. Yet past data seems to indicate that the National League should be an overwhelming favorite. Needless to say, this type of flawed conclusion, based on an obvious statistical perturbation, could be costly to a great many bettors.

Dangerous Idea No. 15: If you can beat one form of poker, you can beat all forms of poker. It is true that certain ideas and concepts apply to all forms of poker. For example, the more people who remain to act behind you, the more selective you should be in deciding which hands to play. But even though understanding these types of ideas is essential to winning play, each form of poker also has its own individual subtleties.

159

Let's compare seven-card stud to Texas hold'em. To the inexperienced player, these two games appear to be very similar: They are both seven-card games, and both have face up and face down cards. But the community-card nature of hold'em makes it strategically very different from stud. For example, kickers in hold'em are much more crucial, since more than one player can have the same basic hand. Specifically, if an ace appears on the board, more than one player can have a pair of aces. This means that if you hold an ace and a bad kicker when an ace is on the board, and someone bets, you can be in trouble. In stud, if you hold two aces and someone bets, your next best card does not have the same impact on your decision.

Consequently, being skilled at one form of poker will not enable you to win at another form. This is why very few players excel at many games, though it can be done.

Dangerous Idea No. 16: There is smart luck and dumb luck. This is an idea that I have seen associated with what I call "pseudo lottery theory," but it also can be applied to other forms of gambling. In addition, it is closely associated with examining large volumes of data, as was discussed in Idea No. 14. The concept, as I understand it, is that examining past results and/or becoming knowledgeable concerning the mechanics of a game, you would be more apt to make lucky decisions. An example might be to pick those lotto numbers that are currently "hot."

However, you must realize that when gambling, there are often many decisions to make. Some decisions count (such as whether to draw two or three cards to a pair in draw poker), and others don't (such as whether to bet red or black on a roulette wheel). If a decision counts, skill and knowledge will help you make it correctly; If a decision doesn't count, no form of luck, either smart or dumb, will help you.

Dangerous Idea No. 17: Winning blackjack and card counting are synonymous. Many years ago, if you mastered a card counting system, you probably could have gone into any casino and expected to be a winner. Unfortunately, this is not true today. Even though a solid count is, of course, required, much more is needed to be successful in the modern casino environment. Today's successful blackjack player not only is an expert at card counting, but also can (1) recognize whether a game is good, (2) manipulate his opponent, the casino, into making the game favorable, or at least assure that the game stays as good as it currently is, (3) manipulate his fellow players in ways that improve the game, and (4) balance factors that will require him to make different decisions at different times. (For example, usually it is better to play heads up, but sometimes it may be better to play at a full table.)

Dangerous Idea No. 18: Play the same in tournaments as at other times. Nothing could be further from the truth. In a regular game, no matter what form of gambling, you want to play your best at all times to assure as large a win as possible. (There are a few exceptions to this. As an example, if a bad player is losing heavily at the poker table, it might be best to ease up a little if you fear that another bad beating might cause this "producer" to quit.) But in a tournament, this is not the case. Your goal should not be to win the most chips, but to maximize your expectation. Consequently, you may at times play more conservatively than what is normal and/or more aggressively than what is generally considered correct. Of course, this depends on the prizes that are offered and the difference between prizes. For instance, on the last hand in a blackjack tournament, depending on whether you are behind or ahead of your opponents, it may become correct to take a tremendous risk, such as doubling down on a total greater than 11, if this gives you a chance to win. Notice that someone playing "correctly" would never do this.

Dangerous Idea No. 19: Use a conservative basic strategy. When playing blackjack, certain plays, such as doubling down with a total of 10 versus a dealer's deuce, are more risky than other plays, such as doubling down with a total of 10 versus a dealer's six. The idea is that to reduce risk, it is often better to make the play that puts less money on the table. The problem is that these plays are more costly in the long run. For example, the reason you split eights against a ten is not to make money, but to lose less money since a total of 16 versus a dealer's ten is such a big loser. The conservative basic strategy that I examined was supposed to lose at a rate of 1.5 percent. Compare this to correct basic strategy, which produces essentially a dead-even game when playing with a single deck and Las Vegas Strip rules. What the conservative basic strategy does is reduce the standard deviation. Unfortunately, this reduction is at a cost you cannot afford.

Dangerous Idea No. 20: Exhibit a wild and aggressive image. This is a poker concept that has become popular with several of the poker writers. The idea is to project an image that will make your opponents think you are a little crazy, thus encouraging them to call a lot of your bets.

This approach makes sense in relatively easy forms of poker, such as high draw, jacks or better to open, where the pots tend to be small and many errors are often obvious (even to the bad players). An example of an obvious mistake in high draw is to call an opener who must have at least two jacks with a pair smaller than jacks. In this game, getting these types of calls can be very profitable in the long run.

But striving for these type of calls is clearly wrong in a game like seven-card stud, where the pots quickly become so large that it is often correct to chase. In a game where it is correct to chase, why would you want to encourage your opponent to call? That is, why make him play correctly in situations where if he folds, you might be able to steal a large pot? Put another way, in most forms of poker, if you act like Bozo the Clown, you are probably playing like Bozo the Clown.

Dangerous Idea No. 21: Bet more with the casino's money than with your own. As silly as this concept is, I see it all the time in the gambling literature. The idea is that if you are ahead, since the money came from the casino, you can tolerate more risk. I've already discussed in detail what makes up a good bet. Specifically, a good bet is determined by your expectation and standard deviation, balanced against your bankroll and how much risk you are willing to assume. The more favorable these parameters are, the more you should want to bet. Notice that a good bet has nothing to do with your current status.

An exception is when you are significantly ahead. In this situation you may want to increase the stakes simply because your bankroll can now tolerate a larger bet, assuming that the standard deviation is relatively constant. However, any money that you have won, even if it is still in the form of chips, is yours and not the casino's. Also, if your expectation is negative on your next bet, you should bet as little as possible (preferably zero), no matter how big your bankroll is.

Similarly, you should not reduce your bets just because you have been losing. (This would be the situation where you are playing with your "own money.") Again, for the same reasons as just given, your bet size should be a function of your expectation, the standard deviation, and the size of your bankroll.

By the way, of all the dangerous ideas I have discussed, this one is clearly my favorite. Now if I could just get my hands on all that casino money, gambling certainly would be a lot more fun and much more profitable.

The Myth of the House Advantage Revisited

One of the strangest articles that I've ever read, which comes under the heading of "pseudo gambling theory," appeared in the August, 1986 issue of *Gambling Times*. The article was titled "The Myth of the House Advantage" and was written by Irving Dlugatch. Although I have no reason to believe the author's intentions were not good, he fell into a trap in which the casinos would like to ensnare many of their patrons. The trap is that short-term results — depending on the game in question — are usually dominated by the standard deviation instead of the expectation, but in the long run, the standard deviation will become insignificant in the way it impacts performance. Let's look at these two parameters in more detail.

As noted previously, the expectation is your win rate if the game can be beaten, or it is your loss rate if your opponent, usually the house, has the advantage. Also, expectation is generally measured in lengths of time. For example, in a particular game, your expectation might be to lose $10 per hour.

The problem is that it is likely for you to perform at exactly your expectation for a short period of time. Sometimes you will do much better, and (unfortunately) sometimes you will do much worse. These fluctuations are measured by the (statistical) standard deviation, and most statisticians agree that your results, for all practical purposes, will be within three standard deviations of your expectation. For example, suppose you expect to be a $10 loser for an hour but your standard deviation for this hour is $100. This means that even though your expectation is negative $10, you could be ahead by as much as $290 or behind as much as $310. No wonder some people walk away from the craps tables big winners. It is not that their expectation has changed, but that the standard deviation is dominating their results.

But it so happens that the effect of the standard deviation tends to "go away" if you gamble for a long period of time. (This is because the standard deviation is inversely proportional to the square root of the sample size.) However, for most gambling games, the standard deviation is large enough that it will take a reasonably long time for its effect to become insignificant. This is known as "getting into the long run," and in some games, it will take at least a lifetime of gambling to get into the long run.

In his article Dlugatch addresses the idea of randomness and claims that "random" is impossible to define. Of course, this is not true. Richard Epstein, in his book *The Theory of Gambling and Statistical Logic,* defines a random event as "an experiment whose outcome is not known a priori."

Let's look at three examples. First, suppose that you are playing craps and throw a seven. Does that seven have any impact on the results of the next throw? Of course not. This means that throwing dice will generate a set of random numbers.

Now suppose you riffle a deck of cards. You do this by dividing the cards into two 26-card stacks and interweaving the two stacks. Notice that the cards which were close together before the riffle are still close together after the riffle. Specifically, suppose you knew that the 5♥ and 10♣ were next to each other at the beginning of this process. If the first card off the top of the deck was the 5♥, you would know that the 10♣ soon would follow. Thus, the shuffling of cards is non-random.

These examples illustrate two other important points. The first is that even though numbers may be generated at random, they do not have to be equally likely. This is easily seen from the dice example by noting that it is much more likely for the shooter to throw a seven as opposed to a three.

The second point is that even though events may be non-random, if you do not have a great deal of specific knowledge of the non-random characteristics that are operating, you should treat these events as though they were random. The best example of this is the shuffling of cards. The typical shuffle is so fast and so complex, especially if a professional dealer is employed, that even the most skilled players have no knowledge as to the distribution of cards in the deck. Consequently, for practical purposes, a shuffle can be considered random.

A statement by gambling writer Mike Caro also addresses this subject: "In the beginning, all bets were even money." What Caro is actually saying is that in the absence of knowledge, events not only can be considered random, but should be considered equally likely as well. Returning to the card shuffling example, even though we know the shuffle is non-random, since we lose knowledge of the distribution of cards, the first card dealt is equally likely to be any card in the deck, and this event can be considered random. Notice that randomness does not have to exist for probability theory to apply. Probability theory will apply as long as the knowledge of the appropriate non-random characteristics is so limited that it cannot be of any aid in the prediction of future events.

However, here is a third example where knowledge of the non-random distribution might help a skilled player. Suppose you are playing a form of poker known as Texas hold'em. In this game, each player receives two downcards and then three cards, known as the flop, are simultaneously spread face up on the table. Two more cards, dealt one at a time, are then added to the community board, producing four rounds of betting. (Good explanations of how hold'em poker is played can be found in David Sklansky's book *Hold'em Poker* and in Doyle Brunson's book *Super/System*.) Let's further suppose you are in a game where the dealer is not shuffling thoroughly, and you notice that one of your cards from the previous hand has appeared on the flop. This may mean that your other card from the previous hand is nearby and is thus much more likely than what conventional probability dictates to appear on the board before the hand is finished. Consequently, playing long-shot hands for which this particular card is needed may now be correct, whereas if the cards were shuffled at random, it would be correct to throw your hand away.

Dlugatch also claims that "you can't tell the difference between random and non-random distributions by the eye alone." Well, this is often true, sometimes it is difficult to tell by the eye alone, but statisticians have developed many tests for randomness. The ones that I am familiar with are known as "run" tests and are well-documented in the book *Statistical Theory and Methodology in Science and Engineering* by K.A. Brownlee. (In addition, see the essay titled "Sequencing" in Part One of this book.)

Dlugatch also states that "counting is useless if the cards are randomly distributed, because the key cards are usually scattered throughout the deck." Of course, this statement is completely inaccurate. Counting cards when playing blackjack provides information about the distribution of the remaining cards in the deck or shoe. When the count indicates that the remaining cards are rich in high cards, the skilled player has a positive expectation. Does this mean that he is guaranteed a win? The answer is no. He is not guaranteed a win because counting cards tells him nothing about the standard deviation, and unless the standard deviation is sufficiently small, there is some probability that a loss will occur.

Another claim appearing in "The Myth of the House Advantage" is that "the non-random distribution makes favorable decks feasible and thus makes it possible to use counting." Again, nothing could be further from the truth. Remember that counting, as just stated, provides information about the underlying probability distribution that governs the remaining cards in a blackjack deck. If these cards were distributed in a non-random manner and the appropriate non-random characteristics were known, there would be no need to count, as we could predict with certainty what the next card would be.

The last part of the Dlugatch essay deals with dice and is more logical than his preceding material. Basically, the theme of this section is to pre-position the dice so that when they are thrown, certain sides are not eligible to come up. In other words, Dlugatch is proposing a scheme that would change the underlying probability distribution that governs the random numbers generated by throwing the dice. Notice that the results still will be random.

The real question is whether this can be done. If it is possible, there is no doubt that a great deal of money could be won on a regular basis at the dice tables. Unfortunately, when throwing dice, the casinos require you to bounce them off the far wall of the craps table. This not only assures randomness, but also assures that the standard probability distribution governs the random numbers that the dice generate. Consequently, I am sure that pre-positioning the dice will have no effect.

But am I right? In Ian Anderson's book *Turning the Tables on Las Vegas,* he describes a dice coup based on exactly this sort of technique. Anderson tells the story of an unidentified player who apparently was very successful at the craps tables. According to Anderson, after many years of practice, this player had learned to throw the dice (based on pre-positioning) so that certain sides of one die did not come up. Of course, this changed the underlying probability distribution and produced gigantic wins. I have no way to verify the truth of this story, but neither can I claim that this phenomenon did not occur.

After reading "The Myth of the House Advantage," I did a great deal of thinking. And even though the article contains ideas that are severely flawed, if it caused other people also to do a great deal of thinking, it has some redeeming characteristics. Nevertheless, I hope this essay will set matters straight.

Bingo System Fallacy

One popular Bingo system suggests that you buy three cards such that each of the 75 possible numbers appears only on one card. The argument goes that for every number called, a spot will be covered, and if one card is "low" on covered spots, then at least one of the other two cards will be "high" on covered spots. Consequently, your chances for a bingo will be higher.

To see what's wrong with this system, let's look at a simple example. (It took me a long time to recognize this fallacy, and that's why this essay is included in the book.) Suppose you are able to find three cards that meet the system requirement and that you pay $1 each for these cards. What are your cards worth after one number has been called? Since this number appears on only one of your cards, that card has increased in value. On the other hand, your other two cards have dropped in value.

According to the system, the location of the covered spot (on your one card) is also important. Sometimes the covered spot will appear in an advantageous location, and your card value will go up a lot; other times it will appear in a poor location, and your card value will go up only a little. On average, however, your card value will go up an amount that will be exactly offset by the loss in value of the other two cards.

In fact, this analysis can be extended to all the cards (in the house) and to every number called. That is, all cards are constantly changing value, but their total value is always constant. Incidentally, their value is always equal to the prize money, and as we all know, since less money is returned than is taken in, your expectation is negative. Thus this system, like all other bingo systems, is worthless.

Another thing this system does is reduce your standard deviation, which is actually bad when playing negative-expectation games. However, taking this to the other extreme — that is, getting three identical cards — also could be futile if one prize is split among all the winners. Basically, since bingo is a negative-expectation game, the more cards you play, the more you can expect to lose.

Pseudo Theory Exposed

Afterthought

Always remember that successful gambling is not easy. The image of the well-dressed player who enters a casino, makes a few quick bets, and then leaves with a wheelbarrow full of money is not anywhere close to the truth. Yet these kinds of illusions constantly appear in the gambling literature.

Another thing to keep in mind is the large amount of risk that is always involved in different kinds of gambling. This occupation is not like a job where you always get paid no matter how you do. Sometimes you make more than you expect, and sometimes you make less than you expect (and perhaps even lose). Moreover, if you perform below your skill level when gambling, you can expect substantial and ongoing losses.

Now you should understand why being able to expose pseudo theory is so important. Staying away from these dangerous ideas is crucial to maintaining a healthy bankroll. Remember, it is your money that you are playing with. If it disappears, your gambling career may be over.

Part Four

Poker Tournament Strategy

Poker Tournament Strategy

Introduction

Poker tournaments are becoming ever more popular and provide many opportunities for the skilled player. However, not much has been written on the subject, with one notable exception: *How To Win At Poker Tournaments* by Tom McEvoy. Although McEvoy is an excellent tournament player and I believe his book should be read by anyone interested in poker competitions, many of the following ideas — which are based on solid mathematical footing — differ dramatically from what appears in his book.

After absorbing the material presented in the five essays that follow, you should discover that you are an expert at tournament play, limited only by your basic poker ability and, of course, the requisite tournament experience.

To Rebuy or Not To Rebuy

Even though poker tournaments have become extremely popular, most players do not play them correctly. The following essays provide some mathematical and strategic concepts that should help in developing a winning approach to correct tournament play. This first essay addresses the subject of rebuys. (I'd like to thank Richard Grenier for supplying the inspiration for some of what follows.)

Concept No. 1: It is correct to rebuy when you are out of money in a tournament with a fixed-percentage payoff. This is an area of tournament play where there is much confusion. Let's look at a simple example. Suppose only three people are competing in a tournament and each has bought in for $1,000. First place pays 75 percent, second place pays 25 percent, and third place pays nothing. In addition, these players are evenly matched in ability. What is the expectation on this initial $1,000 buy-in?

This can be answered by noticing that each player expects to win one-third of the time for a $1,250 profit, each player expects to finish second one-third of the time for a $250 loss, and each player expects to finish third one-third of the time for a $1,000 loss. Consequently, the overall expectation on this initial buy-in is zero. (In this example, I am not considering any additional entry fees that most tournaments charge.)

$$0 = \left(\frac{1}{3}\right)(.75)(3000) + \left(\frac{1}{3}\right)(.25)(3000) + \left(\frac{1}{3}\right)(0)(3000) - 1000$$

Now suppose that one of these players, let's call him Player C, after going all in, rebuys for another $1,000. What is the expectation on this rebuy? If it is positive, then the rebuy is correct. If it is negative, the rebuy actually will be worth less than $1,000 and should not be made.

To answer this question, we need to know the distribution of the money between the other two players. Let's suppose that the first player, call him Player A, has $2,000 and that the second player, call him Player B, has $1,000. Also, let's assume that none of the three players adjusts his playing tactics. This means that the person who just rebought and now has $1,000 has one out of four chances to win the tournament.

What are his chances of finishing second? Figuring this is slightly more complex. There are two cases: when Player A wins the tournament and when Player B wins the tournament. Notice that when Player A wins the tournament — which will happen half the time since he has half the money — Player C will finish second half the time since he has the same amount of money as Player B. Consequently, one-fourth of the time, Player A will win the tournament and Player C will finish second.

$$\left(\frac{1}{4}\right) = \left(\frac{1}{2}\right)\left(\frac{1}{2}\right)$$

Similar reasoning shows that one-twelfth of the time, Player B will win the tournament and Player C will finish second. Consequently, Player C will finish second one-third of the time.

$$\left(\frac{1}{3}\right) = \left(\frac{1}{4}\right) + \left(\frac{1}{12}\right)$$

In addition, Player C will finish last five-twelfths of the time.

$$\left(\frac{5}{12}\right) = 1 - \left[\left(\frac{1}{4}\right) + \left(\frac{1}{3}\right)\right]$$

Now when Player C wins the tournament, his profit on the rebuy is $2,000.

$$2000 = (.75)(4000) - 1000$$

When Player C finishes second, he will break even on the rebuy.

$$0 = (.25)(4000) - 1000$$

And when Player C finishes third, he will lose the entire rebuy of $1,000. Consequently, his overall expectation is a positive $83.

$$83 = \left(\frac{1}{4}\right)(2000) + \left(\frac{1}{3}\right)(0) + \left(\frac{5}{12}\right)(-1000)$$

This means that rebuying is correct. Moreover, rebuying is always correct, as long as Player C has gone broke and no matter how the money is distributed between Players A and B. However, the money distribution does affect the amount of profitability that the rebuy is worth. It turns out that the more even the money distribution is, the less profitable the rebuy is, although it is still profitable nonetheless. You may want to compute a few simple examples to see that this is the case.)

These ideas can be extended to situations where there are lots of players and many places are paid. It is virtually always correct to rebuy. (A few exceptions are discussed later.)

Incidentally, many players probably will be surprised by these results. I certainly was the first time I worked them out. What it means is that if you are leading in a tournament and someone rebuys, the pot is *not* being "sweetened" for you. If that rebuy is correct and profitable for your opponent, it is incorrect and unprofitable for you. Consequently, discouraging your opponents from rebuying when they are broke should be an important part of your overall tournament strategy.

Concept No. 2: Don't rebuy for excessive amounts. This concept is only theoretically interesting, since there are currently no tournaments where excessive rebuys are permitted. To better understand this idea, suppose in the example just given that player C makes a $1 million rebuy instead of a $1,000 rebuy. Now there is virtually no way he can lose the tournament. However, 25 percent of the rebuy will go to his opponents, creating a large negative expectation, even though I've stated that there is virtually no way Player C can lose the tournament. Consequently, although it is always correct to rebuy when you are out of money in a percentage-payoff tournament, since the rebuys are small when compared to the total prize pool, this concept is theoretically wrong if you can rebuy for an excessive amount.

Concept No. 3: Don't rebuy when you have a lot of chips. Again, looking at the example in Concept No. 1, suppose a player can rebuy whenever he has $1,000 in chips or less. This means that at the start of the tournament, all three players in the example have the option to rebuy. As before, if the expectation on this rebuy is positive, it should be made, but if the expectation is negative, it is a mistake and should not be done. Should a player rebuy in this situation?

To answer this question, notice that rebuying immediately is the same as buying in (for this example) for $2,000 while the other players buy in for only $1,000. Even though the large buy-in provides two out of four chances of winning the tournament, one out of three chances of finishing second, and only one out of six chances of coming in last (these calculations are not shown), the expectation is a $177 loss.

$$-177 = \left(\frac{2}{4}\right)(.75)(4000) + \left(\frac{1}{3}\right)(.25)(4000) + \left(\frac{1}{6}\right)(0) - 2000$$

Since we know from Concept No. 1 that the expectation is zero when the buy-ins are equal, this entire $177 loss must be the result of the additional $1,000. That is, the expectation on the rebuy in this situation is negative, and thus the rebuy should not be made.

There are two situations where this concept applies. First, it is usually a mistake to rebuy when your total chips drop just below the rebuy threshold. An exception to this might be when many players already have dropped out and your rebuy will still leave you well behind the leaders. But this is a rare event. That is, in most situations, if you are not broke, or at least almost broke, then it is generally best not to rebuy.

Second, many tournaments allow an optional rebuy — usually at the midway break — for everyone in the tournament regardless of chip position. (A few tournaments even permit players to rebuy twice at this juncture.) From this discussion, it can be seen that if you are among the leaders, it is a mistake to rebuy, but if you are near elimination, rebuying becomes correct.

But what if you are at some point in between? That is, you are significantly behind the leaders but are not in any immediate danger of going broke. To determine whether it is correct to rebuy in this spot would, of course, depend on what the percentage paybacks are and exactly how the money is distributed. However, whether your decision is to rebuy or not to rebuy, it probably will be either marginally correct or marginally wrong. That is, it won't really matter very much in the long run. Consequently, this is a time when you may want to consider the strength of your opponents. If strong players have the chips, lean toward not rebuying. On the other hand, if weak players have the chips — even though the mathematics says that rebuying in this spot is marginally correct at best — their expected poor play may swing your decision toward rebuying. (Remember, the mathematics assumes that everyone plays equally well.)

By the way, this is one of the most common mistakes that occurs in tournaments. Many players, if they have a reasonable amount of chips at this point, will now rebuy for all they can. If they are low on chips, they won't rebuy. They are trying to maximize their chances of winning the tournament when they think they have a shot at it. But they actually are reducing their expectation when they shouldn't or failing to increase their expectation when they should.

Special note. These three concepts illustrate a powerful force that operates in tournament play when the money is distributed on a percentage basis: The value of the chips that are on the table is not constant from player to player. (This is not true in a regular ring game, where each chip has the same value.) Specifically, the more chips you have, the less each individual chip is worth, and the less chips you have, the more each individual chip is worth. This extremely powerful idea, as you will see in the essays that follow, will have a major influence on proper tournament strategy.

However, it needs to be noted that this force becomes significant only late in a tournament. Early in a tournament, it is not that crucial. The reason for this is that early in a tournament, a large stack still represents only a small proportion of the total number of chips, while late in a tournament, a significant amount of the total chip pool can be present in one large stack. This means that early in a tournament, the difference between the value of individual chips, when comparing a large stack with a small stack, may not be very much. But late in a tournament, this difference in chip value can be so significant that it can cause dynamic changes in strategy to become the proper approach.

Concept No. 4: Also consider the side games. Everything that has been written so far applies if you are striving to play a tournament in an optimal fashion. But an exception occurs if you are just interested in the highest positive return on your money and there are some exceptionally good side games that you can get into quickly. Even though it is correct to rebuy — that is, you either rebuy or you are out of the tournament — if the side games are terrific, the correct decision may be not to rebuy.

The reason you would decide not to rebuy is that it is more profitable to leave the tournament than to stay in it, even though your expectation on the rebuy is positive. I don't believe this situation will come up very often, especially at the major tournaments. However, if you play a lot of tournaments, it is bound to happen sometime. Keep in mind that whether it is correct to go to a side game instead of rebuying is a subjective decision.

Concept No. 5: Consider the standard deviation. Remember that when you rebuy after you have gone broke, even though your expectation is positive, your probability of finishing in the money is reduced compared to what it was at the beginning of the tournament. This is because your relative share of the total chip pool is now smaller than it was when the tournament started.

Specifically, suppose you rebuy late in a tournament. Although it is advantageous to do so, your most likely outcome is to go broke again. In other words, if you repeat this scenario over and over again, you only occasionally will finish in the money. However, in the long run, you expect to show a significant profit. Put another way, this is a high-standard-deviation play, which — as has been pointed out — is the type of play the expert players use to increase their win rates.

This book has stressed that to assure survival, high-standard-deviation plays, even if the expectation is positive, should be avoided unless you have a relatively large bankroll. Since rebuying when you have gone broke in a percentage-payback tournament is a positive-expectation play, the conclusion is that if you are not prepared to make four or five rebuys, or cannot afford to make four or five rebuys, you probably should not enter the tournament. This is simply because those people with large bankrolls who can afford to make many rebuys have a significant advantage over those who cannot afford to rebuy or choose not to rebuy. (I know of a major pot-limit Omaha tournament where the winner made seventeen rebuys.)

By the way, speaking of non-self-weighting strategies, positive-expectation plays are frequently accompanied by high standard deviations. This is the price you often must pay to produce a winning strategy. As can be seen, this is applicable to the situation just discussed.

Concept No. 6: Progressive rebuys may not be correct. Some tournaments allow what are referred to as "progressive rebuys." This means that the further along a tournament is, the more your rebuy can be. For example, early in a tournament, you may be allowed to purchase $100 in chips (for $100), while later in a tournament you may be allowed to purchase $1,000 dollars in chips (for $1,000). This enables you to avoid being "outchipped" by your opponents. However, this is not necessarily a good situation to be in. Percentage-payback mathematics clearly shows that the more chips you buy, the less profitable the rebuy is. Depending on what the percentage paybacks are and how the money is currently distributed, if you buy a lot of chips, you may have a negative expectation. The question to ask when determining whether a progressive rebuy is correct is, "How small is the rebuy?" Specifically, if the rebuy is still small compared to the total chip pool and the chip positions of the leaders, rebuying is probably correct; if the opposite is true, the rebuy should not be made. By the way, as has been stated, many people think just the opposite is correct.

Final note. Since the first edition of this book was written, I have discovered that the concept of rebuying is even more misunderstood than I originally thought. If you are still somewhat confused, I suggest that you carefully reread this essay several times. The argument that you need to win the tournament to even show a profit after making a lot of rebuys is not the correct way to analyze the problem. In addition, the idea that when you rebuy late in a tournament, you are too outchipped by your opponents is also not correct. If these arguments were correct, the expectation equations would not produce positive values. It is as simple as that. Remember, your choice is either to walk with nothing or to rebuy. The fact that you already may have gone broke several times has nothing to do with the correct decision. However, keep in mind that this non-self-weighting approach is accompanied by a very large standard deviation. This doesn't mean that you should not rebuy, but that you may have no business playing in the tournament in the first place. Of course, to play or not to play is a personal decision.

Another question directed to me several times since the first edition of this book came out is whether rebuys should be allowed in world-class tournaments. In my opinion, the answer is no as rebuys favor those individuals with large bankrolls. For example, some pot-limit Omaha tournaments have a $5,000 buy-in with rebuys. If you plan to play such a tournament but have only enough money for the initial buy-in, and someone else is prepared to spend $30,000 if necessary, he has a significant advantage over you. His advantage is not just in terms of mathematical expectation on the rebuys. By not being able to rebuy, you will be forced into a survival strategy early, while your opponent can play fast. That is, his advantage is not only mathematical but strategic as well.

Tournament Strategy

From the previous essay, you now know that it is correct to rebuy when you are out of chips but a costly mistake to rebuy when you have plenty of chips. This is because the less chips you have, the more each individual chip is worth, and the more chips you have, the less each individual chip is worth. These ideas can be extended to develop new concepts concerning what is correct for other aspects of tournament play.

Concept No. 1: If you can afford to rebuy, play fast. First, let's define playing fast as squeezing every bit of possible profit from a hand, and then some. It is not the same as playing loose, which is playing too many hands simply for the thrill of playing, even though a large number of these plays will cost you money in the long run. Playing fast will give the tournament player a maximum chance to get a jump on his opposition. All you need to gain a substantial lead is to win one or two hands when squeezing out extra bets from your opponents. If these hands are beaten, you have cost yourself only these extra bets, as you would have played the hands anyway. Moreover, this loss can be made up by an optional rebuy, since the rebuy is almost always profitable. By the way, the fewer chips you have, the faster you should play.

However, some players who understand that playing fast is correct begin to play in a suicidal fashion. As an example, in a small no-limit tournament with a one-hour rebuy period, I watched a well-known player rebuy a dozen times. It is hard to believe this type of play can be correct, even though it probably increased his chances of winning the event.

Concept No. 2: When you can't rebuy, try to survive. You are not permitted to rebuy when you have won enough chips to put you over the rebuy threshold, the time allocated for rebuys has ended, or you are playing in a tournament that does not allow rebuys. Now your emphasis should be on surviving, since the worst thing that can happen to you is to finish just out of the money.

A common misconception held by many players is that survival means to play super tight. But this is not at all the case. Survival means not going for those extra bets and not playing marginal hands in an attempt to make an extra profit. In some spots, you actually can play looser. Also, the further along the tournament is, the more important it is to survive. For example, if the top eight players receive money, it is much more important to be in your survival mode when nine people are left than when fifty people are left. An exception to trying to survive might be when you are above the rebuy threshold but still have lots of time left to rebuy. In this case, you may want to continue to play fast, trying to get a big jump on your opponents.

There is, however, one stream of thought that advocates playing fast, even outright recklessly, early in percentage-payback tournaments that do not allow rebuys. The idea is that every fourth or fifth tournament, you will get lucky, get in a good chip position, and now have a shot at some money or even at winning. Of course, the other times you quickly will go broke. The question arises as to whether this is a better approach.

Let's look at an example. Suppose players A and B enter a tournament over and over again. The buy-in for the tournament is $100, and they each receive $100 in tournament chips. A plays in such a way that after one hour of play, he always has exactly his initial buy-in of $100 in chips. B plays in a much more aggressive and reckless manner. Three out of every four tournaments, he quickly goes broke, but one out of every four tournaments, he manages to have $400 in chips after one hour of play. So the question is, who is better off?

Clearly, each player has the same expectation of $100 in tournament chips after one hour of play. The difference is that the standard deviation around A's expectation is zero, since he always has $100 in chips, but the standard deviation around B's expectation is large, since he usually is broke but sometimes does quite well. However, because of the mathematics that govern percentage-payback tournaments, we know that the less chips a player has, the more each individual chip is worth, and the more chips a player has, the less each individual chip is worth. This means that it is better to have $100 in tournament chips all the time than to have $400 in tournament chips one-fourth of the time and zero three-fourths of the time. Consequently, A's approach of following survival tactics is clearly superior.

A small number of people have amassed good tournament records by playing recklessly early in non-rebuy tournaments. However, I believe this is deceiving. I also believe that in many tournaments, a large number of people start off playing recklessly, even though no rebuy is permitted. It is inevitable that some of these people happened to win a few events. But this doesn't mean that they were playing correctly. (See Concept No. 3 for more discussion on this important tournament subject.)

Concept No. 3: Take advantage of tight play. Many players tend to play extremely tight in tournaments simply because they want to survive. (Note that playing tight is not my definition of survival.) This means that two major adjustments from regular play should be made. On the opening round, as David Sklansky pointed out at one of his seminars, if no one has yet entered the pot, you should open looser, since more antes than usual can be stolen. But if someone playing tight is already in the pot, call less frequently with hands of value, since you most likely will be looking at a strong hand. By the way, if you are in your fast mode, you may want to raise with some of your calling hands.

In the later rounds, these same ideas hold. One world-class player I know put it this way: "You don't win tournaments — you steal them."

I want to point out the importance of this concept. Many tournament players seem to look for any excuse to throw their hands away. In fact, I am convinced that some of the more successful tournament players would be losers if they used the same playing style in a regular ring game — that is, taking advantage of tight opponents. Keep in mind that this concept is consistent with the definition of survival. In other words, you are not really playing loose; you are merely taking advantage of the incorrect strategies that your opponents are using.

Let me give a specific example. When playing hold'em in a ring game, one reason not to call a raiser when you hold a weak hand is that if you don't flop anything, his subsequent bet or bets will force you from the pot, even if there is a good chance that he also has a weak hand. But in a tournament, suppose this same player is less likely to bet when he doesn't flop anything, because he doesn't want to put himself in jeopardy of being eliminated from the tournament. In this case, calling before the flop with a hand that would not warrant it in a ring game may become correct. If your opponent now checks on the flop, indicating that he has missed, you can take advantage of his tight play and possibly bluff him out.

This may be why some less knowledgeable people believe that fast, reckless play is the key to successful tournament strategy. But in reality, they fail to recognize correct bluffs, which normally would not be correct in a regular ring game.

The tendency to play extremely tight is not as prevalent in ladies-only tournaments, because they often draw more than their share of novice players. A highly skilled female player — who understands not only good poker strategy, but proper tournament concepts as well — should be a significant money favorite in many of these contests. Also, for a woman on a small bankroll, ladies-only competitions provide an excellent way to learn tournament poker.

Tight play is also not as prevalent early in a non-rebuy tournament, especially if the players do not perceive the starting stakes as a threat to their initial stacks. For example, with $500 in tournament chips, many players will play loose if the limits are $15-$30, but will significantly tighten up once the stakes are moved to the $30-$60 level. The typical player does not worry about going broke (and being out of the tournament) at the starting betting limits. But this often changes once the stakes are increased and very loose tables suddenly can become very tight. In fact, you sometimes will wonder whether you are at the same table.

Concept No. 4: Don't bluff the large stacks. One reason this concept is included here is that in the first edition of this book, I stated exactly the opposite. My logic was that players with large stacks generally don't mind a small loss, since they still will be one of the leaders, but they don't want a large loss, as they now will become one of the also-rans. Consequently, they are candidates for bluffing.

However, the mathematics of percentage paybacks — that is, the chips change value — totally breaks this idea apart, especially late in a tournament. To bluff a large stack becomes incorrect, simply because it will cost you more to make the bluff, assuming your stack is smaller than your opponent's, than it will cost him to call you. Consequently, bluffing a large stack, especially if your chip position is poor, should not be done unless the probability of a successful bluff is extremely high.

Percentage-payback mathematics also shows the opposite if you are against a small stack. Now it will cost you less to bluff your opponent than it will cost him to call. In addition, as poker writer Mike Caro has pointed out, players on short stacks generally find ways to jeopardize their last few chips anyway, since they usually think the remaining blinds and antes will soon finish them off. This means that they often will play weaker hands than they should, making them even more susceptible to a bluff.

Concept No. 5: Try to get at a table with poor players who rebuy a lot. This may be difficult since many tournaments assign

188

seats, but you could try some seat trading.[18] Even though it is correct for almost all players to rebuy, if some players rebuy a lot and usually give their money away, you want to be in a good position to get it. This way, when your table breaks, if you are still in the tournament, you will have on average more chips than you would if you were at a tight table where no one makes a rebuy.

Concept No. 6: Don't advertise as much. Advertising in the form of outright bluffs and/or image plays (see my book *Winning Concepts in Draw and Lowball*) is not as effective in tournaments, mainly because your opponents are constantly changing as the tournament progresses. It doesn't make much sense to run one of these plays against an opponent who may shortly be out of your game. Notice that one of the reasons to bluff does not apply in a tournament, which is another argument for why tournaments are not the place for wild reckless players.

Special note. Most tournament players will advise you not to rebuy and to play tight. This approach often appears correct, since many tournaments are won by the player who jumps into an early lead that does not require a rebuy and then manages to survive by what appears to be tight play. I hope this essay and the preceding one have shown that the best strategy is to play fast early, with the intention of rebuying if necessary, and then to try to survive. Remember, playing fast is not the same as playing loose, and surviving is not the same as playing tight. In fact, to someone who does not understand correct tournament strategy, surviving can even look like loose play in certain situations.

---

[18]Even though seat trading could be done in a few cardrooms years ago, this practice is not allowed in any of the cardrooms that I am currently familiar with.

Concept No. 7: If you must bluff, do so just before the stakes are raised. This idea, which originally comes from poker writer Mike Caro, is that bluffing just before the stakes are raised will maximize a bluff's advertising effect. This does not conflict with Concept No. 6. What is being said is that if you bluff for advertising purposes, the best time to do so is right before the stakes go up. Needless to say, the worst time to bluff for advertising purposes is just after the stakes have been raised.

Concept No. 8: When playing fast, attack the large stacks. When you are in your fast mode, which is usually early in a tournament, your only purpose should be to win as many chips as possible. This means that you should be willing to get into big confrontations, especially if your hand has potential for a lot of improvement. Should you make a big hand, you are more likely to assure yourself of a big payoff, and you thus may be in an advantageous position for the rest of the tournament.

Concept No. 9: When trying to survive, stay away from the large stacks. When you are in your survival mode, usually after the early stages of a tournament and especially if you have a lot of chips, your purpose should be to maximize your expectation, not to maximize your probability of winning the tournament. This means that you should be reluctant to get into big confrontations, and thus, it is usually best to stay away from opponents who also have strong chip positions. As has been emphasized, often the best strategy is to not play a hand for its maximum value. (There is no contradiction here. Survival means that you frequently give up those small edges that the expert players use in standard games to increase their expectation.) Remember, the price you pay to get maximum value is a much higher standard deviation. When you are trying to survive, it is best to keep your standard deviation as low as possible.

Concept No. 10: Avoid speculative hands when you are low on chips and can't rebuy. Even though this concept should be obvious, it is violated by many players. The problem with playing speculative hands when you are low on chips is that if you complete the hand, you can't always get full value for it because you often will run out of money. Moreover when you cannot rebuy, you should be in your survival mode, and these are not the types of hands that you should try to survive with. Also remember that if your opponents are playing tight, which is generally the case in tournaments, especially after the rebuy period has ended, the value of speculative hands, when they are completed, may not be as great as it normally would be.

Concept No. 11: Don't go out with a bang in percentage-payoff tournaments. We have seen that it is correct to rebuy when you are low on chips and that it is incorrect to rebuy when you have a lot of chips. As has been mentioned, a logical extension of this — which can be shown mathematically — is that in percentage-payoff tournaments, the less chips you have, the more (relatively speaking) each individual chip is worth, and the more chips you have, the less (relatively speaking) each individual chip is worth. This means that going out with a bang is wrong. You should try to go out with a whimper. That is, try to make those few remaining chips last as long as possible.

One of the most common mistakes typical players make in a tournament is to raise on an early round, putting themselves all in, when they have only a marginal raising hand. The correct way to play in this spot is to just call and try to preserve enough chips to play another hand in case this one quickly becomes a loser. (The exception is if you believe the raise will enable you to win the pot or to significantly narrow down the field.) A similar error is raising all in with just a calling hand. A player would be much better off preserving those few extra chips so that he could play another hand should he have to fold the current hand.

Concept No. 12: Overplay hands against short stacks. Even though it is not correct, players on short stacks tend to go out with a bang. In addition, their limited amount of chips often will prevent them from getting full value from their hands. Consequently, against these players, who find ways to put their remaining chips in jeopardy, you sometimes can overplay your hands. Although this should be tempered somewhat if you are currently trying to survive, overplaying your hands against short stacks is often the correct strategy and is not inconsistent with the idea of survival. In addition, keep in mind that your opponents chips are worth more than yours, meaning that you are receiving an overlay on your bets.

Concept No. 13: Play more straightforwardly. One of the keys to poker strategy is to play in a deceptive manner that will cause your opponents to make costly mistakes against you in the future. This includes deliberately playing hands incorrectly and sometimes making totally ridiculous plays. But in tournaments, where your opponents are subject to change at any moment, playing in a deceptive manner is not the best approach. It is usually best to play your hands in a straightforward fashion, adjusting your play only for fast or survival mode.

Concept No. 14: Late in a tournament, you should call liberally if (1) you have good chip position, (2) it won't cost much to call, and (3) you have an opportunity to eliminate this opponent. Late in a tournament, if you are in a strong position and someone goes all in for a small amount, you should call if there is little possibility that someone else will play, even if you are taking slightly (or sometimes even much) the worst of it. Not calling may give this player new life. Note that in this spot, since your opponent is all in, your call won't help him that much. But eliminating this player will help you a great deal, since he can't finish ahead of you if he is no longer in the tournament.

Concept No. 15: Steal less late in a tournament if low on chips. Most players are aware that if you are low on chips, it may be incorrect to try to steal the antes and/or blinds. Even though the play late in a tournament is generally too tight, making it correct to try to steal, some players who normally would not call will now play, hoping to put you out of action. For example, suppose in a hold'em tournament that you have

in a late position and everyone else has passed. If you are low on chips and think that you will be called by someone, no matter what he has, it may be best to see the flop as cheaply as possible. This way, if you don't get a favorable flop, you can still survive to see another hand.

Another reason for not making steal plays late in a tournament is that the chips have changed value. Specifically, when you are low on chips, it costs you a lot more to attempt the steal than your chips indicate, and it may be costing one of your opponents, depending on his chip position, a lot less to call you than his chips indicate.

Concept No. 16: Avoid major confrontations late in a tournament. Even though this idea has already been mentioned, let's look at a detailed example, which is similar to an example that David Sklansky presented at one of his seminars. Suppose late in a tournament that three players are left, call them A, B, and C. Each player has $1,000, and first place gets 75 percent, second place gets 25 percent, and third place gets nothing. Note that each person has the same amount of chips, and assuming that all three are equally skilled players, each has the same probability of finishing first, second, or third, meaning that each has an expectation of winning $1,000.

Now suppose Players A and B go all in against each other. Since we don't know their hands, we assume that it is equally likely for either to win. That is, each player has the same expectation. But what about Player C? Since he still has his original $1,000 and will now be against only one opponent who has $2,000, player C's probability of finishing second will be two-thirds while his probability of finishing first will still be one-third. (Notice that he no longer can finish third, since either player A or player B will have that honor.) This means that his expectation is now $1,250.

$$1{,}250 = \left(\frac{1}{3}\right)(.75)(3{,}000) + \left(\frac{2}{3}\right)(.25)(3{,}000)$$

The point is that by staying out of the major confrontation, Player C made money. Also, if Player C made money, Players A and B had to lose money. By going all in against each other, before the hand is decided, each of their expectations has fallen to $875.

$$875 = 1{,}000 - \left(\frac{1}{2}\right)(1{,}250 - 1{,}000)$$

This is another example of how percentage-payback tournaments really work. Clearly, the person trying to survive is better off, especially late in the contest.

A classic example occurred in the 1987 World Series of Poker. When just three people were left, the two chip leaders, Johnny Chan and Bob Ciaffone, got into a major confrontation with each other. Unless they both held strong hands, one of them was making a serious mistake. Sure enough, Ciaffone, who is an excellent player and had played super up to that point, had a marginal holding. No matter what the outcome of the hand was to be, he had to be making a mistake. His play may have been correct in a normal three-handed ring game, but in a tournament, where the value of the chips does not stay constant, Ciaffone was not getting the pot odds that he thought he was getting.

Incidentally, Chan finished first, and Frank Henderson, the third player left in the contest, who was well behind the two leaders, was able to "sneak" into second place. However, after four days of grueling play, no one can fault Ciaffone for making one fatal mistake.

Concept No. 17: Late in a tournament, if you are in a good chip position, be willing to make bets with seemingly negative expectations against a short stack. David Sklansky shows in his book *The Theory of Poker* that you should make bets on the end only when these bets win the majority of times that they are called. Even though this concept is correct in a standard game, the mathematics of tournaments, where the money is awarded on a percentage-payback basis, changes what is correct. Specifically, it often becomes correct to make bets that will lose the majority of times that they are called.

The reason for this is that chips change value in a tournament, depending on how many you have. Remember, the more chips you have, the less each individual chip is worth, and the less chips you have, the more each individual chip is worth. This means that if you have a lot of chips and your opponent is on a short stack, he actually will be calling you with more money than you have bet, even though he will be calling you with the same number of chips. In other words, in this situation, it becomes correct to make bets that lose the majority of times that they are called (although in a regular game, these bets would be incorrect). This is especially true if your opponent's call will put him all in and will eliminate him from the tournament should you have the better hand. Also, the later in a tournament it is, the more powerful this concept becomes.

By the way, the previous two paragraphs dealt with betting on the end. But this concept applies to all bets. Because of the way chips change value in percentage-payback tournaments, if you are in a good chip position and your opponent is not, many bets that normally would not be correct to make now become the best play. As stated, it does not matter whether more betting rounds are still to come.

Finally, it needs to be pointed out that the opposite is true if you have a short stack and are against an opponent with good chip position. Now for your bet to be correct, you must have far the best of it when you are called, especially late in a tournament. The reason for this is the same as in the previous situation. That is, the chips have changed value in relation to how many you have, and when your stack is short, any bet you make actually costs you much more than what your "healthy" opponent will have to pay to continue in the hand. Notice this concept sates that in certain situations, dependent on chip position, some players can correctly play much looser than other players.

Here's an example. Suppose you are playing in a percentage-payback hold'em tournament. You have made it to the final table and are dealt

in a late position. The pot has been opened with a raise by a solid player in an early position, everyone else has folded, and you think your opponent's most likely hand is something like

The question is whether you should raise or call. Notice that in a standard ring game, it certainly would be correct to raise. But

is this also true in a tournament, especially late in a tournament?

The answer depends on what your chip position is in relation to your opponent's chip position. If you have many more chips than your opponent, meaning that each of your individual chips is worth less than each of his individual chips, you should try to get as much of his money in the pot as possible and a raise would be correct. This probably would be correct even if you thought there was some chance that you were up against two aces or two kings. However, if you have less chips than your opponent, then the chip values have reversed, meaning that the correct play is to just call. If your chip stacks are about the same, it still is probably correct to call, since you are interested in maximizing survival. (You, of course, want to reraise if you think it is likely that there will be other callers unless you make it three bets.)

In an extreme case, you might want to throw the two queens away. For example, let's assume that you are at the final table and that two players have only enough chips left for a big blind. By waiting one round, you probably can gain at least one notch. Thus, even if you are absolutely sure that your hand is best, mucking the two queens might be correct.

Concept No. 18: Tournament speed has little to do with your strategy. In *How to Win at Poker Tournaments* by Tom McEvoy, the former World Series of Poker champion spends a great deal of time discussing tournament speed and its effects on one's overall strategy. Speed refers to how fast tournament limits are increased. Specifically, if the limits go up quickly, it is a fast-action tournament; if the limits go up not quite as fast, it is a medium-action tournament; and if the stakes are raised slowly, it is a slow-action tournament. Even though these descriptions are interesting, I cannot see how tournament speed has any effect on what your approach to correct tournament play should be, since the idea of whether you should rebuy and the appropriate fast play/survival strategies should dominate your overall approach.

What tournament speed does do is restrict the effects of skill on tournament results. This is because, as discussed in Parts Two and Three of this book, the standard deviation is inversely proportional to the square root of the sample size. That is, in tournaments— especially "fast-action" tournaments— the skill difference between players is minimized. This is another reason why survival tactics become so important in tournaments. Essentially, by surviving, you assure yourself of being able to play a few extra hands. This is the one area of gambling where self-weighting strategies are actually superior to non-self-weighting strategies, and for this reason, I do not like tournament play.

Another point of confusion is that the "fast-action" tournaments very often have a proportionately higher total ante in relation to the initial bet than the "slow-action" tournaments do. This means that correct poker strategy now requires looser play (since there is more to win in each pot). This includes — assuming your opponents do not adjust — more ante stealing in the fast-action tournaments, while a tighter style is usually appropriate in the slow action tournaments. However, and this is extremely important, notice that correct strategy is influenced by the ante and not by how fast the stakes are raised. Also notice that even in the high-ante situation, where correct strategy may mean relatively loose play, you still should play fast where appropriate and try to survive where appropriate. As already stated, I just cannot see that how fast the stakes are moved up has anything to do with appropriate tournament strategy. (Note that rapidly rising stakes tend to mean more players are playing with short stacks, and you can adjust to this situation.)

But here's an example that poker writer Mike Caro once suggested to me. Suppose you were playing in a tournament where the buy-in was so large and the stakes were raised so slowly that your chips would not be in jeopardy for months. How would you play? The answer is that you would use your normal best (standard game) strategy and not worry about fast play/survival tactics.

This example also implies that the "faster" a tournament is, the more important the appropriate fast play/survival tactics become. However, the reason I claim that tournament speed has virtually nothing to do with your overall strategy is that even the slow-action tournaments still raise the stakes fairly rapidly, meaning that it is not too long before the number of chips you have seems small when compared to the size of the bet. (The only exception to this might be the $10,000 no-limit hold'em tournament at the World Series of Poker, which usually takes four days to play.)

Settling Up in Tournaments: Part I

In many poker tournaments, a decision is often reached by the few remaining players to negotiate a settlement among themselves concerning the distribution of prize money, rather than playing out the tournament.[19] This is the first of a three-part series that discusses techniques and results in determining a fair settlement among the players. This first essay discusses some of the relatively simple but very important situations that arise in tournaments. Subsequent essays are theoretical and mathematical in some places, and many readers may not care to follow all the details. However, these essays also provide practical tables and guidelines for actual play and settlements.

The analysis in this series is based on two assumptions. First, we will assume that all of the remaining players are of equal strength. Second, we also will assume that all of the remaining players have a substantial number of chips in relation to the antes and/or blinds and the amount they expect to invest in any one pot. The latter assumption will enable us to ignore short-term advantages, such as current position in relation to the button and the money. Unfortunately, this assumption also will prevent us from applying these techniques to pot-limit or table-stakes tournaments.

Winner Take All

The easiest case to analyze is when the structure of the tournament is winner take all (which is rare nowadays). The solution is simple: A fair settlement of the prize money will be in direct proportion to the player's chips. Thus if there are

---

[19]This essay and the two to follow were written by Mark Weitzman.

three players, A, B, and C, with chips of $700, $200, and $100 respectively, and the winner of the freeze-out wins $1,000, then a fair settlement is simply $700, $200, and $100 respectively for A, B, and C. The reason for this is that under our assumptions, poker is a fair (zero expectation) game. Thus none of the players can gain an advantage by continued play, and therefore each player's mathematical expectation in the freeze-out is his current value of chips.

This fact also tells us that player A has a 70 percent chance of winning the freeze-out, player B 20 percent, and player C 10 percent. These probabilities ensure that each player's mathematical expectation is equal to his current number of chips. Thus, in any tournament structure, it is easy to determine the probability of each player winning the tournament. To summarize, in a winner-take-all structure, settle in direct proportion to your chips.

Percentage-Payback Tournaments — Two Players Remaining

Many tournaments are structured so that the top few places receive a certain percent of the total prize fund. Let's analyze the case where only two players are left, first place receives 80 percent of the prize money, and second place receives 20 percent. If player A currently has $700 in chips and player B has $300 in chips, how much should the players settle for?

There are two equivalent methods of solving this problem. The first method proceeds as follows. Player A has a 70 percent chance of winning and a 30 percent chance of coming in second. Hence his mathematical expectation is:

$$(.70)(800) \ [80\% \ of \ \$1,000] + (.30)(200) \ [20\% \ of \ \$1,000] = 620$$

In a similar way, player B's expectation is:

$$(.30)(800) + (.70)(200) = 380$$

The second method of solving this problem is to note that both players are guaranteed $200 and that they are fighting only for the remaining $600. Thus A has a 70 percent chance of winning the $600 and his expectation is:

$$(.70)(600) + 200 \text{ [guaranteed]} = 620$$

Player B has a 30 percent chance of winning $600 — which equals $180 plus a guarantee of $200, for an expectation of $380. The general formula for the two players is fairly simple. If player A has NA chips and player B has NB chips, and first place receives P1 percent and second place, P2 percent, then player A's expectation is:

$$E(A) = (P1)(NA) + (P2)(NB)$$

Player B's expectation is:

$$E(B) = (P2)(NA) + (P1)(NB)$$

This example also illustrates a general point: If you are behind in a percentage-payback tournament, your chips are worth more than their face value, and if you are ahead, your chips are worth less than their face value. For similar reasons, Mason Malmuth has pointed out that the winner of a percentage-payback tournament has in a sense suffered a "bad beat" — he has just won all of the chips, but he gets to keep only a percentage of his winnings.

In a winner-take-all or a two-player percentage-payback tournament, the calculations are fairly simple. In the next part of this series, I discuss methods for determining a fair settlement when there are three or more players remaining in a percentage tournament. The calculations are, unfortunately, fairly complex, since we must calculate the probability of each player finishing in every possible place. (In a two-player contest, we know the probability of winning, and the probability of placing second is simply one minus the probability of winning.)

The calculations given in this series are mathematical in nature. Many other factors will enter into negotiating and deciding on a fair settlement. However, a knowledge of the fair amount often helps a person's negotiating position, and he can strive to obtain more than his fair amount. Thus, the calculations in this and subsequent parts can serve as a baseline from which further refinements can be made.

Settling Up In Tournaments: Part II

In Part I of this series, I discussed techniques to determine a fair settlement in a tournament when only two players remain in the contest. In this part, I present methods applicable to percentage-structure tournaments when three or more players are remaining. This essay is fairly theoretical and mathematical, but the results are presented in easily understood tables in Part III.

Let's proceed by a specific example. Suppose player A has $700 in chips, player B has $200, and player C has $100. We need to calculate the probability of A finishing third and similar probabilities for B and C. Once these are calculated, it is trivial to determine the probability of each player finishing second, since the probability of each winning is known (proportional to each player's chips). After all the probabilities are calculated, we can determine each player's mathematical expectation as in two-player contests, once we are given the payoff structure.

We will use the notation $P(A3)$ for the probability of A finishing third and $P(A1|B3)$ for the conditional probability that A finishes first given that B has finished third, with similar extensions in notation to other players and places. Then we can write the following three equations:

$$(1) \quad P(A1) = P(B3)P(A1|B3) + P(C3)P(A1|C3)$$

$$(2) \quad P(B1) = P(A3)P(B1|A3) + P(C3)P(B1|C3)$$

$$(3) \quad P(C1) = P(A3)P(C1|A3) + P(B3)P(C1|B3)$$

The first equation says that the total probability of player A winning consists of two mutually exclusive events: B finishes third and A wins, or C finishes third and A wins. The probability of B finishing third and A winning is the product of the probability of B finishing third and the conditional probability of A winning given that B finishes third. The other two equations have similar interpretations for B and for C winning.

To solve these equations, we need to determine all of the conditional probabilities. To find $P(A1|B3)$, we note that when B finishes third, he will have lost $200 to players A and C. We assume that he will lose on average half of his chips to A and half to C. That is, there will be no preference on average of his losing chips to A or to C. I believe this to be valid under the assumptions mentioned in the beginning of Part I of this series.

Thus, on average, when B finishes third, A will have $800 in chips and C will have $200 in chips. We then know that A has an 80 percent chance of winning when B finishes third. Thus $P(A1|B3) = .80$. This calculation and those of the other conditional probabilities is illustrated in Table I.

Table I

	Player		
	A	B	C
1. Initial Distribution	700	200	100
2. A finishes third	-	550	450
3. $P(B1|A3)$, $P(C1|A3)$	-	.55	.45
4. B finishes third	800	-	200
5. $P(A1|B3)$, $P(C1|B3)$	.80	-	.20
6. C finishes third	750	250	-
7. $P(A1|C3)$, $P(B1|C3)$	.75	.25	-

We now can substitute these conditional probabilities, along with $P(A1)$, $P(B1)$, and $P(C1)$ — which are .7, .2, and .1 — into the original three equations.

$$(4) \quad .7 = (.8)P(B3) + (.75)P(C3)$$

$$(5) \quad .2 = (.55)P(A3) + (.25)P(C3)$$

$$(6) \quad .1 = (.45)P(A3) + (.20)P(B3)$$

We now have three simultaneous linear equations with three unknowns — P(A3), P(B3), and P(C3). These equations can be solved by the method of determinants, by algebraic elimination, or by computer. The solutions to the three equations are:

$$P(A3) = .087 = (2/23)$$

$$P(B3) = .304 = (7/23)$$

$$P(C3) = .609 = (14/23)$$

This can be verified by direct substitution. With these probabilities and the payoff structure, we can calculate each player's mathematical expectation and thus a fair settlement. Let's assume that first place receives 75 percent, second place 20 percent, and third place 5 percent. Then the calculation proceeds as in Table II.

Table II

		Player	
	A	B	C
1. Current Chips	700	200	100
2. First Place Prize	750	750	750
3. Second Place Prize	200	200	200
4. Third Place Prize	50	50	50
5. Prob. First Place	.700	.200	.100
6. Prob. Second Place	.213	.496	.291
7. Prob. Third Place	.087	.304	.609
8. Expected Value			
a. (2)(5)	525	150	75
b. (3)(6)	43	99	58
c. (4)(7)	4	15	30
d. Total	572	264	163

Thus, for this example, a fair settlement would be $572 for player A, $264 for player B, and $163 for player C. Note again that B and C, who are behind, receive more than their face value of chips, and A, who is ahead, receives less than his face value of chips.

In the next part, I present an alternative approximate method, which is considerably easier to apply in practice, especially to situations involving more than three players. I also present tables that will summarize most situations involving three players.

Settling Up in Tournaments: Part III

In Part II of this series, I presented general techniques for determining settlements in percentage-structure tournaments with three players remaining in the competition. In this part, I present tables for some of the more common situations, as well as an alternative method for computing settlements. This alternative method is easier to implement in practice, although it is less accurate than the technique previously described.

Table I provides settlement values and probabilities of finish for three-player percentage-payback tournaments, under several structures, when one of the players (A) has the lead and the other two players (B and C) are trailing with an equal number of chips.

Table I: Percentage-Payback Tournaments — Three-Player Settlement Value for Player A

Distribution			Probability for A			Settlement			
A	B	C	1st	2nd	3rd	(1)	(2)	(3)	(4)
900	50	50	.900	.073	.027	691	606	562	477
800	100	100	.800	.141	.059	631	561	524	436
700	150	150	.700	.203	.097	570	515	485	430
600	200	200	.600	.257	.143	509	469	446	406
500	250	250	.500	.300	.200	445	420	405	380
400	300	300	.400	.327	.273	379	369	363	353

(1) 1st-750, 2nd-200, 3rd-50
(2) 1st-650, 2nd-250, 3rd-100
(3) 1st-600, 2nd-250, 3rd-150
(4) 1st-500, 2nd-300, 3rd-200

Table I gives settlement values for the leading player — A. To find the values for the trailing players (B and C), simply subtract the value for player A from $1,000 and divide by 2. Thus, under the first structure (750-200-50), the settlement value for player A is $691 and for players B and C it is $154.50.

Table II presents settlement values and probabilities of finish for three players, when two of the players (A and B) have the lead and one of the players (C) is trailing.

Table II: Percentage-Payback Tournaments — Three-Player Settlement Value for Player C

Distribution			Probability for A			Settlement			
A	B	C	1st	2nd	3rd	(1)	(2)	(3)	(4)
475	475	50	.050	.124	.826	104	146	185	227
450	450	100	.100	.208	.692	151	186	216	251
425	425	150	.150	.264	.586	195	222	244	271
400	400	200	.200	.300	.500	235	255	270	290
375	375	250	.250	.321	.429	273	286	295	307
350	350	300	.300	.332	.368	310	315	318	323

(1) 1st-750, 2nd-200, 3rd-50
(2) 1st-650, 2nd-250, 3rd-100
(3) 1st-600, 2nd-250, 3rd-150
(4) 1st-500, 2nd-300, 3rd-200

Table II above gives values for the trailing player — C. To obtain settlement values for the leading players, simply follow the same procedure as for Table I. Thus, under the first structure (750-200-50), the settlement value for player C is $104 and for players A and B it is $448.

An alternative method for computing settlement values has been suggested to me by Mason Malmuth. The method is slightly less accurate than that given in Part II, but it is considerably faster and easier to apply. The alternative method proceeds from the following equations:

(1) $P(A2) = P(B1)P(A2|B1) + P(C1)P(A2|C1)$

(2) $P(B2) = P(A1)P(B2|A1) + P(C1)P(B2|C1)$

(3) $P(C2) = P(A1)P(C2|A1) + P(B1)P(C2|B1)$

Once again, we need to determine conditional probabilities, such as $P(A2|B1)$. (The notation is the same as in Part II.) The problem is that these conditional probabilities are essentially backward; when B wins, we have lost knowledge of the distribution of chips that prevailed between A and C. We can approximate $P(A2|B1)$ by ignoring B altogether. This is illustrated in Table III.

Table III

	Player		
	A	B	C
1. Distribution	700	200	100
2. B Wins	700	-	100
3. $P(A2|B1)$, $P(C3|B1)$	7/8	-	1/8
4. A Wins	-	200	100
5. $P(B2|A1)$, $P(C2|A1)$	-	2/3	1/3
6. C Wins	700	200	-
7. $P(A2|C1)$, $P(B2|C1)$	7/9	2/9	-

These conditional probabilities can now be substituted into the given equations, along with $P(A1)$, $P(B1)$, and $P(C1)$, which we know are .7, .2, and .1 respectively.

$$P(A2) = (.2)\left(\frac{7}{8}\right) + (.1)\left(\frac{7}{9}\right) = .253$$

$$P(B2) = (.7)\left(\frac{2}{3}\right) + (.1)\left(\frac{2}{9}\right) = .489$$

$$P(C2) = (.7)\left(\frac{1}{3}\right) + (.2)\left(\frac{1}{8}\right) = .258$$

The advantage of this method is that we do not have to solve any simultaneous equations. When these computed probabilities are used to compute the settlement values as in Part II, we obtain 578, 263, and 159 respectively for A, B, and C, as compared to 572, 264, and 164 for the exact values computed in Part II. We see that the results are only slightly different from the more accurate and complicated method.

In conclusion, I would like to emphasize again that the calculations in these essays are theoretical in nature. Many additional factors will enter into deciding on how much to settle for. Thus the calculations and tables in this article can serve as a baseline from which further refinements can be made.

Playing in Tournaments

Afterthought

What you have just read are my basic thoughts on poker tournament play. Yes, When you go broke, it is correct to rebuy in tournaments that award the prize money on a percentage basis, and almost all tournaments do this. But if you are in a good chip position in the same tournament, then rebuying is definitely a mistake. Until now, the concepts that tell us when it is correct to rebuy and when it is not correct to rebuy were not widely known. However, they are so important that your entire tournament strategy, as shown by the essays, should be built around them.

A lot of money can be made in poker tournaments, especially in the smaller ones. This is because the typical player has such a poor understanding of correct tournament strategy that he often gives his money away. Many of these people play super tight and pass up numerous opportunities that someone who understands how to survive will take advantage of. Others don't understand how to survive and make no effort to do so. If members of this subgroup get in a good chip position, they will play in such a way that they minimize their expectation. In other words, they usually have confrontations with large stacks that easily could be avoided.

In the major tournaments, this is also true, but to a much smaller extent. Yet there are still many players who give their money away. Another advantage of the smaller tournaments is that there are always some participants who play poker poorly. This is also less prevalent in the majors, because a smaller percentage of bad players can afford the large buy-ins, although some do get in through the satellites.

Another aspect of tournament play that should be kept in mind is the large standard deviation. In other words, to win a tournament, especially a large one, you must be lucky. Specifically, some people with what appears to be excellent tournament records have very little idea of what is correct. In addition, if it were possible to estimate the standard deviation for tournaments and a good tournament record was compared to a poor one, I suspect that a seemingly large difference often would not be statistically significant. This means that some of the current superstars are probably not very good, just fortunate. (I am not saying that all the people with good tournament records are poor players. But I am fairly sure that even those who are excellent tournament players and have managed to compile outstanding records also have been extremely lucky.)

The essays on settling up in tournaments, written by Mark Weitzman, are very important. No doubt many wrong deals have been made in tournaments, especially in big tournaments, and some of these probably were made by expert players. These three essays should give you good guidelines on where to start when figuring a proper split.

As the poker tournament essays have stressed, in a percentage-payback tournament, the less chips you have, the more each individual chip is worth, and the more chips you have, the less each individual chip is worth. This idea is the major force that should govern many of your strategy decisions in a poker tournament. Moreover, it is true that winning a tournament is really a bad beat, since you must give back much of what you have just won.

Part Five

New Games

New Games

Introduction

The California gambling law is not as concise as it should be. This means that even though many of the standard casino gambling games are not allowed, many forms of gambling, with local approval, are legal. In the past few years, several new games have become widely played in many cardrooms throughout California, and new ones are being introduced all the time. Two of these games, pan nine (also known as super pan nine) and pai gow poker — which is now also played at many casinos in Nevada — are addressed in this section.

Preliminary Pai Gow Poker Information

In late 1986, I did some research with Mike Caro on the new game of pai gow poker. The results of this research were then presented by me at a seminar at the Bicycle Club in Bell Gardens, California.[20] Even though these results are termed "preliminary," they are still quite powerful. For those of you who were unable to attend the seminar, the notes from the presentation are reproduced in this essay. However, two cautions are necessary. First, the quality of play has improved since this material was originally put together. This means that even though the expert should still have a positive expectation when playing, this expectation is probably not as high as it once was. Second, pai gow poker should have an extremely high standard deviation. Consequently, unless you have a very large bankroll, be cautious when deciding how much to bet.

Note No. 1: The bank does slightly better than break even. In a 4 percent commission game, when two typical players were programmed to play against each other, the bank won at a rate of one-tenth of 1 percent. This means that being the banker overcomes the 4 percent drop, as there are enough ties in front that go to the banker to make this position slightly profitable to play. However, the banker actually will do better than this, because on multiple decisions (against many opponents), only the net result is taxed. Also, for those who bet very large, the bank has a significant edge. This is because the largest commission that the clubs take is $80.[21]

---

[20]Just to set the record straight, I was not the main speaker at the seminar.

[21]This has now changed. Check with your favorite club for current conditions.

Note No. 2: The player is a loser. As expected, the player is a loser, and in a 4 percent commission game, the player loses at a rate of approximately 2.5 percent. The commission, plus the tie hands going to the banker, is just more than the typical player can handle.

Note No. 3: Bet big when banking; bet minimally when you are the player. Since we know the banker wins and the player loses, an obviously correct, non-self-weighting betting strategy has now emerged: Bet big when banking, but bet minimally when playing. The idea that you want to play against a large bank when you are the player, to assure that your good hands get paid off, is totally wrong. That is, when you are the player, your best bet is to bet nothing at all.

In fact, I know some people who have done well by always playing behind the banker and never playing against the banker. Of course, when this is done, you are not able to set the hands that can hurt you. However, in a typical game with typical players, this approach should show a small overall profit.

Note No. 4: Position matters. Like almost all other forms of poker, pai gow poker is a positional game. Consequently, since you have a disadvantage as a player and would prefer no action, sit where big bettors act before you do. This way, the bank's liability may be absorbed before the action gets to you.

Note No. 5: Encourage opponents to pass the bank. Remember, the bank is the only position where you can expect to make money in the long run. Consequently, the more you get to be the banker and the less your opponents get to be the banker, the better off you are. This is also a good reason to play the small-limit games, where many people will pass the bank. In the high-limit games, bank passing is a rarity. However, as previously mentioned, if you can bet very large (when banker) so that the commission stops, then you are probably much better off in the bigger games.

Note No. 6: Pushes will account for roughly 43 percent of all outcomes. If you were flipping coins, one for the front and one for the back, you would expect to push 50 percent of the time. However, in pai gow poker, due to tie hands going to the banker, the percent of pushes is reduced.

Note No. 7: Win-to-loss ratios are not a correct method for determining the best plays. This is a significant concept that leads to some surprising results (which are presented below). The method with the highest return percentage is usually the correct choice. However, sometimes when many players are covering your bank, you should choose a close alternative with a higher win-loss ratio and a smaller return.

Note No. 8: Select games with inexperienced poker players. This is some practical advice that is not based on the numerous computer simulations that we have done. Simply put, inexperienced poker players sometimes make horrendous mistakes. These include failing to recognize a straight or a flush, or not realizing that the joker also can count as an ace. By the way, when these players are in the banker position, they rarely make these kinds of errors, since the (house) dealer usually will help them set their hands. Also, these players — and unfortunately there are not very many of them anymore — are much more likely to be found in the smaller games.

Note: What now follows is some specific advice on how to play many hands based on the numerous computer simulations that were done. Although many hands in pai gow poker play automatically, enough decisions come up that allow the expert, when he is the banker, to gain a reasonable advantage against the typical player — and to overcome the house take.

Banker Decisions With Two Pair

1. Fours-up and threes-up. Put good jack or better up front; otherwise split. (Note: A good jack is a jack-ten or a jack-nine).

2. Small sixes-up and fives-up. Put good queen or better up front; otherwise split. (Note: Small sixes-up is a pair of sixes with a pair much smaller than the sixes.)

3. Small eights-up, small sevens-up, and sixes-up. Put any king or better up front; otherwise split.

4. Small nines-up, medium eights-up, and large sevens-up. Put good king or better up front; otherwise split.

5. Small jacks-up, small tens-up, large nines-up, large eights-up. Put any ace up front; otherwise split.

6. Small kings-up, medium and small queens-up, medium and large jacks-up, and large tens-up. Put good ace up front; otherwise split.

7. All other two pair. Always split.

You should notice that much of this advice is different from the way the typical pai gow poker participant plays. Specifically, the typical player splits two pair much more often than should be done. It is incorrect to automatically split small and medium two pair. In fact, with small two pair, it is correct to put a relatively weak hand in front to keep both pair in back.

An exception to this occurs when you are at the end of a long line of bettors and action can reach you only with many pushes. Now it can be shown that the banker is much more likely to have a weak hand in front and a strong hand in back. This is determined as follows. For the banker to push a lot, he probably has one weak hand and one strong hand. Assume the weak hand is in back. Since his better hand must be in back, this implies that the front hand also must be weak. Notice that this is a contradiction. Consequently, the banker is very likely to have a strong hand in back and a weak hand in front. In this situation, it may become correct to select a stronger front hand, sacrificing a medium five-card hand.

Player Decisions With Two Pair

1. Needs (slightly) better two-card hand than banker. Since tie hands go to the banker and almost all ties occur in front, the player needs a (slightly) better two-card hand than the banker.

2. Large tens-up and large jacks-up. Always split.

Some Other Decisions

1. Three aces. Always split.

2. Three kings. Unless you can put an ace or a queen in front, split three kings.

3. Other three of a kind. Never split.

4. Small two pair with a straight or a flush. If you have a small two pair with no joker and the hand also contains a straight or a flush, the correct play is to ignore the straight or flush and to split the two pair. An example of such a hand would be a six-high straight, no joker, that also contains an extra six and an extra four. The correct play is to ignore the straight and put the fours in front. If the hand contained the joker, then the small two pair should be kept in back, and the joker and the next highest card should be put up front.

5. One pair. Always put one pair in back, with the highest two remaining cards up front. This means that it is always wrong to split a pair of aces.

6. No pair. Always put your second and third ranking cards up front.

Final comments. In summary, if you follow the advice given in this essay, you should have a positive expectation in the game of pai gow poker. However, this advice includes making very large bets when you are the banker, and since not all of these bets will be successful, anyone following this winning strategy should see his bankroll go through some tremendous fluctuations. That is, you can expect to have a very high standard deviation. Consequently, it is not recommended that you take all your money and head for the nearest pai gow poker game. However, it does appear that the banker can get the best of it, and this should surprise many readers. It certainly surprised me.

A Few Pai Gow Poker Observations

Since pai gow poker became popular, I have taken some time every now and then to just watch the game. And though most of my writings are technical in nature, I thought you might be interested in my observations and a few opinions I have formed about this new game.

Observation No. 1: Pai gow poker has hurt poker. When standard pai gow (played with dominoes) came on the scene, poker players such as myself were happy, because it meant that clubs which might be having financial difficulty would have another source of revenue. In addition, since the people who participated in standard pai gow were not poker players, the game had virtually no effect upon the poker games.

Unfortunately, the same cannot be said of pai gow poker. These games have had a serious impact on the poker games (probably to the delight of some clubs, since they make more money from pai gow poker), because "stuck" players often will go to pai gow poker in an attempt to get even. This means that instead of staying in a poker game and playing desperately so as not to go home a loser, many "live ones" jump to pai gow poker. In fact, some weak players don't even play regular poker anymore — that is, they don't bother with the formality of getting buried at the poker tables like they used to. They still come to the clubs, but they head straight for the pai gow poker games.

Observation No. 2: The game is too slow. I personally find pai gow poker boring. First, it is a card squeezer's delight. It seems that some people take forever to set their hands. Second, once the hands are set, the action does not always get to you, since the banker's money is often completely accounted for before you play against him. My estimate is that (on average) only about 18 hands per hour are dealt, and of these 18 hands, you won't have a chance for a decision on four or five of them. Compare this to draw poker, where you sometimes can play as many as 50 hands per hour.

Observation No. 3: There are too many pushes. In addition to the slowness of pai gow poker, there are too many pushes. It would be all right to tie every now and then, but pushes occur almost half the time. One suggestion that was made was to allow the joker to be completely wild instead of being used only as an ace or to complete straights and flushes. However, this suggestion did not catch on, and the traditional use of the joker is now probably too well-entrenched. Nevertheless, I'm sure that the clubs also would like to minimize the number of pushes, since they don't collect the commission unless money changes hands.

Observation No. 4: Pai gow poker is the big money game. Despite all its shortcomings, pai gow poker is definitely where the money is. And when I say this, I am considering games like craps, roulette, blackjack, and baccarat, as well as games played only in California. (This observation is not true in Nevada. The huge pai gow poker games that are common in Southern California have not yet spread to the Silver State.)

Observation No. 5: Players like to snap off bets. The bet size in a typical pai gow poker game is generally determined by the banker. The more he puts up, the more his opponents usually put up, especially if the banker has been winning. As noted, the correct way to play this game is to bet small when you are the player and bet large when you are the banker, since ties in the front enable the typical player to overcome the house edge when he is banking. However, your large bet when banking can be only as large as the total action your opponents give you. But based on what I have seen, this is never a problem, especially in the biggest games where there always seem to be one or two players willing to snap off the largest banks.

Observation No. 6: Pai gow poker players do not become poker players. I had hoped that some of the patrons of these new games — especially those with a lot of money — would make their way to the standard poker games. Unfortunately, this has not happened. Even though poker players become pai gow poker players, the opposite seldom seems to occur.

Pai Gow Poker Tournament Strategy

Along with pai gow poker, pai gow poker tournaments have grown in popularity. As it turns out, the same ideas that enabled us to develop correct poker tournament strategies also are applicable to pai gow poker tournaments. The concepts discussed in this essay should help you hold your own in these tournaments.

Concept No. 1: In a percentage-payback tournament, it is always correct to rebuy when you have gone broke. For exactly the same reasons as in a regular poker tournament, if the prize money is distributed on a percentage-payback basis, then it is always correct to rebuy when you have gone broke. By the same token, if you have a lot of chips, rebuying is a mistake. (See the essay "To Rebuy or Not To Rebuy" in Part Four of this book.)

This leads to correct playing strategy. Specifically, you should play fast if you can rebuy and are not (much) above the rebuy threshold; otherwise, you should try to survive. The rest of the concepts address this fact.

Concept No. 2: If you can afford to rebuy, bet big. This is true whether you are the player or the banker, even though the banker has a small advantage over the player. The reasons for this are (1) your rebuy will offset any expected loss, and (2) if you manage to accumulate a lot of chips, you will be in excellent position to outlast your opponents. An exception to betting big is when you are still in the rebuy period but are already well above the rebuy threshold. Now you should be in your survival mode.

Concept No. 3: If you can afford to rebuy, set your hands aggressively. Sometimes in pai gow poker, your seven cards can be set in such a way that you have two medium-strength hands, or a weak hand in front and a strong hand in back. (Due to the rules of pai gow poker, playing a strong hand in front and a weak hand in back is not possible.) Early in a tournament, since the emphasis is on accumulating chips and getting a jump on your opposition, your hands should be set as aggressively as possible, even if your overall expectation would be better if you played the hand more conservatively. Remember, you are playing a tournament, not a regular game.

Concept No. 4: When you can't rebuy, try to survive. You are not permitted to rebuy when you have won enough chips to put you over the rebuy threshold, the time allocated for rebuys has ended, or you are playing in a tournament that does not allow rebuys. Now your emphasis should be on surviving, since the worst thing that can happen to you is to finish just out of the money. Basically, this means that you should play the opposite of what was described in Concepts No. 1 and No. 2 above. That is, bet the minimum and set your hands conservatively, even if this means that you may be setting your hands (technically) incorrectly.

Also, the further along the tournament is, the more important it is to survive. For example, if the top eight players receive money, it is much more important to be in your survival mode when only nine people are left than when 50 people are left. An exception to trying to survive might be if you are above the rebuy threshold but still have lots of time left to rebuy. In this case, you may want to continue to play fast, trying to get a jump on your opposition.

Concept No. 5: Try to get at a table with poor players who rebuy a lot. This may be difficult, since most tournaments assign seats, but you could try some seat trading.[22] Even

---

[22]As stated earlier, even though seat trading could be done in a few cardrooms years ago, this practice is not allowed in any of the cardrooms that I am currently familiar with.

though it is generally correct for almost all players to rebuy, if some players do a lot of rebuying and usually give their money away, you want to be in a good position to get it. This way, if you are still in the tournament when your table breaks, you will have on average more chips than you would if you were at a tight table where no one rebuys.

Concept No. 6: Don't go out with a bang in a percentage-payoff tournament. We have seen that it is correct to rebuy when you are low on chips and that it is incorrect to rebuy when you have a lot of chips. A logical extension of this — which can be shown mathematically — is that in percentage-payoff tournaments, the less chips you have, the more each individual chip is worth, and the more chips you have, the less each individual chip is worth. This means that going out with a bang is wrong. You should try to go out with a whimper. That is, try to make those few remaining chips last as long as possible. I realize that in pai gow poker tournaments, you must make a minimum bet. Consequently, this applies only when you have more than the required amount. But when this is the case, make those chips last as long as possible.

Concept No. 7: Set your hands aggressively against an all-in opponent. This is one exception to surviving that you should adopt. If it is (1) late in a tournament, (2) your opponent is all in, and (3) you are in a good chip position, you always should try to maximize your chances of eliminating this player, as the advantage of eliminating your opposition outweighs any small (expected) loss you might take. By the way, the later in a tournament it is, the more important this concept becomes.

Final note. Since you must place your bet before receiving a hand, not much else needs to be said about pai gow poker tournaments. The dominating force is whether or not it is correct for you to rebuy and how fast the stakes are raised has nothing to do with correct playing strategy. If you are not prepared to rebuy at least four or five times, it is perhaps best not to play the tournament at all.

Pan Nine Strategy

One of the new games that has arrived at the Southern California card clubs is pan nine, sometimes called super pan nine. Although a pan deck is used — eight decks (sometimes twelve decks) with all the sevens, eights, nines, and tens removed — the game is actually similar to baccarat.[23] Each player is dealt three cards, and the dealer also acts as banker. That is, the other seven players each individually contest the dealer. The object of the game is to make a total closest to 9. Face cards count zero, and the other cards are counted at face value. If your hand totals 10 or greater, then your hand is valued at the total count minus 10. In addition, each player has the option of drawing a fourth card, with the dealer/banker being last to exercise this option. As you will see, being able to act last is in the dealer's favor (as it is in poker), and this will affect your proper strategy.

First, let's analyze the player's decision of whether to hit. It should be obvious that an additional card should be taken if your total is 4 or less. But what about when you have a total of 5? This is answered by Table I, which shows the probability of improving to different totals. To keep the calculations relatively simple, for this table and the ones that follow, I ignored the three cards in your hand. However, since a pan deck contains 288 cards, the results are accurate enough to produce the information we need.

---

[23]Since this article was written, the composition of the decks used for pan nine has changed some at many of the clubs. However, the conclusions should still be accurate.

Table I: Probability of finishing with different hands when hitting a total of 5

Hit	Prob	Total	Hit	Prob	Total
Ace	.1111	6	Five	.1111	0
Deuce	.1111	7	Six	.1111	1
Trey	.1111	8	Face	.3333	5
Four	.1111	9			

Based on Table I, the expectation when a total of 5 is hit is 5.11.

$$5.11 = (6+7+8+9+1)(.1111) + (5)(.3333)$$

Consequently, it makes sense to hit a total of 5, since on average the total is improved. Similar analysis shows that a 6 on average goes down in value. This means that it is correct to hit a total of 5 or less, but that you should stand on a total of 6 or greater.

Now suppose that you are the dealer. Here the situation is somewhat different, since the dealer gets to act last. That is, he can use the information gained concerning whether his opponent hits or not to influence his decision on whether to hit. The following analysis will show what is correct to do. To keep the calculations workable, only a two-player contest is assumed. However, the dealer usually has many opponents. When this is the case, you should base your decisions on what your major opponent or opponents do — that is, the person(s) with the most money bet, or what the majority of the money does.

First, we will assume that the player is following correct strategy. That is, he will stand on a total of 6 and hit all smaller totals. Table II shows the probability of being dealt different three-card totals. (The appropriate calculations are not shown.)

Table II: Probability of being dealt
different three-card totals

Total	Prob	Total	Prob
0	.1100	5	.1083
1	.0988	6	.1203
2	.0951	7	.0990
3	.0917	8	.0916
4	.0982	9	.0839

Now suppose that your opponent stands. This means that he has a total of 6, 7, 8, or 9. Table III gives the probability of this player having each of these hands, given that he does not take a card.

Table III: Probability of different totals
given that player stands

Total	Prob	Total	Prob
6	.3047	8	.2320
7	.2507	9	.2150

Assume you have a total of 6 and your opponent stands. From Table III, you will tie 30.47 percent of the time and lose 69.52 percent of the time.

$$69.52 = (.2507 + .2320 + .2125)(100)$$

Next, let's suppose that instead of standing, you hit your total of 6. Table IV gives these results. Again, some of the calculations are not shown.

Table IV: Results when you hit a total of 6 against an opponent who stands

Hit Card	New Total	Win Prob	Loss Prob	Tie Prob
Ace	7	.0338	.0493	.0278
Deuce	8	.0617	.0235	.0257
Trey	9	.0874	.0000	.0236
Four	0	.0000	.1111	.0000
Five	1	.0000	.1111	.0000
Six	2	.0000	.1111	.0000
Face	6	.0000	.2317	.1015
Total		.1829	.6378	.1786

We see that by hitting a total of 6, we now win against an opponent who stands 18.29 percent of the time (versus 0 percent when we did not hit). We now lose 63.78 percent of the time (versus 69.52 percent when we did not hit), and we now tie 17.86 percent of the time (versus 30.47 percent when we did not hit). Clearly, when your major opponent stands (or the majority of the money stands), you should hit a total of 6. Also, similar analysis shows that even if your opponent stands, you also should stand on a total of 7 or better, which is what everyone does anyway.

So far, we have seen that it is correct for the player to hit a total of 5 or less and to stand on a total of 6 or more. It also has been shown that the dealer, who is the banker, is correct to hit a total of 6 when his major opponent — that is, the player with the most money — stands pat. Now we will develop the dealer's correct play when his major opponent hits, and later on we will examine the feasibility of a card-counting system.

Suppose your opponent hits. Table V gives the probability of different three-card starting hands for someone who always hits a total of 5 or less, and Table VI gives the probability of different finishing hands when this same player draws a card. Again, the actual calculations are not shown.

Table V: Probability of different starting totals given that a 5 or less is hit

Total	Prob	Total	Prob
0	.1827	3	.1523
1	..1641	4	.1631
2	.1579	5	.1799

Table VI: Probability of different finishing totals given that a 5 or less is hit

Total	Prob	Total	Prob
0	.0988	5	.1509
1	.0951	6	.1109
2	.0911	7	.0906
3	.1068	8	.0725
4	.1273	9	.0550

If the dealer stands on a total of 5, he will win 52.01 percent of the time:

$$52.01 = (.0988 + .0951 + .0911 + .1068 + .1273)(100)$$

He will lose 32.90 percent of the time:

$$32.90 = (.1109 + .0906 + .0725 + .0550)(100)$$

And, he will tie 15.09 percent of the time:

$$15.09 = (.1509)(100)$$

Now let's suppose the dealer hits his total of 5. Table VII presents the results that are needed.

Table VII: Probability of dealer winning when hitting a 5 versus a player who hits 5 or less

Finishing Hand	Prob	Win	Lose	Tie
0	.1111	.0000	.1000	.0111
1	.1111	.0111	.0894	.0106
2	.0000	.0000	.0000	.0000
3	.0000	.0000	.0000	.0000
4	.0000	.0000	.0000	.0000
5	.3333	.1733	.1097	.0503
6	.1111	.0745	.0243	.0123
7	.1111	.0869	.0141	.0101
8	.1111	.0969	.0061	.0081
9	.1111	.1050	.0000	.0061
Total	1.0000	.5477	.3436	.1086

This shows that by hitting a total of 5, the dealer expects to win 54.77 percent of the time (versus 52.01 for standing), to lose 34.36 percent of the time (versus 32.90 for standing), and to tie 10.86 percent of the time (versus 15.09 percent for standing).

So which strategy is better, hitting or standing, when the player hits? This is answered by looking at the expectation for each strategy when one unit is bet. The expectation for standing is 0.1911:

$$0.1911 = (.5201)(1) + (.3290)(-1) + (.1509)(0)$$

The expectation for hitting is 0.2041:

$$0.2041 = (.5477)(1) + (.3436)(-1) + (.1806)(0)$$

This shows that it is clearly better to hit, but the play is very close. In fact, one reason I did this analysis was that it was speculated that when the player hits, the dealer should stand on a total of 5. Even though it's close, it is still better for the dealer to hit.

What we have done so far is develop a basic strategy for the player and the dealer. Simply stated, the player should hit a total of 5 or less and stand on a total of 6 or higher. The dealer should hit a total of 5 or less if the player hits, but also should hit a total of 6 if the player stands; otherwise the dealer should stand.

Clearly, the dealer has a superior strategy over the player. But is it enough to beat the game? To answer this question, I programmed my home computer to play a two-person pan nine game with both the player and the dealer following the correct strategies as given. The results were as follows. For 100,000 trials, the player won 43,745 times, the dealer won 44,964 times, and there were 11,291 ties. But remember, when you win in this game, 4 percent of your bet goes to the house. Consequently, the preceding results are equivalent to about a 0.6 percent overall disadvantage for the dealer. Hence, you are certainly much better off being the dealer than the player, so don't pass the deal. However, unless some other means is employed, perhaps a card counting system, pan nine cannot be beat.

The next question to ask is whether a card counting system, similar to those systems that are successful in blackjack, can beat the game of super pan nine. Let's quickly recap why card counting systems are successful in blackjack, and then determine whether the game of super pan nine exhibits some of the same characteristics as blackjack.

Card counting systems are successful in blackjack for four reasons. First, blackjack is essentially an even game without card counting. Second, there are many decisions to make. Third, in blackjack, your decisions count. And Fourth, and most important, when certain cards are removed from the deck, their removal has a substantial impact on your overall blackjack expectation.

One game where card counting has not proven effective is baccarat, simply because the four reasons just stated are not valid. The game is not even off the top. There are not many decisions to make. Your decisions do not count. And removal of cards from the deck has very little effect on your baccarat expectation. (See Peter Griffin's book *Theory of Blackjack*.)

Now let's examine super pan nine against this criteria. Pan nine is not an even game off the top. It is true that we have developed a superior strategy for the dealer, but all this strategy does is reduce the house edge. It does not eliminate it. Also, the house edge may not be reduced as much under game situations as is theoretically possible, because (1) there is not a "main" opponent (that is, each player has bet approximately the same amount of money) or (2) your opponent(s) may not be playing correctly. For example, you certainly would not want to hit a total of 6 against someone who stands on a total of 5.

In addition, even though your decisions count in super pan nine, there are not very many to make. This means that unless a large edge can be found, small edges here and there will not enable you to become a winner.

Finally, let's look at what happens when different cards are removed from the deck. Table VIII gives these results, based on 100,000 computer simulations for each situation, assuming the player and the dealer are both playing the proper strategies as given earlier in this essay.

Table VIII: Results when different cards are removed

Card Removed	Player Wins	Dealer Wins	Ties
None	43,745	44,954	11,291
Ace	43,897	44,648	11,455
Deuce	44,012	44,994	10,994
Trey	44,276	44,858	10,866
Four	44,035	44,973	10,992
Five	43,776	45,248	10,976
Six	43,595	44,932	11,473
Face	42,886	44,020	11,094

Table IX gives similar results, with the difference being that the dealer stands on a total of 5 when the player hits.

Table IX: Dealer stands on 5 if player hits

Card Removed	Player Wins	Dealer Wins	Ties
Ace	43,947	44,358	11,695
Deuce	43,922	44,872	11,206
Trey	43,949	44,857	11,194
Four	43,168	45,752	11,080
Five	43,742	44,703	11,465
Six	44,133	44,091	11,776
Face	43,149	43,316	13,535

Notice that the largest advantage for the dealer occurs in Table IX when all the fours are removed from the deck. But even this most optimal situation gives the dealer an edge after the house take of only about three-fourths of 1 percent. That is, a situation that seldom occurs will produce only a very small advantage.

The conclusion is that card counting systems for the game of super pan nine probably will not be effective. (By the way, I have already seen one published system and it was completely wrong.) This is because favorable situations will appear only rarely when you are the dealer, and at best, they will be only slightly positive, not enough to realistically make up for all the times when you are at a disadvantage. (This includes when you are not the dealer.) Consequently, super pan nine can be played for fun, but don't expect to make a living off this game.

New Games

Afterthought

As can be seen, the game of super pan nine should be played for fun, not for profit. But pai gow poker is another matter. This game can be beaten, although it is not easy to do. First, you will need a large bankroll to withstand the enormous fluctuations of the game, and second, you will need tremendous patience, since you will be able to make only two or three big bets an hour.

There also are opportunities to make money in the tournaments involving the new games, simply because the typical tournament player has no idea of what correct tournament strategy is. If you adhere to the concepts on tournament play that are discussed in this section and in Part Four of this book, you should be a money favorite in any tournament you enter.

Part Six
Gambling Fantasy

Gambling Fantasy

Introduction

Now we come to what most readers will consider the fun section of this book. However, what follows also should be read on a more serious level. You should try to determine where some of the concepts already discussed apply, and why they caused either success or failure. Notice that much of what follows concerns actions that took place far away from the "very exciting gaming tables," but nevertheless much gambling still occurred.

The World's Greatest
Semi-Bluff

Semi-bluffing is one of the many tools that the expert poker player uses to increase his profits. Semi-bluffing is when you bet hoping your opponent will fold, but if he calls, you still have some chance of winning the hand. Consequently, it is not a complete bluff, but it is not a bet for value either. The proper time to use a semi-bluff is when you are against an opponent who won't fold often enough to make an outright bluff worthwhile, but who still won't call every time. Semi-bluffing is applicable to virtually every form of poker.

Two examples of semi-bluffs are as follows. First, suppose in lowball draw that you raise the blind with a two-card draw. Needless to say, you are hoping the blind will fold. But if he doesn't, you still have a chance to win the pot. Second, suppose in seven-card stud that you have a four flush and an ace-king showing. (You just caught the ace). If your opponent bets, you may want to raise as a semi-bluff. Notice that if your opponent does not fold, you still have a good chance to win the pot.

What follows is an example of this poker technique that was applied away from the poker table. As you will see, appropriate poker strategy can be applied to many adversarial situations. (For those more interested, an excellent discussion of semi-bluffing appears in David Sklansky's book *The Theory of Poker*. I also need to reference Bruce Caton's book *Terrible Swift Sword,* from which most of the following information was obtained.)

The world's greatest semi-bluff took place approximately 132 years ago in June of 1862. The location was just outside of Richmond, Virginia, where a huge Union army was poised, preparing a final advance on the Confederate capital. The Confederate army, which was much smaller than its Union foe, was even more handicapped in that it could not match or defend against the huge siege guns that the Army of the Potomac (North) possessed. All the Union army had to do was move forward and capture Richmond, and because of the defeats that the South already had suffered in the West, the Civil War probably would have ended quickly.

In addition, the commander of the Southern forces in Virginia, General Joseph E. Johnston, had just been severely wounded at the bloody but indecisive Battle of Seven Pines. (In poker, we would say that the pot had just been split.) To replace him, Jefferson Davis named his military adviser, General Robert E. Lee, to take over the defense of Richmond. Lee took on the task and quickly developed a plan, based on the semi-bluff, that not only would risk everything on one hand, but also had the potential to win the whole war in one quick stroke.

Actually, the semi-bluff was already started under Johnston. Acting on Lee's advice, he had sent General Thomas J. "Stonewall" Jackson north into the Shenendoah Valley (of Virginia) with a small force in the hope that Jackson would cause enough trouble that the North would not commit all of its troops to the Richmond area. This Jackson quickly did in one of the most spectacular campaigns of the war. Not only did his small army outmarch and outfight its opponents, but the Northern authorities, including President Lincoln, became convinced that an invasion of Washington, D. C. was imminent. Consequently, 30,000 troops were withheld from the "on to Richmond" offensive, while Jackson turned around and headed south to help defend the Confederate capital.

This was the first indication that the North was playing too tight. At the poker table, players who just play tight tend to win small amounts against weak opponents. But when these "rocks" move up to the bigger games and run into expert players, who play tight but aggressive and are capable of running creative plays, the rocks may not go broke as fast as the loose players, but they eventually end up that way. And when they do, many of them believe they have been exceptionally unlucky and virtually never change their style, because the loose players are always telling these rocks how well they play.

The first thing Lee did was name his army "The Army of Northern Virginia," even though it did not appear that they would ever see Northern Virginia again. These image plays are common in poker. It is rare to find a winning player who does not convey confidence, and this is exactly what Lee was doing. When your opponents are intimidated by an aggressive image, they will play in a much more predictable manner. If Lee could make his opponent "play" conservatively, he could take the kind of chances that poker experts take in their regular games, with reduced risk. Notice that Lee was not only increasing his expectation, but lowering his standard deviation as well.

Next, Lee gave orders instructing his army to dig a massive defensive works (trenches and so forth) in front of the city of Richmond. Lee knew that his opponent, General George B. McClellan, would not move until everything was perfect. In other words, McClellan played too tight and would not make a bet unless he had an absolute lock. This gave the South the time it needed to dig its trenches, which Lee hoped would "free" his army for battle. That is, Lee wanted his opponent to think he was just as conservative. At the poker table, when your tight opponent believes you play similar to the way he does, he becomes more susceptible to bluffs.

During this time, Lee also instructed his cavalry to find out exactly where the enemy was. General J.E.B. Stuart and his troopers managed to ride clear around the Army of the Potomac and supplied Lee with the information that was needed. The "eyes" of the Army of Northern Virginia informed Lee that McClellan had about 80,000 troops in front of Richmond, and in addition, on the North's right flank, there were another 30,000 troops just north of the Chickahominy River.

Lee now finalized his plans. He would take most of his army out of the trenches, have them join up with Jackson's men, swing around to the rear of the Army of the Potomac, and attack the exposed right flank. In all, he would put about 55,000 men on this offensive and leave only 25,000 men to face the main Union force. (If McClellan moved against these Richmond defenders, it would be only a short time before he occupied Richmond. But as stated, Lee knew that his opponent played too tight and figured that his gamble had a good chance to pay off.) The plan was to fight a battle north of the Chickahominy River and to "bluff" a battle in front of Richmond. Notice that this is a classic semi-bluff. Lee wanted McClellan to fold. But if McClellan didn't, the Confederate army might still do well enough north of the Chickahominy to carry the day.

Lee moved quickly, but Jackson was surprisingly slow, and the battle (which took place in early June) began without Jackson's army. Commanding the Confederate troops in front of Richmond was General John B. Magruder, who was known as an amateur actor in the old army. He put these skills to work. The Confederates staged mock charges, shuffled men around in obvious view (but out of range), fired their guns and cannons at regular intervals, and did everything but fight. At the poker table, these kinds of tells come under the general heading of "when weak, act strong." They are commonly seen, especially in draw poker and at the lower limits, and are one of the tools that the expert player uses to read his opponent. Unfortunately for the North, its commander was not an expert poker player.

McClellan became convinced that he was being attacked by superior numbers on both sides. The facts that 80,000 of his men actually saw no action and that there were casualties on only one of the two fronts seem to have completely eluded him. His orders were to hold ground at all costs. Just as expected, General McClellan had been bluffed out of action by General Lee. The semi-bluff was working.

By the second day, Jackson was finally in the right place, and the Confederate attack against the now crumbling right flank of the Army of the Potomac continued. Yet McClellan sent no reinforcements and made no attempt to move into Richmond with the main body of his army. (Magruder kept up the bluff, and his troops continued to march around, fire guns, and shout out orders, but not really do any harm to anyone.) Finally, at the end of the second day, with his right flank smashed, McClellan ordered a retreat. The semi-bluff was successful, as the man with the "best cards" folded his hand.

There was fighting for a solid week in what became known as the "Seven Days" battles. The Union army continued to retreat, even after finally winning a victory on the seventh day at Malvern Hill. Their commander just played too conservatively and could not understand why his "chips" were disappearing.

Robert E. Lee did not accomplish everything that he set out to accomplish, which was total defeat of the Union army, but he did manage to win a great victory for the South, and he turned a short war into an all-consuming one. Lee clearly showed that the skill needed to play the game is sometimes more important than the strength of your hand.

There are not many poker players who have the heart and the courage to put their total bankroll on the table trying to achieve the ultimate win. Yet General Lee, was to do this not only at Richmond, but also at other significant junctures in the Civil War. In addition, Lee had an excellent understanding of the game; he was a superb judge of the character of his opponents and often knew exactly what they were thinking. Fortunately, there are not many poker players with these same skills. But when you run into one, as General McClellan found out, the games are very tough to beat. In other words, playing tight may beat a weak home game or the smaller games in a major cardroom, but when your opponents are tough, tight predictable play will be almost as expensive as loose reckless play.

The World's Greatest Gamblers

When someone mentions great gamblers, names like Nick the Greek and Amarillo Slim come to mind. But gamblers appear in many other fields. To qualify for the list of great gamblers discussed in this essay, the following criteria were used. First, the individual had to be willing to risk everything for the chance to win it all. Second, his judgment had to be sound and correct. Third, his judgment had to go against what was generally considered to be correct. And fourth, his strategy had to cause his opponent to become confused and mistake-prone. The list is, of course, not complete, and I am sure that many other individuals could be added. However, the following men are examples of truly great gamblers.

Robert E. Lee. Perhaps the greatest of all American gamblers, this southern Civil War general would again and again risk everything in the hope of possibly winning the war, thus creating an independent southern nation. One example was discussed in the preceding essay, the "World's Greatest Semi Bluff." Here are two additional examples of Lee's gambling exploits.

The first occurred immediately after the Battle of Sharpsburg, fought near Antietam Creek in Maryland. A copy of Lee's orders had been lost and were found by Union forces. General George B. McClellan, the Union commander, now knew exactly where his enemy was, and he confronted the Army of Northern Virginia near Sharpsburg, Maryland. Worse for Lee, his whole army had not yet crossed the Potomac, and he had only 40,000 men to face more than 100,000 Union soldiers. (Sort of like a top professional gambler leaving half his playing stake at home.) Nevertheless, Lee ordered his army to stand and fight in an effort to gain that "final" victory.

After a terrible fight, in which each side suffered more than 12,000 casualties, the Southern army was still together, but there was no way it could stand another day of fighting. Lee had an escape route across the Potomac River. However, it was not a good one, and he would be badly harassed by the pursuing Union army. Hence, Lee decided on a great gamble. He would hold his ground and attempt to bluff his opponent out of an attack.

Lee knew that General McClellan was extremely conservative — he played too tight and was very predictable — and Lee thought that his tactics would confuse his opponent into making the mistake of letting him survive. For a solid day, both armies, battle lines drawn, were just a short distance from each other, but no orders were given by either side to continue the battle. That night, Lee and his army retreated unharassed. (He had successfully bluffed his opposition out of betting.)

Another gamble that General Lee pulled off occurred in the spring of 1863 at what is now known as the Battle of Chanslerville. A huge Union army of 120,000 men, under the command of General Joseph Hooker, was moving south to engage Lee's army of only 60,000 men. If Lee fought like he was supposed to, the South slowly and surely would be defeated. But Lee decided to gamble everything and split his army into three units, a tactic that all other military experts at the time would say was virtual suicide in the face of the enemy. With the help of General Thomas J. "Stonewall" Jackson, the largest portion of Lee's army made a spectacular flanking march.

After a day's marching, during which time the rest of the Army of Northern Virginia could have been destroyed had Hooker reacted properly, all of a sudden, the South had its enemy caught in a crossfire. (Sort of like being caught between two raisers in a lowball poker game.) Despite this, the Union army was still in fairly good shape. But Lee had correctly judged that his opponent, General Hooker, would not be able to understand what had happened. Hooker thought only of defeat — similar to the big-time gambler who has lost his heart

— gave orders to retreat, and the South won another spectacular victory.

Winston Churchill. World War II had gone badly for England. The pacifist government of Neville Chamberlain had failed, the allies were defeated in Europe, and the German Air Force was systematically destroying its military targets on the British mainland. To make matters worse, it did not appear that the Royal Air Force had enough planes or enough trained pilots to successfully defend its country. The German strategy was working.

Then in August, 1940 the British staged an air raid on Berlin. Churchill had made the ultimate gamble. For a chance to win the war, he was now willing to risk the entire civilian population, as well as the military targets. The German response was to go along with this change of rules. The Germans shifted their bombing emphasis from military to civilian targets, which were much farther away. Of course, as we know, the gamble paid off. Even though the amount of civilian suffering was high, the Royal Air Force became more powerful and England was never invaded. This ultimate gamble, which raised the stakes of World War II, gave England the chance it needed to defeat the axis countries.

Daniel Webster. In the 1840s, Daniel Webster had become one of the most important men in the United States. A former secretary of state and presidential candidate for the ill-fated Whig Party, Webster was now the leading spokesman in the Senate for the anti-slavery North. In fact, he had a good chance of winning the presidential nomination again, a goal he very much wanted.

But Webster was also a man of vision. He could see that the country was on a disastrous course. The union was in jeopardy, and he knew that with no union there was nothing. Consequently, on that fateful day in 1850, Webster decided to make the ultimate gamble. He rose in the Senate and gave a speech. But instead of blasting the South and its "peculiar institution," he gambled his career, aspirations, and reputation by arguing that the union was more important and must be preserved at any cost. Webster was finished, a disgrace to his constituency, but the union was saved (at least for a while). The compromise of 1850 was worked out, and it would be another ten years before the union was dissolved.

John F. Kennedy. Anyone who has participated in or watched a no-limit poker game is aware of the tremendous tension and pressures that develop, especially if the game is large. For example, suppose in a no-limit game that you hold a good hand and an opponent unexpectedly bets. Here are your options and what can happen.

First, you can fold. Even though you hold a good hand, your opponent may have a better hand. But this is not necessarily the case, so folding may cost you the pot. Second, you can call. Perhaps your opponent is bluffing and you will win, but you also may discover that you are a loser. Your third option is to raise. If your opponent has bet a hand that is better than yours but is still not great, you may get him to fold. But if he holds a great hand, which you may not have anticipated, you jeopardize all your chips.

In October of 1962, the Kennedy administration discovered that the Soviet Union was building a missile base in Cuba that would handle offensive nuclear weapons. Kennedy, like the player in a no-limit poker game who finds himself facing an unexpected bet, had three choices. First, he could ignore and/or downplay the importance of the missile site. This is equivalent to folding. Second, he could try to make a deal with the Soviets, perhaps making some unpopular concessions to get the missiles removed. This is equivalent to calling. Kennedy chose to raise.

A blockade of Cuba was announced — and like a no-limit poker game — the tension was tremendous. Kennedy was jeopardizing all his chips. If the Soviets attempted to break the blockade, it could lead to a thermo-nuclear exchange.

Anyone familiar with no-limit poker is aware that a great deal of time is sometimes required to make decisions in

251

pressure situations. Pressure was mounting in the Kremlin and time was running out, as the Russian ships slowly approached the blockade line. Finally, the Soviet Union folded and orders were given to turn back their ships. Kennedy probably held the stronger hand, since in 1962, the United States was much stronger militarily than its foe. But by raising with the blockade, Kennedy never had to face a showdown.

There is, of course, a significant difference between this situation and no-limit poker: Both opponents, that is, the United States and the Soviet Union, could have lost. Even in 1962, there were probably enough nuclear weapons on both sides to destroy civilization.

William T. Sherman. The year was 1864, and General Sherman had his Union army deep in Southern territory. The problem was that even though Sherman was close to Atlanta, he had failed to bring his Southern host to that final decisive fight. The Confederate commander, General Joseph E. Johnston, was an extraordinary defensive tactician who knew that as long as his army survived, the Southern nation would survive. In addition, Johnston also knew that if his army could survive a few months longer, the ultimate victory that the North so badly needed would not occur until after the elections (in the North) and Lincoln might be defeated at the polls. This was literally the best chance the South had.

Unfortunately for Johnston, Jefferson Davis, the Confederate President, did not see things quite the same way. Consequently, since Davis wanted the invader brought to battle and defeated at the outskirts of Atlanta, Johnston was relieved of his command and was replaced by the aggressive and courageous fighter General John B. Hood.

A curious thing now happened. One of Sherman's subordinates related a story to his commander about Hood playing in a poker game many years before the Civil War began. Apparently, Hood had bet $2,500 with "nary a pair" in his hand. Sherman used this information to help formulate his strategy for attacking Atlanta. He now knew that instead of being against a defense-oriented opponent, whom he was continuously pursuing, the Union Army should brace itself for an attack. As suspected, the attack came soon. After several vicious battles, including the Battle of Atlanta, Sherman — who had correctly predicted his opponent's intention all because of a poker game held many years before — finally achieved the decisive victory that the North and President Lincoln so badly needed.

Abraham Lincoln. Thanks to a Southern general named Robert E. Lee, the Union war effort was in trouble. This alone was not enough to make President Lincoln want to gamble. The problem was that it appeared both England and France were close to recognizing the Southern Confederacy as a country. If this happened, the Northern cause would be lost.

Lincoln recognized this, and in 1863 decided to issue the Emancipation Proclamation, which freed the slaves in only those territories that currently were in rebellion. Both France and England now had to abandon recognizing the South as a sovereign nation. This act was a gamble because the population of the North — especially the Northern Democrats who had volunteered so patriotically for the war cause — was not fighting to free the slaves; it was fighting to preserve the union. And at a time when many more volunteers were needed, the administration feared that the Emancipation Proclamation might dramatically affect its military manpower. Fortunately, this did not happen.

However, many forms of gambling come with a cost referred to as the vigorish or rake. This was true of Lincoln's great gamble. The "vig" on the Emancipation Proclamation came approximately two years later in the form of a bullet.

Anwar Sadat. Sadat was in a similar situation to Lincoln. His war effort against Israel had essentially failed, and Egypt's prospects in a future war appeared dismal. In addition, Egypt's economy was in terrible shape. So Sadat decided to take a great gamble. He would go to Jerusalem and try to make peace at the risk of alienating the population of Egypt and bringing down his regime. Sadat accomplished his goal. The Sinai Peninsula has been returned to Egypt, and peace was established between the two countries. Unfortunately, Sadat also had a "vig" to pay. Like Lincoln, Sadat was assassinated. His great gamble cost him his life.

The World's Worst Gamblers

The preceding essay gave some examples of the world's greatest gamblers. To qualify, a person had to risk everything to win it all, often go against conventional strategies and thought, use correct judgment, and maximize his expectation. This essay discusses a different group of people. They also took great risks, yet hindsight has shown that in most cases, they were very foolish, or exhibited other characteristics of unsuccessful gamblers.

Neville Chamberlain. Chamberlain, who was prime minister of England in the late 1930s, was willing to gamble for peace. He recognized that the Treaty of Versailles, which had ended World War I, was very unfair to Germany, and he was willing to rectify the situation. Consequently, at the Munich Conference in September 1938, Chamberlain, along with Edouard Daladier, the premier of France, agreed to let Hitler's Germany expand into the Sudetenland. (This is after previous German expansions.) Chamberlain thought his great gamble would bring "peace in our time," but in just a few short weeks, Hitler would attack Poland, and World War II would begin.

A top poker player must be a good judge of the character of his opponents. Obviously, Chamberlain did not have this ability. Some poker players, usually because of excessive egos, are never satisfied with a win. That is, they always want to win more and play bigger. Needless to say, this is the type of person that Chamberlain ran into. All he accomplished was to give Hitler more chips, enabling him to go to a bigger game.

Jefferson Davis. The year was 1864, and the Civil war was now going badly for the South. The North had a large army, deep in Southern territory, under the command of the highly skilled general William T. Sherman. Opposing Sherman was a much smaller Confederate army under the command of the defense-minded general Joseph E. Johnston. However, Johnston's strategy was correct. He was willing to pick up small wins and would fight only when he had the best of it. Moreover, Johnston knew that if he and his army could survive a little longer, Lincoln might be defeated in the presidential elections, as the North still desperately needed that ultimate victory.

Unfortunately for Johnston, he had to work for Jefferson Davis, whose actions remind me of the desperate gambler who is on a losing streak and is willing to take foolish risks in an effort to get even. Instead of being satisfied with small wins and being willing to "grind his chips back," Davis replaced Johnston with the aggressive and courageous fighter General John B. Hood, who immediately brought his army out of the trenches. After much vicious fighting, Atlanta was lost and the North had its ultimate victory. Davis now discovered that instead of getting even, he was just about broke.

Benito Mussolini. Benito Mussolini, the Fascist dictator of Italy before and during most of World War II, reminds me of the ultimate "live one." A live one can be defined as a person who gambles more on hope than on skill, and consequently makes many bets whether he has the best of it or not. He is always looking for an excuse to stay in action, even if he has been losing heavily. Such was the case with the "Duce."

During the summer of 1943, Mussolini met with Hitler in Northern Italy. The purpose of the meeting was to discuss the war, which no longer was going very well for the Axis Powers. The Russians were making spectacular advances on the Eastern Front, and the Allies were now completely victorious in Northern Africa. In addition, the American and British operation to invade Southern Italy had begun. Mussolini understood this and proposed that Hitler sue for peace with the Russians, which would enable the Axis Powers to reinforce the Southern European Front. But Hitler would have none of it. He told the Duce of "fantastic new weapons" that were being built and convinced Mussolini of great victories still to come.

Mussolini, with spirits revived, was now eagerly ready to resume the war effort. Unfortunately for him, the Allies' invasion of Sicily was moving along successfully. In a few days, the Duce found himself not only the disposed dictator of Italy but imprisoned as well. That is, he finally had run out of chips to bet.

Davey Crockett. Davey Crockett was a Tennessee frontiersman and a politician who had served several terms in the United States Congress. However, in 1836, Crockett lost his congressional seat and decided to seek his fortunes elsewhere.

I'm reminded of the poker player who has become "hometown champion" and is now dissatisfied with his regular game. He heads to Las Vegas so he can take a shot at the big time. Unfortunately, he fails to realize that the skills needed to become the best local player are still not good enough for success against top players in Nevada.

Well, Crockett didn't head to Nevada, but he did go to Texas (where the action was) with a small group of followers and decided to help with the Texan effort to gain independence from Mexico. Crockett was gambling that he could re-establish himself as a frontier hero and return to the United States, where he could then run again for office. Unfortunately, the stakes he played for were more than he could afford. He and his small band got involved in a no-limit game at the Alamo, and Crockett never had a chance. He did become a legendary figure, but when the defenders of the Alamo finally ran out of ammunition, Crockett lost his great gamble — and his life.

Earl Van Dorn. In 1862, after suffering some initial reverses in the West, the Southern Confederacy laid plans for a great counteroffensive. The first step was for General Earl Van Dorn to lead an army west of the Mississippi into Missouri. This Van Dorn did, and the great Battle of Pea Ridge was fought. Even though this battle is not as well-known as other Civil War battles, primarily because a total of only 25,000 men took part, it was still strategically significant and meant that the state of Missouri would be safe in Union hands.

What was unusual was that part of Van Dorn's army consisted of American Indians (two regiments of Cherokee and one regiment of Creek). Apparently, the Confederates had sold the Indians on the doctrine of states rights. Van Dorn took the great gamble that with little training, the Indians would stay in their battle lines and not revert to traditional Indian fighting methods.

But when the battle began and the bullets started to fly, the Indians broke from their lines and ran behind some trees a short distance away. It was not that the Indians were afraid, but that this was the way they had been taught to fight.

Despite this, the Battle of Pea Ridge lasted all day, but Van Dorn could not pull off a victory with only half an army. The first round of the South's great counteroffensive had been lost.

John Burgoynne. "Gentleman Johnny" Burgoynne was an English general who tried to lead an invasion force down from Canada into New York during the Revolutionary War. Part of Burgoynne's army was made up of Mohawk Indians. Early in the expedition, he gave a speech to the Mohawks in which he explained that they were now part of a civilized army and would not be allowed to scalp their victims, rape the women, and torture the children. On hearing this, the indians quit, leaving the invading English force much weaker. Burgoynne had gambled that people would be willing to behave differently from what they were accustomed to. He also did not understand that many people who gamble do so because they crave action. If they are forced to be more prudent — that is to play tight — a lot of them will simply stop gambling, because they won't have any fun. Obviously, Burgoynne's gamble failed.

Special note. One key to successful gambling is game selection. Specifically, you want to play in a game that is as easy to beat as possible. For example, it doesn't do much good to be the eighth best poker player in the world if you always get in games with the seven better players. In blackjack, game selection includes considering bet variation tolerances and deck penetration, as well as the rules a particular casino offers, which can make the difference between being a winner and a loser.

The next three gamblers were all highly skilled at what they did. But they made the mistake of taking on opponents who were too tough for them. The first two misjudged a man, the third misjudged a country.

Stephen A. Douglas. Stephen Douglas was perhaps the most prominent politician in the United States during the 1850s. He was the principal architect of the 1854 Kansas-Nebraska Act and was considered to be the favorite for the presidency in 1860. However, in 1858, Douglas had to run for re-election to his Senate seat and accepted a challenge from his opponent, Abraham Lincoln of the newly-founded Republican Party, to a series of debates that probably brought stump speaking to its peak.

In life, as in poker, it is a critical error to underestimate an opponent, and Douglas completely underestimated the tall, awkward-looking man who out debated him. (They must have made an interesting pair, as Douglas, also known as the "Little Giant," was almost a foot and a half shorter than Lincoln.) Lincoln got Douglas to admit that slavery was not an inherent right, but just a law that "unfriendly" legislation could repeal. This cost the Little Giant the support of the South, as well as the presidential election of 1860. A more prudent gambler never would have allowed himself to get into this situation.

Stanley Ketchel. In 1909, Stanley Ketchel was the popular middle-weight champion of the world, and he signed to fight Jack Johnson, the first black heavyweight champion of the world. Johnson apparently had agreed to one condition set by Ketchel's manager: to carry the "Michigan Assassin" for 20 rounds to protect Ketchel's reputation as middle-weight champion.

But Ketchel had other ideas. In the twelfth round, Ketchel caught Johnson with an overhand right and dropped him to the canvas. Stunned but unhurt, Johnson jumped to his feet and immediately hit Ketchel so hard that not only did he knock Ketchel out cold, but the film of the fight clearly showed Johnson scraping some of Ketchel's teeth out of his gloves.

When a reporter asked Jack Johnson how he had felt when Ketchel had dropped him to the canvas, Johnson replied, "Better than Ketchel did 30 seconds later. He crossed me, and I made him pay for it."

Ketchel's great gamble had failed. In fact, it had no chance. Ketchel had misjudged the ability and ferocity of his opponent. He also failed to understand that when you move up in stakes, the competition generally gets tougher.

Tojo Hidecki. Tojo was the premier of Japan during the early 1940s and had been a chief proponent of the Japanese military expansion in the 1930s and early 1940s. Tojo's great gamble was to attack the United States by directing the Imperial Navy to destroy the U.S. Pacific Fleet at Pearl Harbor. The idea was to knock the United States out of the war before the United States got into it, which would allow Japan to accomplish whatever objectives its expansionist government wanted in the Pacific.

Tojo reminds me of the winning gambler who believes he will never lose again, or if a loss does occur, it will be easy to recover from. This type of person tends to become careless until a costly mistake (sometimes) snaps him out of it. Needless to say, this is what happened to Tojo. Attacking the United States at Pearl Harbor, even though it appeared at first to be spectacularly successful, was one gamble that did not pay off.

Self-Weighting Disasters

One of the themes of this book is that correct non-self-weighting strategies are the way to success. Does this mean that self-weighting strategies are the path to disaster? Well, sometimes this is certainly the case. This essay provides some examples from history of disasters that were caused by self-weighting strategies. You should notice that all of these disasters could have been avoided if appropriate non-self-weighting strategies had been followed.

Disaster No. 1: The Spanish Armada. In 1588, Philip II of Spain decided to do something about England, which had become an irritant to Spain in the Atlantic Ocean and in the New World. Consequently, Spain sent a great fleet to England for the purpose of destroying the English fleet and then invading the British Isles. This fleet, known as the Armada, was to be defeated in one of the most one-sided battles in naval history.

Up until the battle, the Spanish had been successful by fighting at close range with large, slow-moving ships, and they planned to continue this tactic. Notice that this was a self weighting strategy. The Spanish planned to engage the English ships and slowly, mainly by force of numbers, devastate their opponents.

Unfortunately for the Spanish, the English adopted a different strategy, one that was non-self-weighting. They built smaller, faster ships with long-range guns. Their plan was to maneuver into position out of range of the Spanish guns, to take a few shots, and then as the Spanish fleet came toward them, to quickly move out of range and take some more shots.

Notice that the Spanish were playing every hand, while the English were playing only, when they had an advantage. Needless to say, the battle was one-sided, and when the great Armada tried to take refuge off the coast of France, the English changed tactics. They set fire to many small boats and allowed them to drift into the harbor where the Spanish fleet had moved, causing much of the Armada, in its effort to escape, to be destroyed first by fire and later by bad weather.

The result was a dramatic victory for Sir Francis Drake and the English. Spain would now go into decline, while Britain would slowly become the dominant power in the world.

Disaster No. 2: The 1929 stock market crash. The market was going up, and everyone was buying stock. The typical investor didn't care what stock he bought. The idea was just to accumulate stocks, and the more he had, the better. In addition, ways were created, such as buying on margin, that allowed the typical investor to accumulate even more stocks. Of course, this was done at tremendous leverage. Needless to say, this type of self-weighting approach doomed the typical investor to disaster, and in the fall of 1929, the market crashed and the country was plunged into depression.

Disaster No. 3: World War I trench warfare. Most of World War I was fought in the trenches, due to the fact that the machine gun had become such a potent weapon. Each side had adopted the same strategy. They bombarded their opponent's lines, and when the shelling stopped, the next step was an attempt to move forward. Of course, the soldiers in the trenches were protected from the bombardment, and when the enemy tried to move forward, the side remaining in the trenches would again demonstrate how effective the machine gun was.

This pattern of shelling, trying to move forward, and being machine-gunned down continued for several years. Notice that each side was playing many hands with similar size bets. That is, self-weighting strategies were followed, and millions of soldiers were killed and wounded.

A correct non-self-weighting strategy would have been to stay in the trenches (not play so many hands) and wait for some development that would finally allow penetration of the enemy's defensive lines. Eventually, something like this did happen. The British developed crude tanks (allowing them to move forward), the United States joined the war effort, and Germany became exhausted.

Disaster No. 4: The Battle of Fredericksburg. The year was 1863, and this was one of the major battles of the American Civil War. The Union Army of the Potomac, under the leadership of General Ambrose Burnside, met the Confederate Army of Northern Virginia, under the command of Robert E. Lee, at the town of Fredericksburg. Lee had his army well entrenched in excellent defensive positions on high ground. Burnside, in his desire to be on the offensive, launched many repeated attacks, but each attack easily was beaten back by the Confederate forces.

Instead of stopping the attacks after the first one failed, General Burnside adopted a self-weighting strategy and kept up the attacks for a full day, suffering almost ten times the number of casualties as the Confederates. In fact, Confederate General Peter Longstreet announced during the battle, "We can kill them all." Finally, after a full day of fighting, Burnside had endured enough, and he called off the self-weighting massacre.

Disaster No. 5: George Foreman versus Mohammed Ali. In 1973, George Foreman appeared to be the most devastating boxer there ever had been. Not only had he knocked out almost all of his opponents, but he also had destroyed such formidable adversaries as Joe Frazier and Ken Norton. Foreman literally hit too hard for anyone to stay with him. It seemed that after a few punches, his opposition would just fall. Now it appeared that in Zaire, Africa, he also would destroy Mohammed Ali, who was trying to regain his title.

The fight began as expected. Foreman threw the punches, and his opponent seemed helpless as he just covered up. But Ali did a better job of covering up than anyone who was watching the fight realized. After a few rounds, Foreman was too tired to keep punching, and the former champion was not only unhurt, but fresh as well. Notice that Foreman had followed a self-weighting strategy. Constantly throwing punches led to his defeat. Ali, on the other hand, had followed a correct non-self-weighting strategy. He fought only when it was to his advantage, mainly at the end of each round when Foreman was most tired, and stayed out of trouble when fighting would have been to his detriment. This strategy, coupled with Foreman's incorrect self-weighting approach, produced a stunning victory for Mohammed Ali.

The Adventurer in Action

Following are two more stories about the Adventurer. Even though both of these tales discuss errors that the Adventurer made, be assured that as of this writing, there is no question that he has become one of the top poker players in the world, no matter what the game.

Story No. 1: The Adventurer meets Doyle Brunson. After a spectacular 1986, the Adventurer decided that it was time to expand his horizons. The game he wanted to tackle was no-limit deuce-to-seven lowball, even though he had never played this particular game before. So the Adventurer packed his bags in January 1987 and headed to Las Vegas for Amarillo Slim's Super Bowl of Poker, which was being held at Caesar's Palace Hotel and Casino.

After warming up at the craps and baccarat tables, the Adventurer finally was ready to play some big-time no-limit poker. The problem was that sitting in this game was legendary poker player (and two-time world champion) Doyle Brunson. Now a player of Brunson's skill isn't going to stop someone like the Adventurer from playing, even though players of Brunson's caliber should make most skilled players at least think twice about sitting down.

However, the Adventurer did seek some last-minute advice from gambling authority David Sklansky, who just happened to be in the area. "Suppose I have a 7-5-3-2 to draw to, I open for $1,000 and Brunson raises me $3,000 or $4,000. What should I do?" asked the Adventurer. "Well, you probably should go all in," answered Sklansky. "Doyle will likely fold, but if he doesn't, you still have a premium draw."

Since there was an open seat, the Adventurer immediately sat down. On the first hand he was dealt, he picked up a one-card draw to a 6-4-3-2. Notice that this is a very different hand from the one he had discussed with Sklansky. The reason for this is that if the Adventurer should happen to catch a five, he will have a straight, which counts as high in this game. In other words the draw to the six is not nearly as good as the draw to the 7-5.

Nevertheless, the Adventurer opened for $1,000 and was promptly raised $4,000 by Brunson. Following Sklansky's advice and believing in "fate," the Adventurer promptly went all in for a total of $10,000, and his legendary opponent, instead of folding, promptly called. (Sklansky pointed out later that (1) with a draw to a six in this game, the proper play would have been to fold, and that (2) a new player who is totally unknown to the Vegas pros should not have tried this sort of play on the very first hand, since someone like Brunson might call thinking this person was crazy.) Needless to say, the Adventurer caught a three giving him a pair, while Doyle Brunson surprised everyone by showing down a rough 10-9-8-7-4. (By the way, I know many players who will have trouble believing that the Adventurer did not draw out on his opponent.)

To finish this story, the Adventurer later said to me that he had thought, since he was unknown to these high-limit players, that they would throw some money his way. "They did," I said. They did!"

Story No. 2: The Adventurer meets Mike Caro. This poker confrontation took place in a $75-$150 ace-to-five lowball game at the Bicycle Club in Bell Gardens, California. One of the things this story will show is that poker is much more than a game of cards.

What happened was that after the Adventurer opened the pot, poker writer Mike Caro promptly raised and was immediately called. The Adventurer drew one card and Caro stood pat.

Now came the fun part. "Before you look," said Caro, "I want you to know that I have an 8-7-3-2-A." This created a big problem for the Adventurer. Not only had he drawn to this hand, but he had made it perfectly. (The Adventurer was doubly surprised since he had opened looser than normal.) In

266

addition, the Adventurer knew that despite what Caro had said, there was a good chance that he was "snowing" (playing a hand that had no value and could win only if his opponent threw his cards away). Notice that this creates a dilemma for the Adventurer. If he bets and Caro is on a snow, he will lose a bet, but if he checks and his opponent is not on a snow, he also will lose a bet. In addition, if Caro really had an 8-7-3-2-A, by betting, the Adventurer "might steal half the pot."

The only thing the Adventurer really knew was that it was very unlikely for both him and his opponent to each have the same hand. Whether to check or bet was just not clear, but the Adventurer decided to go ahead and bet. "Take the pot," said Caro. "I'll show you my hand if you will show me yours," said the Adventurer. "OK," replied Caro, as he spread a full house.

Final note. I want to re-emphasize that even though the Adventurer made these mistakes, he is a world-class player who ordinarily makes very few errors. I don't expect these types of errors to be repeated in the future. On the other hand, as the essay shows, in a game as complex as poker, even the best of us can misplay a hand every now and then.

Some Creative Bad Beats

Introduction. Most of my writings are designed to be both instructional and informative. This essay deviates from that pattern and attempts to show one of the "lighter" sides of serious poker play.

You do not need to spend much time in public, or private, cardrooms before you are subjected to what are known as "bad-beat" stories. Most players, including myself, quickly get tired of hearing about impossible drawouts that have just cost the "best" player at the table, if not in the whole club, "half his stake." But sometimes what you hear is very creative and thus is worth repeating. What follows are some bad-beat stories from California poker before the legalization of stud and hold'em. Only forms of draw poker were legal, and the deck used contained 53 cards that included a joker. In high draw, the joker counts as an ace or can be used to complete straights or flushes; in lowball, the joker becomes the lowest card not already in your hand.

Bad Beat No. 1: The ultimate snow hand. This story involves one of the very best California players, Art Sathmary, also known as ASQ. The game was a $30-$60 lowball straddle (that is, no ante but multiple blinds), and ASQ was dealt four aces. Now most players would be discouraged if they picked up four aces in a lowball game, but not someone as creative as Sathmary. ASQ raised the blinds and was called, and he and his opponent each drew a card. After the draw, Sathmary bet, but unfortunately (for him) was called. To everybody's amazement, ASQ then spread five aces. Later Sathmary told me that he thought his opponent may have seen his fifth card, a king "in the window" (before the draw), and thus ASQ was forced to draw instead of rapping pat, which is probably the preferred way to play a snow hand. (I can't help but suspect, however, that the opportunity to draw to five aces was too strong to

268

resist.) Anyway, ASQ is the only player I know of who drew one card to four aces, caught the fifth one, and still lost the pot.

Bad Beat No. 2: Going all in. This play supposedly occurred in one of the Gardena clubs. It was a $20-$40 draw game, and the pot was being contested by two people, who each drew one card and who each had about $1,000 in chips. After the draw, the opener bet, was raised by his opponent, and then reraised. The before-the-draw caller then paused and suggested, "Why don't we just put them all in?" This player had made a straight flush and thought he was against a live one who just might agree to this proposition. "Sounds good to me," said the opener, who then pushed all his chips to the center of the table and was, of course, matched by his opponent. The opener then turned over five aces and won a gigantic pot. This was a truly bad beat for the holder of the straight flush. Imagine asking someone with five aces if he would like to go all in.

Bad Beat No. 3: Hopping out of five aces. One of the players whom I sometimes played against in the bigger draw games in the Los Angeles area was supposedly dealt five aces pat in a $25-$50 draw game. Everyone passed to him, and of course the pot was immediately opened. To this person's delight, he got three callers who all backed in and drew one card. Since it was likely that there were straight and/or flush draws out against him, the opener decided to "smartly" throw away one of his aces and hoped to check-raise after the draw if one of his opponents hit. Well, this is exactly what happened. Except that the player who was check-raised, raised again. It turned out that four aces was not the winner, as a straight flush took the pot. The opener had "hopped out" of the winning hand.

Bad Beat No. 4: The *Book of Tells* in action. This is, without a doubt, my favorite bad-beat story, since I was involved in the pot. I was in a $25-$50 jacks-or-better-to-opendraw game, and it was now the second round. That is, no one had opened, so everyone had to ante again. Since in this game it is still only

$25 to open on the second round, the high ante structure means that it makes sense to open much weaker than what would be normal. Consequently, I opened with the minimum pair of jacks, an unknown player to my left called, and poker writer Mike Caro, who was in the dealer's position, also called. Everyone else folded. I took three cards, the unknown player drew one card, and Mike Caro also drew three cards. Well, I was somewhat lucky and caught a pair of deuces, giving me a medium two pair. Not strong enough to bet, but perhaps strong enough to win the pot in a showdown. Therefore, I checked.

Unfortunately, the opponent to my immediate left, who had drawn one card, bet. I now could win only if he was bluffing. A moment later, Caro called. I started to throw my hand away, because jacks and deuces is not strong enough to overcall, but then I had second thoughts. Anyone who has read *Mike Caro's Book of Tells* would know that Caro is supposed to be an expert at reading his opponents. Consequently, it seemed to me that if Caro called, I had a "high percentage tell" that the bettor was "surely" bluffing. Since Caro obviously would call someone who was "definitely" bluffing with anything, I overcalled. Well, as if it can't be guessed, the one-card draw was bluffing. Mike Caro had a pair of tens. He also was going to try to steal the pot, but this other bet disrupted his plans, and I was the winner with jacks up. (In hindsight, and since the pot was fairly large, Caro should have raised to make sure that I didn't overcall.) A few hands later, I asked Caro if he knew why I had called. "Yes, I do," he said, "You called because I called." This is an example of how someone's expert play can cost him a pot. What turned out to be a good win for me became a bad beat for my opponent. By the way, the bluffer, after being called by a pair of tens and then overcalled by jacks and deuces, threw in his hand and immediately walked out of the card club in complete disgust. I have never seen him again.

Bad Beat No. 5: Hit the road, Jack. One of the most annoying players that I have ever played against was named Jack. An older man with a foghorn-like voice, Jack played exceptionally slowly and complained constantly. He literally drove most of his opponents crazy. However, he did have one redeeming characteristic. Jack was a habitual loser. In fact, he was one of the worst players I have ever seen. Jack would show up at the card club at the beginning of the month, just after receiving his pension check, play for two or three days without sleeping, until he was broke, and then go home to wait for the next check to arrive.

Anyway, one day I was playing in a game that had one open seat. Even though all six other seats at the table were taken, one of the players was away and only his chips were present. I had just sat down, and in a couple of minutes, an eighth player arrived. This person immediately began to explain that he had been playing at the club down the street but had to leave because of an exceptionally irritating player. It turned out that his antagonist was an older man with a foghorn-like voice, who played exceptionally slowly and complained constantly. Of course, some of us recognized that Jack was being described, and we understood how this guy felt. A few minutes later, the player who I had not yet seen returned to his chips. To my surprise, it was Jack! Apparently, shortly after the first person left the other club, Jack decided to do the same thing. As slow as Jack was, he somehow got to the club where I was playing before the player he had driven out of the other game arrived. Without a doubt, this is one of the worst beats to have ever happened at the poker table. Needless to say, our newly arrived opponent, after seeing Jack, immediately went on tilt and quickly lost all of his money.

Bad Beat No. 6: Brotherly love. This bad beat supposedly occurred many years ago at a card club that is no longer in operation. A large argument erupted at the table among several players who were disputing the pot. Since all the games at this time were hand dealt (today there are professional dealers in almost all games), arguments were not uncommon. But this argument was exceptionally spirited, and soon the whole table became involved. Finally, the shift manager arrived and announced that he would make a decision that would be final and could not be disputed. He then pushed the pot to one of the players at the table, thus settling the matter. However, the player who got the pot was not even in the hand, although he took an active part in the theatrics. The catch was that the winner was supposedly the brother of the shift manager. Talk about a bad beat. Imagine arguing for forty-five minutes with absolutely no chance of winning.

Bad Beat No. 7: The brutal beat. This last example really isn't a bad beat, but it is still an example of the misery that can prevail at a poker game, especially if it is a lowball game. Two players, whose names I won't mention, were up against each other in what appeared to be a typical lowball hand. What was interesting about this situation was, to put it mildly, that these players were not the best of friends. After the draw, the first player bet, was immediately called, and without any hesitation crumbled up his cards, to the utter joy of his opponent. However, before the dealer pushed the pot, the initial bettor flipped the crumbled cards up one at a time. First an ace appeared, then a deuce, then a three, then a four, and then — very slowly — a five. He had made a wheel and just wanted to watch his "buddy's" joy turn to sorrow. Not exactly a bad beat in the classical sense, but I'm sure that the losing player didn't feel any differently from someone who had just lost with a terrific hand.

Final comments. Even though these stories all occurred in California, where only draw poker was legal at the time, I'm sure that equally creative stories exist no matter what type of poker is being played. As mentioned earlier, bad beat stories can get old very quickly, and I don't even know whether some of these are completely true. But I think you will agree that the seven bad beats in this essay are exceptions worth repeating.

Building Pyramids

This essay is for those of you who are big winners. Consequently, there probably will be only a small number of people who actually need to read it. However, since many readers have the goal of being a big winner, they may want to read and study what follows. In addition, the following is applicable only to those of you who play games where chips are used, particularly poker and blackjack.

When playing, you always should be conscious of the opportunity to build pyramids. To do this requires two basic considerations. First, the skilled pyramid builder always knows what the smallest practical chip (in terms of monetary value) to play with is, and he usually will buy in for more chips than most other opponents, so he can have a decent start on his architecture. In fact, the correct amount to buy in for will produce exactly 100 chips. The skilled pyramid builder will start with five stacks of twenty chips each and will place two stacks in the front and three stacks in the back, with the two-stack row being centered in relation to the three-stack row.

Notice that you are very close to starting with a completed pyramid. As you win chips, add them to a new stack, placed in a third row centered in the middle of the two-stack row. If you keep winning and complete the pyramid, start a new stack on the right hand side of the row closest to you. (This is the row that began with three stacks.) Once this stack is completed, start the next stack on the right hand side of the next closest row to you. Continue this process until a new pyramid is finished, and then start the whole process again as you keep winning chips.

But what happens if you manage to lose some chips? The thing to keep in mind when this occurs is what I call "pyramid integrity." That is, always remove chips from the stack that is on the right hand side of the row that is furthest away from you. When that stack is gone, start removing chips from the right-hand stack on the row that precedes this row. For example, if you start with five stacks of chips and lose forty chips, which make up two stacks, you will now be left with a three-stack pyramid. Of course, this is not as desirable as a six-stack pyramid, but your pyramid integrity has been maintained.

A few other things to keep in mind are first, immediately change any larger chips that you may get into the appropriate smaller ones so that pyramid building will be continuous. (An exception would be blackjack players who are interested in "rainbow betting." See my book *Blackjack Essays* or Steve Forte's book *Read the Dealer*.) Second, any small miscellaneous chips must be kept in their own stack on the right-hand side of the row closest to you. You should make an effort to dispose of these chips as soon as possible. Third, and most important, when someone asks you what you do for a living, your reply should be, "I build pyramids." Don't tell them something silly like, "I am a professional gambler."

Here are a few don'ts. First, don't build pyramids made up of stacks that are not exactly twenty chips in height. Twenty is the optimal number not only for tabulation purposes, but for intimidation purposes as well. Second, don't start to build a pyramid on top of the one that you have just completed. Always remember that nothing is better than for your pyramid to become so big that it begins to crowd your neighbors. If they complain, tell them that they are just jealous of your architectural skills. And third, never sit down to play unless you plan to follow these guidelines. This doesn't mean that you have to build a large pyramid. It just means that you must set your chips up in the appropriate manner and follow all the correct rules on adding and removing your chips, even if you plan to stay only a short period of time.

Finally, I need to mention that this is another advanced concept that I learned from the Adventurer. For those of you who might be curious about who the Adventurer is, just look for the person with the largest pyramid. He won't be hard to find.

Gambling Fantasy
Afterthought

There probably is not a serious gambler alive who at one time or another has not wondered who the very best gamblers are or were. A good example is David Sklansky, who has published very interesting rankings of players according to their skill at certain games and their knowledge of gambling in general, and these rankings have generated a lot of discussion and interest. Of course, these rankings take into account only those people who actually sit down at the "very exciting gaming tables." In reality, it is probably a rare person who doesn't take part in at least some form of gambling, even if he never knows it.

You also should notice that successful gambling is the result of a proper mix of many attributes. These include knowledge, judgment, courage, and patience which produce an appropriate non-self-weighting strategy. Isn't it interesting to see which people in the previous essays had the right mix and which did not?

In addition, keep in mind that all the great gamblers were somewhat lucky. No decision of the kind that they made was guaranteed to work. That is, even though they got the outcome they sought, there was still great risk involved. However, their decisions were clearly correct.

Conclusion

Even though this book is a blend of many diverse topics, the overall theme of appropriate non-self-weighting strategies should shine through. In addition, as many of the essays show, these strategies apply not only to many different facets of gambling, but also to many different situations away from the "very exciting gaming tables."

Another related concept that constantly comes up is that of statistical fluctuations, which are measured by the standard deviation. Remember, as stated earlier, statistical fluctuations are the skilled gambler's friend. By enabling the unskilled player to win every now and then, statistical fluctuations become the hook that keeps the bad players producing.

Another idea emphasized in the text is that successful gambling is not easy. Not only will many hours of study be required, but many additional hours gaining experience at the "very exciting gaming tables" also will be needed. Progress can be slow at times, but once the proper skills are mastered, gambling can be quite rewarding. Consequently, if you are new to gambling, it is probably best to start small and gradually work your way up to bigger stakes. Another reason to start small is to make sure any initial success that you may have is the result of a positive expectation and not from being on the right side of the standard deviation.

Speaking of expectation and standard deviation, also keep in mind that the strategies with the highest expectation are often accompanied by the highest standard deviation. This is simply because they are usually more non-self-weighting than a less profitable approach, and this higher standard deviation may not be a price that all of us want to pay. This means that if you are on a limited bankroll, it may not be a price that you can afford to pay.

Finally, the most important concept that the text attempts to emphasize, though not always directly stated, is that the highly skilled gambler does a great deal of thinking. This is the key to developing that intangible quality that some people call "heart" or "courage." It is the real reason why some risk takers continually take chances that do not appear to be justified and why these people seem to have much more than their fair share of success. It is also the reason that the world's greatest gamblers were successful, and it is the key to successful non-self-weighting strategies.

Appendix A

Opinions of Various Books

Following are my opinions of a few gambling books I have read. Unfortunately, most books about gambling are not worth the paper they are printed on, but a small number should be studied in detail by anyone trying to achieve success in this field. The following list is not supposed to be all-inclusive, but it should give you a good idea of what is available in those areas with which I am familiar.

In addition to a narrative description of each book, I have included a numerical rating from 1 to 10, with 10 being the best and 1 being the worst. These numerical ratings appear in parentheses after each title. The only books I have not rated are those written or co-written by me, but I believe they are of the highest quality.

My numerical ratings require a little more explanation. Only those books that have had a major impact on me or on gambling itself were eligible for a rating of 10. This means that some of the books that received a rating of 9 are every bit as good as some of the 10s. In addition, the highest rating given a book that I read mainly for its entertainment value was a 7. If a book received a rating of 1, I consider it to be exceptionally terrible, and the advice that it contains will prove costly to anyone who regularly ventures to the gaming tables.

Poker

1. *The Theory of Poker* (10) by David Sklansky. In many ways, this is the best book ever written on poker. Moreover, it is written by a top professional player. Unlike other books on poker, this is not a "how-to"book, but rather a book on theory that discusses in-depth strategy and many sophisticated concepts. Serious players who do not study this book will lag behind those players who do. I reread my copy every three or four months and always find it helpful to my game.

2. *Hold'em Poker* (10) by David Sklansky. The first definitive work on the game of Texas hold'em. This book is in many ways the best and is absolutely must reading for anyone planning to play in California, Nevada, or elsewhere. The book covers the basics, such as which hands to start with, plus discusses concepts pertaining to very sophisticated play. The only criticism I have is that the book has become slightly outdated in the sense that most games today are structured differently from what this text is geared toward. However, even with this being the case, anyone who reads and studies this book will be way ahead of those who don't.

3. *Sklansky on Poker* (10) by David Sklansky. This text is a combination of *Sklansky on Razz* and *Essays on Poker,* with some new material added. Specifically, the book provides the definitive work on the game of razz (seven-card stud played for low), many essays on general poker concepts, and a short section on tournament play. Anyone who reads and studies this book not only will improve his overall play, but also should be able to play razz virtually perfectly.

4. *Hold'em Poker For Advanced Players* by David Sklansky and Mason Malmuth. Since I co-authored this book, I decline to give it a numerical rating. However, rest assured that this is the strongest strategy for the game of Texas hold'em ever put into print. Anyone who studies this text, is well-disciplined, and gets the proper experience should become a significant winner. Some of the topics discussed include play on the first two cards, semi-bluffing, the free card, inducing bluffs, being beat on the river, staying with a draw, playing when a pair flops, playing trash hands, fourth-street play, playing in loose games, playing in short-handed games, and much more.

5. *Seven-Card Stud For Advanced Players* by David Sklansky, Mason Malmuth, and Ray Zee. Again, since I am a co-author, I won't give this book a numerical rating. However, the same comments given for the hold'em text apply to this book. Some of the subjects covered include the cards that are out, ante stealing, playing big pairs, reraising the possible bigger pair, playing small and medium pairs, playing three flushes, playing three straights, playing weak hands, fourth street, pairing the door card on fourth street, fifth street, sixth street, seventh street, defending against the possible ante steal, playing against a paired door card, continuing with a draw, scare-card strategy, buying the free card on fourth street, playing in tightly structured games, playing in loose games, playing in short-handed games, and much more.

6. *High-Low-Split Poker, Seven-Card Stud and Omaha Eight-or-Better, For Advanced Players* (10) by Ray Zee. Although this is the third book in the "For Advanced Players" series, it is actually books three and four in the progression, since two different games are covered. Among the topics discussed in the seven-card stud eight-or-better section are starting hands, disguising your hand on third street, when an ace raises, fourth street, fifth street, sixth street, seventh street, position, bluffing, staying to the end, scare cards, and much more. Some of the subjects covered in the Omaha eight-or-better section include general concepts, position, low hands, high hands, your starting hand, how to play your hand, play on the flop, multiway versus short-handed play, scare cards, getting counterfeited, your playing style, and much more.

7. *Super/System — A Course in Power Poker* **(10) by Doyle Brunson.** This text is considered a classic work on most major limit games played, as well as on no-limit hold'em. The book was written by two-time World Champion Doyle Brunson in collaboration with some of the best players in the world, including Mike Caro, David Sklansky, Chip Reese, and Bobby Baldwin. Most serious poker players, myself included, will literally wear the covers off their copies. My only criticism of the book is that as the years have gone by, the text has become outdated. For instance, most high-low split games are played today with a qualifier for low, and the excellent high-low split section in this book does not discuss this concept. In addition, the structure used for limit hold'em in most cardrooms today is different from the structure discussed in the limit hold'em section of this book.

8. *According to Doyle* **(6) by Doyle Brunson.** A collection of folksy stories, advice, and anecdotes from Doyle Brunson. Although this book probably won't help you much in your poker play, it is still entertaining and worth reading.

9. *Winning Concepts in Draw and Lowball* **by Mason Malmuth.** Since I am the author, you know my opinion of this book will be favorable. However, I don't believe I am alone in that opinion, and I think this work will be of major benefit to anyone trying to excel at these games. This book is for both the recreational and the professional player. It is partitioned into sections that are designed to help players improve their games, and teaches you how to think like a top player, which is absolutely essential to winning play. However, one problem is that these games are not as widely played as they used to be. With the legalization of hold'em and stud in California, high draw has virtually disappeared, and lowball draw is slowly experiencing the same fate.

10. *Poker Essays* **by Mason Malmuth.** This text is a collection of articles that I have written, most of which appeared in *Card Player* Magazine. Topics include general concepts, technical ideas, structure, strategic ideas, image, tournament notes, cardroom improvements, and poker quizzes. If you are interested in playing stud or hold'em, this text should be of benefit.

11. *Fundamentals of Poker* **by Mason Malmuth and Lynne Loomis.** This is a beginners book that I co-wrote. It provides general poker guidelines, and major sections on Texas hold'em and seven-card stud, as well as a section on six other forms of poker. If you are new to poker and are looking for something to get you started, this book should be ideal.

12. *Caro's Book of Tells* **(10) by Mike Caro.** The definitive work on "tell" play, that is, how to interpret the body language of poker. Absolutely must reading for all serious poker players. More than 250 photographs, as well as detailed descriptions of what is happening and the motivation behind the tells.

13. *Poker For Women* **(6) by Mike Caro.** An interesting work for beginning players. Special emphasis on the advantages female players have in a mostly male game. This book should be read by most serious players, even though it is written for someone just starting out in poker.

14. *New Poker Games* **(5) by Mike Caro.** An entertaining and informative book for those of you looking for new poker games to add to your Friday night home game. The book contains some insights to strategy but is written at a fairly basic level.

15. The Mike Caro Reports. As of this writing, Mike Caro has issued six professional-level reports:*Caro's Advanced Strategies for Draw Poker* (10), which includes both high draw and lowball; *Caro's Professional Hold'em Report* (3); *Caro's Professional Seven-Stud Report* (7); *Caro's Poker Plan 3* (7), which is on the

283

psychology of poker; *11 Days to 7-Stud Success* (7); and *12 Days to Hold'em Success* (8). All of these reports should be read by the serious player.

My rating for the hold'em report requires a little more explanation. The charts that it contains have you playing many hands that have the potential to trap you for a great deal of money. Specifically, after someone has raised, automatically playing hands like KQ, KJs, KJ, K10s, K9s, QJs, Q10s, Q9s, J10s, J9s, J8s, 109s, 98s, and 87s, usually playing hands like Q8s, J7s, 108s, 97s, 86s, and 76s, and occasionally playing hands like 99, 88, 77, 66, A10, A5-A2s, K10, QJ, J10, 106s, 96s, 95s, 85s, 75s, 65s, and 54s will not be good for your bankroll. Ironically, in the text, Caro correctly advises to play very tight in early position. I agree that in this game, occasionally playing a hand wrong is proper strategy. But calling raises with numerous hands, as the charts recommend, will prove very expensive.

16. *Mike Caro's Fundamental Secrets of Poker* **(9) by Mike Caro.** I don't agree with everything this text contains, but many of Caro's best concepts are discussed. At the very least, this book will give you a lot to think about, and at best, it definitely will improve your game. Topics covered include general winning advice, seven-card stud, Texas hold'em, tells and psychology, and tournament advice.

17. *Bobby Baldwin's Winning Poker Secrets* **(5) by Mike Caro.** A simplistic book discussing the life of Bobby Baldwin through his World Series of Poker win in 1978. Also included are some poker tips for each major variation of poker. I found this book to be entertaining, but it won't help very much with your poker play unless you are just beginning.

18. *Tales Out of Tulsa* **(5) by Bobby Baldwin.** This book is a collection of columns that first appeared in *Poker Player*. Many of the columns are interesting, and most serious players will want to eventually read this book. However, it won't help much with your poker play.

19. *The Biggest Game in Town* **(7) by A. Alvarez.** An extremely entertaining book about the World Series of Poker and some of the more famous players who regularly participate in this tournament. This book won't help you play any better, but I found it to be very enjoyable reading.

20. *Complete Guide to Winning Poker* **(4) by Albert Moorehead.** A completely out-of-date classic that covers many poker games. If you like to read gambling books, as I do, you may want to look at this one, but it won't help you to win against today's sophisticated players.

21. *The Computer Guide to Hold'em Poker* **(2) by Robert Zahrobsky.** This book is a good example of how a little knowledge can be dangerous. There is much more to poker, especially hold'em, than computer simulations. Even though this book does contain some interesting facts, the advice it offers will cause most players to become losers. For example, Zahrobsky says that two overcards on the flop that also provide an inside straight draw are marginal hands at best. He needs to read Sklansky's hold'em book to find out how strong these hands really are.

22. *Eight or Better, High-Low Split, Seven Stud* **(1) by K.A. Coddington.** If you want to lose your money fast, this is a good book to read. The author has very little understanding of stud eight-or-better.

23. *Omaha High-Low Eight or Better* **(?) by K.A. Coddington.-** I haven't read this book, but I did read his stud eight-or-better book. I suspect that this text is of the same quality.

24. *Free Money (How to Win in the Cardrooms of California)* **(7) by Michael Wiesenberg.** A well-written and detailed book for someone starting out in the poker world. The book contains a simplified version of *Mike Caro's Advanced Strategies for Draw Poker*. It won't help the advanced player very much, but if you enjoy reading gambling books, you may want to pick up this one.

25. *Hold'em Poker Bible* (4) **by Dick Davis.** A very simplistic approach to hold'em poker. There is nothing really wrong with this book, but you need much more than what it provides to win in most public cardrooms. However, its format is entertaining, and from that perspective, it should have a higher rating.

26. *Hold'em Poker for Winners* (1) **by Carl Anderson.** Without a doubt, this is one of the worst books ever written on the game of poker and on hold'em in particular. I found much of the book totally unintelligible and parts of the book just plain silly. As an example, the author talks about opponents who bet with a "three count." For some reason, this book has received much favorable publicity, and for the life of me, I can't understand why. The game situations described in this book are totally ridiculous, and anyone who follows the advice offered will surely go broke very quickly.

27. *Play Poker, Quit Work, and Sleep Till Noon* (8) **by John Fox.** A controversial book that is now out-of-date due to the changed conditions in many California cardrooms. Even though the book covers only high draw, I consider it must reading for all serious players, no matter what their game. This is because aspects of poker strategy are discussed in this book that are not discussed in many other places. One caution, though. I think there is too much emphasis on angle shooting, and some of the plays border on outright cheating. In addition, keep in mind that many of the ideas on image that work in this game are not correct in most other forms of poker.

28. *How to Hustle Home Poker* (7) **by John Fox.** In some ways, I like this book better than the previous one, yet many of the same comments apply.

29. *How to Win at Poker Tournaments* (6) **by Tom McEvoy.**
Although Tom McEvoy is a former World Series of Poker champion and has a great deal of tournament experience, I think some of the advice in this book is actually the opposite of what is correct. For example, McEvoy usually advises against rebuying, especially late in a tournament when, he says, you will be "taking much the worst of it." Of course, this is not true. However, there are many good observations given in McEvoy's book, and since so little literature on this subject is available, I think it should be read by all serious tournament players.

30. *Insurance for Hold'em and Omaha Poker* (6) **by Herb Coddington.** A well-organized book for those no-limit players who are concerned with insurance situations. Unfortunately, a small number of the calculations are incorrect.

31. *Money Poker* (1) **by Mr. X as told to Walter Gibson.**
Definitely one of the worst books ever written on poker. Mr. X has no idea of how the game is played. On the other hand, if I made four of a kind as often as he did, I wouldn't need to know how to play either.

32. *Omaha Hold'em Poker (The Action Game)* (8) **by Bob Ciaffone.** An excellent book written by a professional player. It currently offers the most accurate advice for the relatively new game of Omaha and also includes a section on Omaha high-low split eight-or-better. My only complaint is that Ciaffone did not divulge more secrets. Nevertheless, anyone who studies this text, is well-disciplined, and does not play too big should have no trouble winning.

33. *Cappelletti on Omaha* (3) **by Mike Cappelletti.** I was very disappointed with this book. It contains little strategy, and I disagree with most of the (few) concepts that it does discuss. For example, the author states that you should follow up a bet on the flop with a "come-bluff" on fourth street if a harmless card hits on a board that has both straight and flush potential.

While this is a strong play in pot-limit Omaha, in limit play, which this book is about, you simply will be called.

34. *Poker Faces — The Life and Work of Professional Card Players* **(9) by David Hayano.** A fascinating account of the lives and experiences of professional card players written by a top player. The book won't help you play better, since it does not address strategy, but it is must reading for anyone interested in taking up the game of poker seriously.

35. *Poker Strategy, Winning With Game Theory* **(9) by Nesmith Ankeny.** This is an excellent book on draw poker based on a game-theory approach. Many strategic concepts are discussed, and I think this book is must reading for serious players.

36. *Programmed Poker* **(1) by Jim Glenn.** Another book whose advice will cause you to go broke quickly. The author has no conception of even the basics of the game, such as position.

37. *Properties of Hold'em Hands* **(2) by Chip Johnson and Ray Tayek.** Another worthless book that is merely a large set of tables showing the probability of every starting hand maturing to a finishing hand after all the cards have been dealt. Even though the work appears to be accurate, I don't see how this information can do anyone any good. It certainly won't help in forming an accurate strategy for playing this very complex game.

38. *The Railbird* **(6) by Rex Jones.** A very entertaining book. It won't help you play any better, though.

39. *Scarne's Guide to Modern Poker* **(4) by John Scarne.** A classic but completely out-of-date book. There are much better sources for learning how to play poker.

40. *Total Poker* **(7) by David Spanier.** Another very entertaining book, but it won't help you improve your game.

41. *Winning California Poker* **(1) by Vern Albery.** I find it hard to believe that this book was written by a professional player. How can you write a book on draw poker and never mention sandbagging? Obviously, I don't think it is worth reading.

42. *Winning Poker Systems* **(9) by Norman Zadeh.** Absolutely must reading for all serious players. I think some of the opening tables are too loose, but this excellent work discusses many strategic concepts that are not well-discussed in other books. An excellent source for poker theory as well.

43. *Wins, Places, & Pros* **(6) by Tex Sheahan.** Another very entertaining book that contains a few hints on strategy.

44. *How To Win at Stud Poker* **(2) by James Wickstead.** An old, outdated book on five-card stud. Contains almost no worthwhile information.

45. *Secrets of Winning Poker* **(4) by George Coffin.** Another outdated book. Somewhat more interesting than the preceding book but also contains little worthwhile information.

46. *Winning Methods of Bluffing and Betting in Poker* **(1) by L. Taetzsch.** Another silly book. Some authors need to learn that in a typical poker game, every player does not play every hand to the end.

47. *The Education of a Poker Player* **(8) by Herbert O. Yardley.** This is another ancient book that contains much outdated advice. But I believe Yardley was a very good poker player, and some good insights are provided in this book. Read it if you like, but learn the specifics on strategy from another source.

48. *Poker, California Lowball, Hi-Low Split Poker with a (Joker) as played in Home Games, How to Play Like the Professional For Pleasure and Profit* **(1) by Robert Quisenberry.** I'm not sure what the exact title of this book is, but all these words appear

289

on the front cover. Much of the information provided, what little there is, is inaccurate. Not at all worth reading.

49. *Seven-Card Stud, The Waiting Game* **(7) by George Percy.** A reasonably well-written book for someone starting out in seven-card stud. The information that the book contains won't be enough to win at the medium and high stakes, but it is very good for the beginning player.

50. *Intermediate Hold'em: Seven Ways to Win* **(6) by Andy Nelson.** The author claims to be an intermediate player who has written a book to help someone play in intermediate games, such as the $10-$20 limit at the Golden Nugget.[24] Unfortunately, to win at the tough games in Las Vegas, you must go way beyond the advice offered in this book. However, for someone starting out, the book does provide some helpful information. Even though many concepts, such as semi-bluffing, are left out, the author emphasizes avoiding the types of errors that many inexperienced players make. Consequently, for someone new to poker, this book may be worth reading.

51. *Hold'em: Book One* **(5) by Andy Nelson.** This book is supposed to be read before the one I just reviewed. Unfortunately, it is not as good. Some of the advice is all right for a beginner, but this small text contains some major errors. For example, when you flop a small flush draw, the book advises you to throw it away unless there are at least two other players putting money in the pot. This advice is much too tight.

52. *Omaha, Book One* **(5) by Andy Nelson.** A short text written for someone completely new to this game. But the advice is reasonably good, even though the author probably recommends play that is a little too tight.

---

[24]The Golden Nugget closed their cardroom in 1988.

53. *Omaha, High/Low Split — Book One* (4) by Andy Nelson. Most of the preceding comments apply. The reason I rate this book lower is that it contains some juvenile drawings. In addition, the chapter on reading the board is identical to the chapter on reading the board that appeared in *Omaha, Book One*.

54. *Seven-Card Stud, High/Low Split, Book One* (5) by Andy Nelson. Another book similar in size and format by the same author. The reason I don't rate it higher is that Nelson overvalues the high hands. However, if that fact is kept in mind, this text should be of help to someone starting out.

55. *Seven Ways To Win* (3) by Andy Nelson. A short book that discusses patience, position, hand selection, handling bad beats, handling losing, and staying too long with a hand. This advice should be useful to someone starting out who plays in low-limit games. Again, the author recommends play that is too tight. For example, when playing limit hold'em, always throwing away hands like K♣Q♦ from a late position just because you are running bad is silly.

56. *Seven More Ways To Win* (3) by Andy Nelson. This text is similar in style and format to the preceding one. The author discusses preparation, playing well, table image, dangerous hands, getting maximum returns, what raising means, and record-keeping. Even though some of this material may prove helpful to someone starting out, I disagree with much of it. For example, Nelson's advice on how to play when a pair flops in hold'em is much too timid, and I believe he overrates the value of image in hold'em and stud. Contrary to what the author says, it is often correct to call heads up with three suited cards in seven-stud, and it is usually correct to play a flush draw in hold'em when a pair flops. However, this small text might still be useful for those of you new to poker.

57. *Play Poker to Win* **(6) by Amarillo Slim Preston.** This book was difficult to rate, since the stories and color are great but the advice is weak. Consequently, this book should be read mainly for entertainment.

58. *Poker, A Guaranteed Income For Life by Using the Advanced Concepts of Poker* **(4) by Frank Wallace.** A carefully written book that is much too vague. However, it contains some interesting advice if you are just trying to hustle people. While this book should be read, you won't learn much of real value.

59. *Mixed Nuts* **(2) by Michael J. Barry.** This is another book of computer simulation strategy. Unfortunately, the game is not played at all like these computer simulations assume. Specifically, players do not always call to the end no matter what appears on the board. Also, most players adjust the quality of the hands they play, depending on whether the pot has been raised (before the flop), and on their position. This book also contains several pages of concepts. Although most of the concepts are reasonably correct, there are enough errors — along with the recommended playing hands — to cause someone to go broke. As an example, the author recommends not to play draws against one opponent. He needs to read Sklansky's books. Then he might learn about semi-bluffing, getting free cards, implied odds, and so on.

60. *Omaha Express* **(7) by Michael J. Barry.** I was surprised by this book, since I did not like the hold'em book written by the same author. The text is only a small part of the book, which contains mostly tables. I don't see the value in most of the tables, but the advice on how to play is fairly good. For example, the author warns about queen-high flush draws, bottom sets, bottom two pair, and the danger of having some of your outs in your hand.

61. *Poker According to Maverick* (6). I'm not sure who wrote this completely outdated classic, but I found it very entertaining. However, it won't help you with your play.

62. *Seven-Card Stud, High-Low Split 8 or Better, "The Player's Bible"* (3) **by Michael D. Spencer.** A small and very weak book on the game of stud eight-or-better. This author has only a limited understanding of the game, and like many inexperienced eight-or-better players, he significantly overvalues the strength of high pairs in the first three cards. But if you are just starting out, this book might be worth looking at.

63. *Winning at Poker in the Cardrooms of California* (7) **by Michael Wiesenberg.** An enjoyable and informative collection of essays dealing mainly with the games of draw and lowball as played in California cardrooms. The discussions on cheating and scams are well worth reading.

64. *The Elements of Seven-Card Stud* (3) **by Konstantin Othmer.** Although this text is a major effort, I found much of it to be extremely inaccurate and silly. There are several problems with the book. First, many topics, such as ante stealing and the meaning of scare cards, are not even discussed. Second, much of the advice on what to play is wrong. For example, the author advises you to give up on small pairs and three flushes much too soon. And third, the advice to project a loose, wild, and aggressive image will prove costly to readers. Poker writers need to learn that in a complex game like seven-card stud, where the pots are very large and it is often correct to chase, assuring that your opponent calls you — meaning that he is now playing correctly in the vast majority of situations — is a disastrous strategy to pursue. The reason I don't rate this book lower is that the author does recognize the value of playing live hands. In addition, I found some of the simulation data that it contains to be interesting. However, the approach to stud that this book advises will prove unprofitable to those who follow it.

65. *Omaha Hi-Lo Poker (Eight-or-Better), Playing for Profit & Pleasure* (5) by Shane Smith. This was a difficult book to rate. If you are new to this game, it is *almost* a very good beginners book. The reason I don't rate it higher is that the text contains many errors. For example, the book implies that hands like K♠2♠3♦4♣ and 8♥8♦9♥9♠ frequently should be played. However, these hands generally should be thrown away in this game. I also think some of the affirmations in the book are silly. (At the time of this writing, I understand that a new version of *Omaha Hi-Lo Poker (Eight-or-Better), Playing for Profit & Pleasure* is in the works and that many of the errors have been corrected. If this is the case, this text should be very good for someone just starting out.)

66. *Poker Tournament Tips From the Pros* (6) by Shane Smith. This book is a compilation and summary of many poker tournament ideas that other writers have put into print. I think the book will be most helpful to those of you who play mainly in small-limit tournaments.

67. *Texas Bill's Winning a Living, The Professional's Guide to Poker Profits* (8) by William Melms. This is a fairly good book if you are an intermediate player who is trying to improve his game. Melms also discusses some unusual topics, such as how different drugs can affect you at the poker table and how to handle different types of players.

68. *Poker (Las Vegas Style)* (7) by Bill "Bulldog" Sykes. I have always considered the Bulldog to be one of the most entertaining writers in the gambling field and this book holds true to form. If you are a fan of "Uncle Muley" or just want to get a feel for what low-limit Las Vegas poker is like, this is the book to read. It's not a strategy book, so it won't help you improve your game. Nevertheless, I recommend this text.

69. *High-Stakes Poker, The Sky's the Limit* (7) by Doug Young. Doug Young is a high-stakes poker player who decided to put some of his thoughts about the game and his experiences into print. The real value of this book is that it examines the inner personality of the poker player and what it takes to become successful. The text also contains some strategy hints.

70. *Winning Poker for the Serious Player* **(5) by Edwin Silberstang.** This text is geared for the intermediate player, and it contains a fair amount of worthwhile advice. The problem with the book is that it also contains some erroneous information. For example, Silberstang states that when playing hold'em, "If you are on the flush or straight draw, and you miss on fourth street, then throw your hand away unless you figure to get the nut straight or flush on the river." This advice will prove to be very expensive.

71. *Poker, Sex, & Dying* **(8) by Juel Anderson.** This book is mistitled, but I found it very interesting. The book provides a variety of different personality profiles and discusses how these personality types might perform at the poker table. Trying to classify different people, including myself, and place them in the different categories was entertaining. However, the reason I don't rate this book higher is that I don't believe these ideas are practical when at the table. But I enjoyed reading the book and think all serious players should read it.

Blackjack

1. *Beat the Dealer* **(8) by Edward O. Thorp.** The book that started it all. Even though the strategies are out-of-date by today's standards, this book is still absolutely must reading for anyone interested in playing blackjack.

2. *Blackbelt in Blackjack* **(10) by Arnold Snyder.** An excellent book on the game. Includes Snyder's Zen count, which is one of the best modern-day counts, and much practical advice for current casino play. Absolutely must reading for any serious player.

3. *The Blackjack Formula* **(9) by Arnold Snyder.** One of the most important tools for the serious blackjack player. This book provides a formula for computing your expectation in any blackjack game that is available. Many readers will discover that some of the games they have been playing in are not worth their time.

4. *Blackjack for Profit* **(9) by Arnold Snyder.** Another useful text for the serious player. This book compares different count systems and also offers valuable advice on determining which are the best games.

5. *Blackjack Essays* **by Mason Malmuth.** This is another book that will get a good review, because I wrote it. The book explores myths and realities of playing blackjack in today's casino environment. Discusses theory, application, biases, fallacies, practical advice, and much more. I believe that this book is must reading for any serious blackjack player.

6. *Fundamentals of "21"* **by Mason Malmuth and Lynne Loomis.** This is a beginners book that I co-wrote. It provides the basics of "21," an overview of basic strategy, and an introduction to card counting, as well as other useful advice.

7. *Blackjack: A Winner's Handbook* **[1981 edition] (7) by Jerry Patterson.** A good overview of most count systems in use today. Also contains some reasonable advice on actual casino play.

8. *Blackjack's Winning Formula* **(6) by Jerry Patterson.** An honest, straightforward approach to the game of blackjack, this book is a good place to start for someone just beginning to play blackjack seriously.

9. *Break the Dealer* **(1) by Jerry Patterson and Eddie Olson.** It's hard to believe that one of these authors also wrote the two preceding books. Much of what appears in this book is completely bizarre. I don't agree with the theories on non-random shuffles, and I was very disappointed with the chapter on their TARGET strategy, which is really just an advertisement with no new information on why this system supposedly works.

10. *Blackjack: A Winner's Handbook* **[1990 edition] (1) by Jerry Patterson.** Even though this book has the same title as one of the preceding books, it is completely different. A great deal of emphasis is placed on "winning strategies for today's player." This includes things like using card clumping for table departure and explanations of why traditional card counting is no longer always effective. Needless to say, most of this is totally inaccurate.

11. *Blackjack Super Gold* **(6) by Lance Humble.** A well-written book more for the beginner than for the advanced player. Discusses the basic strategy and gives much practical advice.

12. *Blackjack Your Way to Riches* **(6) by Richard Albert Canfield.** A reasonably well-written count book that also contains some good practical advice. Most serious players will want to eventually read this book, although it promises more than blackjack can deliver.

13. *How To Play Winning Blackjack* (7) **by Julian Braun.** An excellent book by the man who did most of the computer work for today's modern systems. Gives an excellent analysis of the basic strategy and also provides analyses of many other systems. Unfortunately, the advice on money management is silly. I would give the book a higher rating if it did not contain this section.

14. *Million Dollar Blackjack* (10) **by Ken Uston.** One of the best books ever written on the game by one of the best players to ever play blackjack. The book contains excellent count systems, as well as a great deal of practical advice. Absolutely must reading for all serious players.

15. *Playing Blackjack as a Business* (8) **by Lawrence Revere.** This book first appeared in 1969, but it still makes for excellent reading. The book contains some of the best point counts ever devised, although it has now been shown that some of these counts are more complicated than necessary.

16. *Power Blackjack* (3) **by Bryan Thibodeaux.** A book that contains some good advice and some very bad advice. Many of the ideas on streaks, cycles, and selecting a betting system don't make sense to me.

17. *Professional Blackjack* (9) **by Stanford Wong.** One of the premier books on card counting. Absolutely must reading for all serious players. The text includes the High-Low count, which many professional players use.

18. *Blackjack Secrets* (10) **by Stanford Wong.** If you want to know how to win the maximum at blackjack, read this book. It includes some of Wong's best material and is extremely good.

Topics discussed include how to win without getting kicked out, winning faster, tokes, comps, turning pro, and much more.

19. *Winning Without Counting* (7) by Stanford Wong. I think this controversial book is somewhat outdated. The section on warps is excellent, but I believe the opportunity for warp play is limited in today's casino environment. I also believe the section on tricks can get many players in trouble. On the other hand, there are ideas discussed in this book that are not covered in other blackjack texts. Consequently, the book should be read by all serious players — that is if you can obtain a copy. I believe it is currently out of print.

20. *Basic Blackjack* (9) by Stanford Wong. Another top book. If you are interested in how some particular rule affects blackjack or how some unusual betting option works, this is where you'll find that information. The text also includes some material that originally appeared in *Winning Without Counting*.

21. *Read the Dealer* (10) by Steve Forte. A book for the serious blackjack player who is trying to get every extra edge. The book is well-written and well-thought-out. However, many players may get in trouble using these powerful techniques, since they will see tells because they want to and not because they are there. Absolutely must reading for all serious players.

22. *The Theory of Blackjack* (10) by Peter Griffin. A mathematical text that analyzes the game of blackjack. Most of the complex math is separated from the main material. Absolutely must reading for serious players.

23. *Turning the Tables on Las Vegas* (7) by Ian Anderson. A good study of how to use some of the psychological factors available to the skilled player to assure a win. Well-written and definitely one of the better books on casino blackjack.

24. *World's Greatest Blackjack Book* **(8) by Lance Humble and Carl Cooper.** One of the better texts on card counting, this book is filled with a great deal of practical advice. All serious players should have a copy of this book. However, the authors are too paranoid about cheating.

25. *Winning Blackjack* **(5) by Stanley Roberts.** An outdated book that contains a simple-to-use system that I don't believe will be very effective in today's casino environment. It does include some good advice on practical play.

26. *Winning Blackjack Without Counting Cards* **(1) by David Popik.** One of the silliest books available. Anyone who follows this advice can expect to go broke quickly.

27. *So You Wanna Be a Gambler — Card Counting* **(1) by John Patrick.** Another amazingly bad book. His basic strategy is wrong, his emphasis on finding hot tables is wrong, and his money management advice is silly. This is another book whose advice can prove to be very expensive. By the way, there are six books, along with lots of videos in this series, all with the title "So You Wanna Be a Gambler." I suspect that all are of equal quality.

28. *Julian's No-Nonsense Guide to Winning Blackjack* **(2) by John F. Julian.** Although this book contains reasonably good discussions of basic strategy and card counting, I give it a low rating because it also contains something ridiculous called the "sprint strategies." This is advice that encourages you to overbet your bankroll and to compensate this overbetting with incorrect strategies. For example, the author advises that once you have a five-unit bet out, do not double down with a total of 11 against a dealer's ace, 10, 9, 8, or 7. Advice like this will cause you to quickly go broke.

29. *Blackjack For Blood* **(7) by Bryce Carlson.** This is a relatively new blackjack book that I consider to be vastly overrated. The text includes something called the "Omega II" system, which is a standard two-level count. There is nothing wrong with this count. However, if you are interested in learning how to count cards, I would recommend a much simpler system that will perform nearly as well. The book also includes some crude attempts at humor, which some readers might find offensive. On the other hand, Carlson is a serious player, and his chapters on how to conduct yourself in a casino and some of the tricks that he uses are well worth reading.

30. *Card Counting for the Casino Executive* **(9) by Bill Zender.** This is an excellent blackjack book written by a knowledgeable casino executive. It includes a simple plus/minus count that will perform essentially as well as the more sophisticated counts and also discusses some of the other techniques of beating blackjack. The discussions on countermeasures and barring players are must reading.

31. *Fundamentals of Blackjack* **(9) by Carlson R. Chambliss and Thomas C. Roginski.** Another very good blackjack book that discusses many different aspects of the game. If you are new to card counting, the discussion of different card counting systems should prove to be most valuable. Absolutely must reading for all serious players.

32. *Blackjack: A Professional Reference* **(8) by Michael Dalton.** If you like to read book reviews, then this is the book for you. I didn't rate it higher, because it doesn't help your game. But I found it enjoyable reading. Moreover, if you want to do research on the game but don't know where to find reference material, this is where you should start.

Other Topics

1. *Getting the Best of It* (10) by David Sklansky. Another marvelous book by David Sklansky. Absolutely must reading, no matter what area of gambling you are interested in. Includes an excellent section on sports betting, as well as essays on both poker and blackjack. Also included is one of the best descriptions in print of the mathematics of gambling for non-mathematicians.

2. *Caro on Gambling* (9) by Mike Caro. A very good and readable book about gambling in general. The best parts of the text are the three crash courses for different poker games, the video poker advice, and the advice (similar to my own) on money management. This book contains some of Caro's best material.

3. *The Gambling Times Quiz Book* (5) by Mike Caro. An interesting set of quizzes designed to teach a beginner something worthwhile about gambling. Not the most sophisticated book in the world, but it looks nice in a collection.

4. *Caro's Professional Pai Gow Poker Report (and Banker Guidelines)* (9) by Mike Caro. Since I helped put this report together, it receives a good rating. Moreover, the information that this report provides — which was developed by computer simulation and was based on how we thought typical opponents actually play — will enable the reader to overcome the house commission and obtain an edge in the game of pai gow poker. This report tells you exactly how to set every hand. If you play pai gow poker for high stakes, you cannot afford to be without this work.

5. *Optimal Strategy For Pai Gow Poker* (9) by Stanford Wong. This is clearly the best work on pai gow poker to appear to

302

date. Topics discussed include getting an edge, optimal strategy, approximate strategy, and miscellaneous details. If you master this material, you should do quite well at this game.

6. *How To Play Pai Gow Poker* **(7) by George Allen.** A small book designed to give you the same kind of information that is available in the Caro report. However, many of the conclusions and breakoffs are different. I'm not sure how the author came up with his plays, since in one place he states that they are "based on probability theory," and in another spot says that "Dr. Allen made a computer analysis." However, this book should enable you to play better than the typical player.

7. *Billy Woo's Pai Gow Poker* **(4) by Billy Walsh.** A simplistic book that shows different recommended ways to play a few hands. This text also gives alternate ways to play some of the hands. Unfortunately, in a few cases, the alternate strategy is superior to the "Billy Woo" way.

8. *The Gambling Times Guide to Casino Games* **(1).** Not worth bothering with.

9. *The Gambling Times Guide to Winning Systems and Methods (Vol 1)* **(1).** Not worth looking at.

10. *The Gambling Times Guide to Winning Systems and Methods (Vol 2)* **(1).** Not worth looking at.

11. *The Gambling Times Guide to Systems That Win (Vol 1)* **(1).** Not worth looking at.

12. *The Gambling Times Guide to Systems That Win (Vol 2)* **(1).** Not worth looking at.

13. *The Gambling Times Guide to Winning Systems (Vol 1)* **(1).** Not worth looking at.

14. *The Gambling Times Guide to Winning Systems (Vol 2)* **(1).** Not worth looking at.

15. *How To Win at Casino Gaming Tournaments* **(1) by Haven Haley.** A completely worthless book that contains virtually no information on how to win at casino gaming tournaments.

16. *The Mathematics of Gambling* **(9) by Edward O. Thorp.** A well-written book discussing many interesting gambling topics. Well worth reading. The advice on "bet sizing" is extremely valuable.

17. *The Eudaemonic Pie* **(4) by Thomas Bass.** The story of how a group of physicists tried to beat roulette. I found the subject matter interesting but the book very boring.

18. *How To Play Pai Gow* **(?) by George Allen.** A short but well-written book on the game of pai gow. Unfortunately, I don't know enough about pai gow to know whether the strategy advice in this book is any good.

19. *Theory of Gambling and Statistical Logic* **(10) by Richard Epstein.** I consider this to be one of the most amazing books in the gambling field. It is a graduate-level text for someone with a sophisticated background in math and statistics, and it contains a wealth of information.

20. *Extra Stuff: Gambling Ramblings* **(9) by Peter Griffin.** This text is a collection of various articles that Peter Griffin wrote during the 1980s. Also included is his paper "Mathematical Expectation for the Public's Play in Casino Blackjack."

21. *The Psychology of Gambling* **(9) edited by Jon Halliday and Peter Fuller.** I found this strange book to be very interesting reading. The reason I refer to this book as "strange" is because psychologists have some bizarre ideas about people like you and me. However, if you are interested in what someone like

Sigmund Freud had to say about gamblers, I recommend this book, although it is not always easy reading.

22. *Casino Tournament Strategy* **(10) by Stanford Wong.** A terrific book by a knowledgeable expert. This book details the optimal playing strategy for craps, blackjack, baccarat, and keno tournaments and will enable you to obtain a significant edge over the typical player. Absolutely must reading for anyone interested in these tournaments.

23. *Gambling and the Law* **(10) by I. Nelson Rose.** An extremely well-written and interesting book about gambling law by the leading authority in the field. This book should be read by all serious gamblers, as well as by anyone who has a management position in the gambling field.

24. *Psyching Out Vegas* **(5) by Marvin Karlins.** A well-written, enjoyable book to read. However, many of the ideas, which fall under the heading of money management, are either naive or just plain silly. This book won't help you win, but it sure can help you lose.

25. *The Casino Gambler's Guide* **(10) by Allan Wilson.** One of the first legitimate books on gambling. The blackjack system is out-of-date, but the discussions on systems and biased roulette wheels are still terrific. It is also the original source of the Oscar's Grind craps system. Most serious gamblers will want to read this book, especially if they are just starting out. Unfortunately, at the time of this writing, I believe it is out of print.

26. *The Fundamentals of Craps* **by Mason Malmuth and Lynne Loomis.** This is another book in the *Fundamentals* series. If you are new to craps or are having difficulty understanding this fast casino game, this book offers excellent instruction. Also included in the text is the famous system "Oscar's Grind."

27. *Dr. Z's 6/49 Lotto Guidebook* (9) **by William Ziemba.** This is the complete book on lotteries, and it is excellently written. Moreover, unlike many other lottery publications, it tells the truth. Included in the text is advice on playing the unpopular numbers, which can produce a positive expectation.

28. *Lem Banker's Book of Sports Betting* (8) **by Lem Banker and Frederick Klein.** An interesting and informative book by one of the most knowledgeable people in this field. I do think Mr. Banker bets more games than he should. However, many of the approaches to successful sports betting presented in this book seem logical to me.

29. *Covering the Spread, How To Bet Pro Football* (4) **by Gerald Strine and Neil D. Isaacs.** Another interesting book that is enjoyable to read. However, I don't see how this book will help the typical bettor.

30. *Sports Betting, A Winner's Handbook* (1) **by Jerry Patterson.** One of the more bizarre books on sports betting. Patterson claims that his methods will produce about 1,000 good bets a year. Unfortunately, just about everything that he claims is either worthless or already reflected in the line. In addition, the book contains much conflicting information, such as a four-point move either way in the over/under line would not have changed the results in 85 percent of all NFL bets. This may be true, but it also may mean that what was a good bet before the four point move is no longer a good bet, and vice versa.

31. *Pro Football Over/Under Wagering* (3) **by Dana Parham.** A well-written, but badly flawed example of trend analysis. If the author had computed the appropriate standard deviation, he would have seen that virtually none of his results is statistically significant. This book may be an example of looking at enough data until something is found that seems to work. Also evident are other basic statistical mistakes. For example, the author points out that the majority of games go under 52 points. He seems to be saying that any 52-point game is probably a good under bet. Of course, this would be true only if most games with 52-point totals go under, and if the proportion that goes under is statistically significant.

32. *Gambling Scams* **(10) by Darwin Ortiz.** An extremely well-written book by a knowledgeable expert on many different forms of cheating in all sorts of gambling games and environments. This text is absolutely must reading for all serious gamblers.

33. *On Casino Gambling* **(8) by Darwin Ortiz.** I found this material to be somewhat tedious and much too detailed for all but the most sophisticated readers. On the other hand, Ortiz is certainly one of the foremost experts in this field, and this book is a good overview of most of the games that the casinos offer.

34. *Knights of the Green Cloth, The Saga of Frontier Gamblers* **(9) by Robert K. DeArment.** Normally, the highest rating that I give a book read only for its entertainment value is a 7, but this book is so good that I rated it much higher. The work contains fascinating stories about some of the most interesting characters of the Old West including Wyatt Earp, Wild Bill Hickok, and Poker Alice.

35. *Professional Video Poker* **(10) by Stanford Wong.** If you want to learn how to play video poker virtually perfectly and want to obtain a significant edge over the casino, this is the book to buy. Wong provides professional-level strategies that are relatively easy to master. Absolutely must reading for anyone interested in these games.

36. *America's National Game of Chance — Video Poker* **(8) by Lenny Frome with Maryann Guberman.** This text is a collection of some of the best articles that Lenny Frome has written. If you want to learn more about video poker this is an excellent place to start. The reason I don't rate the book higher is that some of the advice concerning "hot and cold" machines is flawed.

37. *Winning Strategies For Video Poker* **(10) by Lenny Frome.** If you want to learn how to correctly play almost any form of video poker then this is the book for you. The book actually is a collection of tables that illustrates how to play correctly in every conceivable situation. An absolute must for video poker enthusiasts.

38. *Fundamentals of Video Poker* **by Mason Malmuth and Lynne Loomis.** This is another book in the *Fundamentals* series. If you are new to video poker, this book provides excellent instructions for the basic game. Machines discussed include jacks-or-better, tens-or-better, deuces wild, and joker wild.

39. *The Mathematics of Games and Gambling* **(9) by Edward Packel.** An excellent discussion of the mathematics and probability that are important to gambling. The book is enjoyable to read and is filled with many helpful examples. Highly recommended for those of you who are weak in this area.

40. *Guerrilla Gambling: How to Beat the Casinos at Their Own Games* **(2) by Frank Scoblete.** According to this author, a guerrilla gambler is someone who can beat the casinos using hit and run tactics. For example, he states that "Craps and roulette are two fine examples of *seemingly* random games that can be exploited by skill and perception." Well, if you believe that, don't expect your money to last very long. My favorite quote from the book comes out of the roulette section where Scoblete states "The Big number strategy is designed to take advantage of short term fluctuations in probability; that is, certain numbers repeating simply due to randomness." The reason I rated this text a 2 instead of a 1 is that it is well written and some of the material such as blackjack basic strategy is reasonably well presented.

41. *Bargain City: Booking, Betting, and Beating the New Las Vegas* **(9) by Anthony Curtis.** If you are new to gambling or haven't spent much time in Las Vegas, then this book should do you a lot of good. Not only does it contain sections giving good basic advice on various types of gambling, but it also has chapters which instruct you how to get the best room rate, how to take advantage of casino coupons, where the best buffets are, and much more.

42. *Comp City: A Guide To Free Las Vegas Vacations* **(10) by Max Rubin.** If you liked the ideas which were presented in the essay titled "Free Bets and Other Topics" then this is the book for you. The author tells you everything that you will ever need to know about how to squeeze the maximum in comps out of the casinos, what it will cost you to do so, and how much risk you will be taking. I suspect that this book will impact many casinos in Las Vegas and other locations. However, I don't believe the impact will occur quickly, so there should be many opportunities for those of you interested in living the good life.

43. *Gambling Theory and Other Topics* **by Mason Malmuth.** This is the book that you are reading. I happen to like it and I hope you've enjoyed it.

Appendix B

Maximum Likelihood Estimator for the Mean and Standard Deviation

The normal probability density function is

$$N(u_i, \sigma_i) = \frac{1}{\sigma(T_i)^{1/2}(2\pi)^{1/2}} e^{-\left[\frac{(x_i - uT_i)^2}{2\sigma^2 T_i}\right]}$$

where x_i is the result for the ith session, σ and u are the parameters, and T_i is the length of time of the ith session.

First, form the likelihood function L:

$$L = \prod_{i=1}^{n} \left[\frac{1}{\sigma(T_i)^{1/2}(2\pi)^{1/2}} e^{-\left[\frac{(x_i - uT_i)}{2\sigma^2 T_i}\right]} \right]$$

$$= \frac{1}{(2\pi)^{n/2}\sigma^n} e^{-\left[\frac{1}{2\sigma^2}\sum_{i=1}^{n}\frac{(x_i - uT_i)^2}{T_i}\right]} \prod_{i=1}^{n} T_i^{-1/2}$$

Next, take the log of the likelihood function L:

$$\log(L) = -\log(2\pi)^{n/2} - \frac{n}{2}\log\sigma^2 - \frac{1}{2\sigma^2}\sum_{i=1}^{n}\frac{(x_i - uT_i)^2}{T_i} + \log\prod_{i=1}^{n}\frac{1}{T_i^{1/2}}$$

Differentiating with respect to u and setting the resultant expression equal to zero, we get:

$$0 = \frac{1}{2\sigma^2}\sum_{i=1}^{n}\frac{2T_i(x_i - uT_i)}{T_i} = \frac{1}{\sigma^2}\sum_{i=1}^{n}(x_i - uT_i) \Rightarrow$$

$$\sum_{i=1}^{n}x_i = \sum_{i=1}^{n}uT_i = u\sum_{i=1}^{n}T_i \Rightarrow$$

$$u = \frac{\sum_{i=1}^{n}x_i}{\sum_{i=1}^{n}T_i}$$

Also, differentiating with respect to $2\sigma^2$ and setting the resultant expression equal, to zero we get:

$$0 = -\frac{n}{2\sigma^2} + \frac{1}{2\sigma^4}\sum_{i=1}^{n}\frac{(x_i - uT_i)^2}{T_i} \Rightarrow$$

$$\sigma^2 = \frac{1}{n}\sum_{i=1}^{n}\frac{(x_i - uT_i)^2}{T_i}$$

$$= \frac{1}{n}\sum_{i=1}^{n}\left[\frac{x_i^2}{T_i}\right] - \frac{u^2}{n}\sum_{i=1}^{n}T_i$$